LOCAL GOVERNMENT MANAGEMENT

The rhetoric and reality of change

LINDA KEEN
AND
RICHARD SCASE

OPEN UNIVERSITY PRESS

Buckingham · Philadelphia

Open University Press
Celtic Court
22 Ballmoor
Buckingham
MK18 1XW

email: enquiries@openup.co.uk
world wide web: http://www.openup.co.uk

and
325 Chestnut Street
Philadelphia, PA 19106, USA

First published 1998

A catalogue record of this book is available from the British Library

ISBN 0335 19893 7 (pb)   0335 19894 5 (hb)

Library of Congress Cataloging-in-Publication Data
Keen, Linda.
    Local government management:the rhetoric and reality of change /
Linda Keen and Richard Scase.
        p. cm.
    Includes bibliographical references and index.
    ISBN 0–335–19894–5 (hb). – ISBN 0–335–19893–7 (pb)
    1. Local government–Great Britain.   I. Scase, Richard.
II. Title.
JS3111.K43   1998
352.14′0941–dc21   97–44088
                                                                          CIP

Typeset by Graphicraft Typesetters Ltd., Hong Kong
Printed in Great Britain by St Edmundsbury Press,
Bury St Edmunds, Suffolk

LOCAL GOVERNMENT MANAGEMENT

This book is for Alison Walsh. It is dedicated to her late husband, Professor Kieron Walsh, who died in 1995 at the early age of 46. It is written in memory of his contribution to local government studies, and his commitment to the development of local authorities which would be truly accountable to their citizens and communities.

Contents

Acknowledgements

The support received from a number of sources during the completion of this book is gratefully acknowledged, including, most importantly, the managers of 'Barset County Council' (who cannot be identified for reasons of confidentiality), the Local Government Management Board, and the Institute of Local Government Studies at the University of Birmingham. We would also like to thank Chris Skelcher for his detailed comments on an earlier draft of this book.

1 The 'new managerialism' in local government

Local government has experienced an unprecedented rate of change during the 1980s and 1990s, which has been precipitated mainly, but not exclusively, by the policies of successive Conservative governments. An increasing volume of public sector literature has identified the development of a 'new managerialist' approach within local government, involving, essentially, a move from bureaucratic and professionally dominated 'administration' to a more flexible, customer-orientated, private sector style of management and service provision. However, there has been little research into the extent to which prescriptions have been put into practice. The evidence suggesting the adoption by local authorities of this 'new managerialism' has been derived predominantly from the accounts of senior managers. Beyond this, little is known. How far, then, is there a rhetoric which fails to be effected in reality? The purpose of this book is to explore this question on the basis of a review of the relevant literature and a detailed analysis of a particular local authority. As a case study, this is used to illustrate what may or may not be broad ranging and 'transformational' processes of change in the ways in which local government managers execute their tasks. Certainly, they are subject to growing pressures for change, forcing them to adopt innovative approaches in response to both internal and external organizational requirements. These are likely to continue despite the election of a Labour central government in 1997. This government's policies, too, seem to have embraced many elements of the 'new managerialist' approaches extolled by its Conservative predecessors. Thus, there is little likelihood that the scale and scope of the predominant prescriptions for local government reform will decline in the future. But the question remains as to the 'fit' between rhetoric and reality. In order to analyse this, it is first necessary to identify some of the key features of local authorities in terms of how they operate as *organizations*.

Local authorities as organizations

All contemporary local authorities share a common heritage which origin-ated in the nineteenth century, including an institutional framework, en-shrined in the legislation which set them up and in the numerous statutes which empower them to carry out their functions. Greenwood and Stewart (1986) identify five key institutional features of local government which continue to distinguish local authorities from other public, private and voluntary sector organizations.

First, each authority operates with a focus on a specific local geographical area, and (until the 1980s) on the assumption that it be self-sufficient: that it should have the skills and resources needed to provide all the various required services. Second, they have discretion in the scope of their service provision within a statutory framework of national legislation. Third, local authorities have the right to raise taxes locally. Fourth – and a most critical characteristic – they have a local electoral base, legitimating their decision making and ensuring accountability to the local community. Fifth, they are *not* all-purpose public authorities – they are responsible only for certain func-tions, and therefore have to collaborate and cooperate extensively with other agencies (such as health authorities) to ensure effective planning for the local community as a whole.

These key institutional features (which remained largely unchanged until the early 1980s) continue to influence the structure and management systems of contemporary local authorities (Knowles 1977). For example, Morris, writing in 1990, comments on the extent to which, in today's very different world, the original Victorian constitutional rules, procedures and standing orders remain 'instantly familiar in their language and in daily application' (Morris 1990: x). The traditional characteristics of local authority structures include: (a) committees of elected members (councillors), responsible for particular functions and services, who are accountable to the electorate for the authority's policies and activities; (b) bureaucratic administration sys-tems with an emphasis on standardized and formalized procedures, rules and activities; and (c) a culture of professionalism, derived largely from externally provided training and socialization and established initially to combat local corruption and nepotism (Greenwood and Stewart 1986; Stewart 1986; Laffin and Young 1990). This operates to ensure that there is elected member/political control over the authority's activities, uniform-ity of service provision and a high degree of procedural and substantive integrity and probity (Hood 1991).

Challenges to the traditional management structures of local authorit-ies began in the early 1960s. Increases in rate levies, combined with staff shortages, stimulated interest in productivity gains and improved levels of administrative efficiency. There was an increase in the general use of 'management services' such as work study and operations research, aided by new (mainframe) computers. The Local Government Training Board (LGTB) and the Local Authorities Management Service and Computer Committee were both established in 1967 to help local authorities to improve their management system. (These merged in the early 1990s to form the Local Government Management Board (LGMB).) There was also a growing emphasis on 'management' rather than 'administration' in the texts of the time (Keeling 1972).

A second phase of management reform in local government began in the mid-1960s (Cockburn 1977). This was concerned not just with efficiency gains, but also with promoting integrated or corporate management systems upon what were highly differentiated and decentralized forms of organization. The pressures for such reforms emanated from a variety of sources. Council boundaries had become inappropriate for changing population distributions, especially in the wake of post-war housing reconstruction and with the advent of large-scale car ownership. It was difficult for smaller councils to manage efficiently the increased number and complexity of functions allocated to them. The division and fragmentation of service responsibilities, both between departments of each authority and between different authorities, made coordination and effective planning extremely difficult. There was also increased public concern about the rising level of public expenditure (Hepworth 1980). Thus, the Maud Report, commissioned in 1964 and published in 1967 in response to these problems, recommended greater organizational integration within local authorities, together with fewer committees, sub-committees and departments (Cockburn 1977; Greenwood *et al.* 1980).

The Maud Committee's concern with corporate *management* began to give way in the late 1960s to a greater emphasis on corporate *planning*, derived initially from the US Planning-Programming Budgeting System (PPBS), which focused on the effectiveness of local authorities for meeting the needs of their local communities. This trend was stimulated by a variety of developments. These included central government innovations in the control of public expenditure; a plethora of government reports on urban problems hinting at the need for more integrated approaches; growing opposition to the professional dominance and control of so many public services (Laffin 1986); and a large number of new councillors elected between 1966 and 1972 who had challenged traditional practices. Information about the new system was disseminated by the Institute of Local Government Studies (INLOGOV), through various management consultancy reports commissioned by several local authorities and through a series of articles published in 1971 by the *Local Government Chronicle* (Hambleton 1978).

The Bains Report, published in 1972, made a significant observation about the purposes of local government: 'Local government is not, in our view, limited to the narrow range of provision of a series of services to the local community ... It has within its purview the overall economic, cultural and physical well-being of that community' (Bains 1972: 6). It recommended the replacement of the traditional 'departmental' approach by a more integrated and wider-ranging corporate planning strategy. Other key developments during the 1970s included the end of 'the era of growth' in public expenditure in 1974/5, together with growing levels of popular disillusionment with 'public services which appeared to be provided by insensitive, monolithic bureaucracies in conformity with rigid and apparently unnecessary rules' (Elcock 1993: 154). This, in addition to the wave of public sector strikes which occurred at the end of the 1970s, contributed to the electoral success of the Conservative Party in 1979, which came to power committed to reform of the public sector, including local government. Successive Conservative central governments have since made significant changes in the external environment and the institutional framework within which local authorities must operate. One hundred and twenty-four pieces of legislation with implications for local government were enacted between 1979 and 1990 (Local Government Information Unit 1990). The overall impact of such laws was to reduce the level of local authorities' autonomy over the nature and scope of their spending and service provision (Stoker 1988). Three main trends can be discerned since 1979.

First, central government has subjected local authorities to increasingly stringent controls over the level and patterns of their expenditure (Cook 1993). The 'cap' on permitted spending levels now includes limits on the amount which can be raised from the local council tax, the non-domestic (or business) tax base has been removed from local authorities' control and they may spend only a limited proportion of any capital receipts obtained from selling assets such as council houses. Less than 20 per cent of local authority expenditure is now financed locally, with consequent severe reductions in local accountability. Arguably, these constraints mean that 'Effectively, it is the Minister and a small group of civil servants, rather than elected members, who are deciding the absolute and relative growth of budgets in local authorities' (Gibson 1992: 21). Such constraints have compelled local authorities to look for ways to improve the efficiency and effectiveness of their management and service delivery systems. In addition, the Audit Commission was established in 1983 with powers to compel local authorities to improve the three 'Es' – their economy, efficiency and effectiveness – through its auditing role and its publication of comparative performance data.

Second, local government has been subjected to the 'establishment of market conditions, through transferring services or assets to private ownerships, encouraging competitive tendering for services, or creating internal markets'

(Elcock 1993: 155). Under compulsory competitive tendering (CCT) and other legislation, local authorities are required to distinguish between the 'purchasers' and the 'providers' of services. Services are no longer expected to be provided solely, or even primarily, by local authorities themselves. Instead, local authority provider units are required to compete on the open market with providers from the voluntary and private sectors to obtain service delivery contracts. Originally focused towards manual services, such as refuse collection, these market systems are being extended to professional services such as engineering, finance and computer services, although the new Labour government is at the time of writing considering the removal of the 'compulsory' element of competitive tendering for all services in 1999 (Vize 1997).

Third, there have been moves towards the development of a ' "public service" orientation, focusing on the public as clients, customers and citizens, with a move away from supply-led to demand-led services, no longer dominated by professional providers but responsive to the needs of those being served' (Farnham and Horton 1993: 239). This has arisen partly as a result of government policies, and partly as a result of demographic and socio-economic changes. Central government launched the Citizen's Charter in 1991, which required local authorities to adopt a number of 'public service principles' that all citizens were entitled to expect from public organizations (Spencer 1992: 88). These include entitlements to standards of service provision, to more involvement in decision making, to information provision, to more clearly specified complaints procedures. This initiative reflected the growing demands of more highly educated citizens, with higher expectations about public service quality standards and with growing suspicion of the 'expert' judgement of professional groups (Gyford et al. 1989; Prior et al. 1995; Elcock 1996).

A number of major socio-economic and demographic changes have also occurred. These include an ageing population, an increase in single person households, significant levels of unemployment and homelessness, and a continuing increase in middle-class jobs at the expense of traditional working-class occupations. Thus, local authorities have needed to focus their increasingly scarce resources more effectively towards those most in need, while at the same time meeting the demands of more prosperous and discerning groups for sophisticated and effective services in areas such as leisure and education (Radley 1992).

In terms of their internal features, post-1974 local authorities vary considerably in size, from a few hundred staff to over 50,000 (Audit Commission et al. 1985). They are generally labour-intensive organizations, with staff as a percentage of total costs ranging from around 55 per cent for a large county to 65 per cent for a small district. National staffing levels across all local authorities in England and Wales are estimated to have fallen between 1975 and 1993 by about 13.3 per cent (about 278,000 full-time equivalents). Trends differ, however, within different functional/service areas, with a general decrease in manual staff levels (arising largely from CCT initiatives), and increases in some administrative, technical and professional staff categories, including police, social services and computing functions. While many texts on local authority organizations stress the pre-eminence of professional cultures, Stewart (1992) draws attention to the diversity of work systems and processes that exist within each authority. These range from the highly complex and non-routine activities of the professional social or housing worker to the more standardized and routinized work of council tax collection, street cleansing or refuse collection. The growing use of computerized work systems and management information systems is also affecting the nature of work processes within many local government occupations.

Greenwood *et al.* (1980) use the term 'public accountability' to characterize the nature of a local authority's external control system. This incorporates two key aspects. First, there is the extent to which the councillors 'formally organise themselves into identifiable political groupings: this is the extent of *political organization*'. Second, there is the *complexion* of the controlling political party: whether it is Labour, Conservative or some other party (pp. 120–1). The external political control of local authorities means that decisions about the provision of services are made within a statutory framework on the basis of balancing resource availability with essentially political (value-based) choices about how to define and meet local needs and demands. Since the Widdicombe Report (1986) and subsequent legislation, the extent of *political organization* has increased: 'Partisan conduct is rapidly becoming commonplace, with members of both major parties increasingly bound by (political) group decisions and reflecting this changing expectation in more partisan voting both in council and – a notable change this – in committee meetings' (Young and Davies 1990: 60).

The nature of the *political complexion* or party control is also a significant contingency factor. This has been a response, in part at least, to the increasing polarization of political debate at central government levels during the decade (Butcher 1990). Thus, there have been important ideological differences between political parties about the role of local authorities and the nature of their structures and management systems. Stoker (1991), for example, identifies several key factions within local government political ideologies, such as the Conservative 'urban ideologues' who dominated Wandsworth and Westminster Councils in the late 1980s and early 1990s, and Labour's 'urban left' in other London boroughs. Even within the current context of increasing central government restrictions over the level of autonomy granted to local authorities, it is clear that key local political actors can still make choices about the particular strategic direction to be taken by their authority. Thus, Greenwood (1987) was able to classify various local authorities according to which one of four strategic styles they had chosen to adopt: the prospectors who seek innovation, the defenders who seek stability, the analysers who combine innovation with stability and the reactors, who have no coherent strategy (Miles and Snow 1978).

As a consequence of these changes in both their external and internal characteristics, growing numbers of local authorities are changing their internal operating processes, moving away from the traditional bureaucratic form to what is often described as a 'new' public sector management model (Hood 1991).

Traditional and 'new' forms of local government

Traditional bureaucratic model		*New public sector model*
self-sufficiency	⟶	the enabling authority
near-monopoly	⟶	the competitive council
hierarchical and central control	⟶	management by contract and influence
direct management of services	⟶	devolved management
uniform and standardized services	⟶	customer orientation, quality and choice
stable employment	⟶	flexible employment structures

(From Stoker (1989: 7).

The direction of change is from the traditional 'self-sufficient' local authority, which enjoyed a near monopoly in service provision, to the 'enabling', 'competitive' and 'mixed economy' authority (Leach *et al.* 1994). Local authorities, acting as purchasers, are responsible for specifying and then enabling, rather than directly providing, the services to be delivered by separate providers – by private and voluntary sector organizations as well as authorities' own workforces (Brooke 1989). Traditional management systems, based on hierarchical, and relatively centralized, control systems, are seen as giving way to 'arm's length' negotiated relationships between groups of managers. More decentralized control systems focus on clear specification of performance outcomes within the context of strategic and devolved management processes. Systems for organizational regulation move from hierarchies to markets and, possibly, to networks (Walsh 1995). These are characterized by longer-term collaborative partnership arrangements between purchasers and providers in an almost 'boundaryless' organization (Thompson *et al.* 1991; Peters 1992; Flynn 1994; Francis 1994: 79).

Devolved management involves 'managers at the lowest possible level having: more authority over resources; greater scope for decisions; accountability for achieving agreed targets' (Stoker 1989: 33). They operate within a

corporate-wide mission and 'core-value' statements and strategic
⌐⌐g systems, incorporating resource utilization and service delivery
targets against which each manager's work unit performance is assessed
(Caulfield and Schulz 1989). Considerable emphasis is placed on tailoring
local service provision more specifically to particular individual and community needs through the use of various 'quality' management and marketing techniques, together with an increasing emphasis on 'empowering'
the consumer (Walsh 1989; Prior *et al.* 1995; Hood *et al.* 1996). The
extensive implications of these changes for local authority staff correspond,
broadly speaking, to moves from personnel to more flexible human resource
management strategies (Fowler 1988b; Storey 1992; Sisson 1994). Professional staff are expected to acquire resource management responsibilities
and to be subject to central management's 'policing role, encroaching on
professional activities through such techniques as cost-centre budgeting
and performance indicators' (Lawson 1993: 74; Watkins *et al.* 1992).

Overall, these changes can be seen as representing moves towards the
'reinvention' of government thesis developed by Osborne and Gaebler
(1992), with the emphasis on structures which are 'mission rather than
rule-driven', 'decentralized' and 'entrepreneurial' (Gray and Jenkins 1995:
85; Young 1996). They involve a move from cultures 'dominated by traditional public service values to ones attuned to the market, business and
entrepreneurial values of the "new" public service model' (Farnham and
Horton 1993: 238). Advocates of the new model claim that it 'increases
accountability, fosters efficiency and improves organisational performance
. . . by stressing the management of resources, providing better information
on which decisions can be taken, and hence leads to greater control' (Gray
and Jenkins 1993: 22). Semi-autonomous business units, operating within
a clear strategic framework, become more responsive to local customer
and community needs. In addition, workforce motivation is strengthened
through the use of coherent organizational cultures emphasizing 'commitment' rather than 'control' strategies for regulating performance (Walton
1985). Critics of the new model, however, claim that this is largely 'hype' or
rhetoric in that, apart from the terminology used, little has in fact changed;
that it promotes the interests of an elite group of 'new managerialists',
rather than customers or lower level staff. The main result, according to
these critics, has been 'a rapid middle-level bureaucratisation of new reporting systems' and the weakening of 'elementary but essential competences
at the front line' (Hood 1991: 9). They also query the claims that the new
model can be seen as a purely technical or 'neutral' mechanism, suitable
for the achievement of goals set by elected representatives – local or national.
They argue that the peculiar characteristics of local government continue
to distinguish it from the private sector. These include differences in basic
goals and purposes, the criteria for assessing organizational effectiveness
and the nature of external ownership and control (Greenwood and Stewart

1986; Stewart and Ranson 1988; Broussine 1992). Key differences between local government and private sector organizations include the former's concern with matching provision to publicly defined needs, and with ensuring equity of provision to all those entitled to particular services, compared with private sector concerns with product demands at a price in the market. Public accountability is 'required for both means and ends . . . to explain and justify actions taken' (Stewart and Ranson 1988: 4), rather than private sector accountability to the market. The political process is an integral condition of public sector management according to which collective needs are defined, and ways of meeting them chosen. Thus, despite arguments that public–private sector differences are becoming blurred, most authors continue to support the view that 'the two sectors have features which are unique and not shared with the other', each requiring different forms of structure and management systems to ensure maximum effectiveness (Broussine 1992: 6).

Despite this claim, most of the local government chief officers included within Broussine's (1988) research also felt that many private sector management techniques were applicable, at least in part, to local government. He argues that there is a trend away from the purely 'public administration is unique' approach to the view that 'Public service management needs to change, but retain and strengthen its distinctiveness' (Broussine 1992: 7–11). The Audit Commission *et al.* (1985) publication *Good Management in Local Government* is a good early example of this philosophy, as is the first of many papers produced by the LGTB (Clarke *et al.* 1985) which note the limitations, but also the possibilities, of applying the attributes of the successful companies outlined in *In Search of Excellence* (Peters and Waterman 1982) to local authority management systems. Thus, under 'close to the customer', the authors noted the problems in local government of adopting the private sector approach to the customer or the market as the authoritative judge of what products are required. Nevertheless, they suggest using the concept of 'customer' to develop greater responsiveness to local community needs. Similarly, Stewart and Ranson's use of the term 'market', which would have been almost unknown in local government circles until the 1980s, acknowledges its relevance for local government management. Thus, the private sector marketing framework has been used to reaffirm the importance of public accountability through, for example, 'learning from citizens about their understanding of needs' (Stewart and Ranson 1988: 3), rather than assuming that councillors somehow know best. Although public sector marketing 'cannot be modelled on the private sector alone' (p. 3), the inference is clear that the concept does, albeit in a different way, have a role in local government.

In the context of the Bains Report's definition of the purposes of local government, the ultimate output or 'product' of local authorities is difficult to identify or measure in quantitative terms. The criteria for assessing their effectiveness remains essentially a politically-based value process, in contrast to the economic goals (ultimately profitability) of the private sector. The external political control exercised by members over local authority organizations – legitimated by direct elections – and their statutory obligation to provide equity of service provision requires a critical degree of central coordination by senior management who are accountable to these elected members, and ultimately to the local electorate. This suggests that local authorities are compelled to retain, albeit in amended and more flexible forms, elements of a hierarchical bureaucratic structure within their 'new' management approaches.

Since the emergence of a generic new 'public management' during the 1980s, a number of sub-models or 'ideal types' have been identified, each placing a different emphasis on the various elements contained within this perspective. Thus, for example, Leach et al. (1994) differentiate between three approaches: *residual enabling*, based on a private sector style business orientation; *market enabling*, which emphasizes a customer orientation; and *community enabling*, with a focus on promoting citizenship values such as equality, accountability and fairness. Similarly, Ferlie et al. (1996: 12–15) identify four different 'ideal types', each with a different emphasis on particular 'new' management traits: *efficiency drive*, comparable with Leach et al.'s first model; the *downsizing and decentralization* approach, focusing on the idea of the fragmented local authority with a small strategic core and considerable contracting-out of operational functions; the *in search of excellence* approach, with an emphasis on ideas derived from the series of popular 'excellence' management texts which were produced during the 1980s (see Chapter 2); and *a public service orientation*, which is comparable with Leach et al.'s 'community enabling' model, and which places a strong focus on local accountability. All of these variants require fundamental changes in managerial roles.

Managerial roles

Job roles in local government have traditionally been tightly prescribed, involving relatively inflexible employment contracts, detailed and activity-based job descriptions, and work study specifications for manual/clerical workers. Relying on the extensive use of written rules and procedures, a centralized personnel function exerted a high degree of control over the duties, numbers and grades of all staff (Kerley 1994). Nationally prescribed conditions of service and grading structures, with a long hierarchy of numerous grades with narrow salary ranges, reinforced tendencies towards a high degree of job specialization associated with the characteristics of machine bureaucracy. Professional jobs were narrowly defined on the basis of particular expert skills. In general, such staff had no responsibility for, or control over, resources – personnel, finance etc. – necessary to deliver services. These tended to be controlled by centralized management.

Since the 1980s, local authorities have been exhorted to adopt more flexible patterns of role specialization in order to achieve more flexible and innovative service provision that is more responsive to customer needs (Audit Commission 1988, 1989a, 1990, 1991, 1995; LGTB 1990a, b; LGMB 1993a; Fowler 1995). Such initiatives include: more flexible employment contracts and staffing/grading structures (linked to flatter organizational hierarchies); increased use of temporary and part-time staff; the introduction of performance appraisal schemes; and, in a small number of authorities, withdrawal from national pay bargaining and/or the adoption of performance-related pay systems (LGTB/LACSAB 1990; Donaldson 1992; Farnham 1993; Young and Mills 1993; Young 1996). Patterns of numerical, functional and financial flexibility have reflected private sector style moves from personnel management to human resource management, which encourage individuals to 'go beyond contract' – to focus on the achievement of performance outputs within a context of rigorous performance control systems (Storey 1992). Moreover, under the impetus to win tenders under CCT legislation, traditional rigid job demarcation in direct service organizations has increasingly given way to more flexible, multi-skilled workgroups and working practices and conditions. These pressures are likely to extend to other sections of authorities' work, with the extension of CCT to professional services (Farnham and Giles 1996).

Professional jobs are also being redesigned: the Audit Commission (1989b: 9) urges reassessment of the skills required to perform 'professional' tasks, and to identify those which require 'limited professional expertise'. Such tasks, requiring lower levels of individual discretion and judgement, can be allocated to non-professional staff, or be contracted out to the private/voluntary sectors. The job roles and responsibilities of professional staff and managers are becoming broader. They are taking on responsibilities for new functions such as resource management and, while retaining their own professional specialism, are likely to be working increasingly within multidisciplinary project teams and work groups. This is the case both across professional and departmental boundaries within authorities and with other agencies, in the context of the 'enabling', 'competitive' and 'mixed economy' council (Watkins et al. 1992). Professional jobs are also being redesigned according to the different roles required within the functional purchaser/provider split. Other recent initiatives address issues of culture – of ensuring the adoption of the appropriate beliefs, values and attitudes required to ensure effective changes in behaviour (Flynn 1994). Thus, increased emphasis has been given to the need to nurture specific corporate values, visions and goals. An LGMB survey (Young and Mills 1993) found that about 80 per cent of the 285 responding authorities had already adopted, or were considering the adoption of, core value or mission statements. Many of these are derived from *In Search of Excellence* (Peters and Waterman 1982), and include references to the need for more risk-taking, innovation, customer orientation and concern for staff. A typical example is presented in Appendix 2.

In combination with training policies, such corporate cultures represent attempts to limit the 'cosmopolitan' orientation of professional staff to their national/professional association ethics and values in favour of the adoption of a 'local' orientation to the particular service policies and objectives of the professional's own employing authority (Gouldner 1957; Laffin and Young 1990). However, attitudes and values are not easily changed. Staff with traditional departmental loyalties and professional service ideals may view with scepticism commitment to the 'customer' as espoused through the official corporate culture, especially if they have to restrict the scope of their own service provision because of expenditure constraints (Clarke 1988; Harrow and Willcocks 1990). In any case, specific sub-cultures will still tend to develop within many of the differentiated work units of local authorities. Indeed, increasing devolution to performance or cost centres will reinforce the need for the development of strong corporate cultures to limit 'local' sub-cultural variations.

The effective dissemination of corporate cultures and the effective operation of new formal standardization methods requires appropriate training, communication and employee involvement systems. LGTB/LACSAB (1990) reported an increase in these, including: suggestion schemes; improved communication systems (including staff attitude surveys); staff welfare programmes (to promote the 'caring' employer image); and improvements in workplace and social facilities. The reasons for the introduction of such measures are diverse, but they certainly correspond to the measures being adopted in the private sector to increase corporate commitment. Training provision is an important method, not just for developing personal skills, but also for socializing employees into the norms and values of an organization. Local authorities have traditionally relied on external training provision for their professional staff, which contributed significantly to their predominantly 'cosmopolitan' service orientation rather than to a 'local' commitment to a particular organization's policies and values. Several studies (LGTB 1988b, 1990b; Leach *et al.* 1993) have urged the adoption of management training and development programmes to develop corporate managerial role identities, as opposed to the professional role identities of service managers. Such programmes emphasize the need to develop managers 'who are capable of working with the organisation's future priorities. For example, the challenge of competitive tendering, the changing roles and relationships between councillors, officers and the public, the moves towards a more market-centred approach, the importance of inter-agency working' (LGTB 1988b: 45). Local authorities are increasingly being urged to develop into 'learning organisations', with their staff involved in continuous improvement, change and adaptation (Stewart 1986; Clarke and Stewart 1988; Clarke 1996).

Some processes of organizational change

In relation to departmental structures, the professional employees of local authorities have traditionally tended to work in fairly small work units or teams, which were traditionally grouped together within specialist service departments. Since the 1980s, there have been moves towards grouping different professional service staff together on the basis of location or geographical *area*. This decentralized, area-based, approach has been particularly pronounced among social services and housing departments (Young and Mills 1993). Some authorities have taken the geographical dispersal of service provision beyond traditional departmental boundaries, with area-based 'neighbourhood' offices providing a range of interdepartmental services (Lowndes 1992; Lowndes and Stoker 1992a, b; Stoker *et al.* 1988). These initiatives are underpinned by a philosophy of 'getting closer to the customers' to improve the identification of, and response to, their needs. They are aided by developments in new information technology, reflecting similar moves in the private sector towards market-based groupings.

The introduction of internal market systems – required by central government CCT and other service-specific legislation – is also making a profound impact on departmental structures. The split required between purchaser and provider functions has involved restructuring along these functional lines between and within service departments (Fowler 1988a; Young and Mills 1993; Young 1996). Thus, for example, many authorities, in response to CCT requirements, have set up a separate department with its own chief officer to manage and run all the manual contracting service provision subject to CCT. One district council envisaged a purely functional division of just two principal departments for the whole authority – one for the purchaser/client role and one for the contractor/provider role. In response to the 1990 NHS and Community Care Act requirements, almost half the authorities' social services departments in Young and Mills's (1993) survey had reorganized around a purchaser/provider division, while the remainder were either planning or considering such a split. Under 'mixed economy' service provision, provider functions are also carried out by provider agencies located outside, as well as inside, local authorities, in private or voluntary sector organizations. These arrangements have significant implications for both the nature and the quantity of 'horizontal' linkages required to ensure cooperation and coordination between functions.

Virtually all authorities have established chief executive posts as recommended by the Bains Report, and most authorities have a senior management team, composed of departmental chief officers led by the chief executive (Audit Commission 1989c). Developments since Bains include the increased attachment of various support functions to the chief executive's department, such as public relations, corporate planning, personnel, management services and administration. The number of departments has tended to decrease, with functions regrouped within a smaller number of larger departments or directorates, together with flatter departmental structures (Young and Mills 1993). An LGTB/LACSAB survey (1990) reported that one-third of all authorities had reduced the number of management layers within their organizations, and a further 5 per cent were planning to do so. For example, one district council replaced its 'fossilized' departmental structure (with as many as 16 layers between the top and bottom) by a flatter structure with no more than three layers between 'the heads of functions and the people on the ground' (Tighe 1992: 14).

Elected member structures have also changed. The Audit Commission (1990) recommended fewer and larger service committees and increased numbers of smaller sub-committees or informal work groups to improve decision making and maximize member involvement. Reflecting these recommendations, Young and Mills (1993: 13) and Young (1996) reported a general trend towards streamlining management and decision-making structures, with a 'slimming-down in the number and frequency of committees and sub-committees' and 'a complementary trend towards use of member working parties'. In combination with the area structures described above, a few authorities have also developed multi-service area committees (Stoker et al. 1988; Lowndes 1992).

Adopting a strategic approach

Many councils are also adopting various features of strategic management to service planning and delivery (Issac-Henry and Painter 1991; Buckland and Joshua 1992; Leach et al. 1994). In an attempt to discover the extent to which these authorities 'conduct themselves in a strategic manner' as opposed to simply reporting the existence of a strategic planning system, Young and Mills (1993: 25–6) reported that half the county council chief executives claimed that their teams spent at least half their time on strategic issues, with much more uneven practices reported by other authorities. In addition, 38 per cent of all the authorities had established specialist strategic management posts. Even so, Caulfield and Schutz (1989), in examining local authority strategic planning systems, claim that many represented little more than the simple bringing together of service plans, with little systematic performance review. They tended to conclude that many of the problems experienced in the 1970s with corporate planning were resurfacing: 'Above all there does appear to be a lot of emphasis on the mechanics, and a relative neglect of the underlying culture . . . the moral is clear: the style, approach and vision of the local authority are more important than the bare achievement of producing a strategic plan' (ibid.: 94). Similarly, Jackson (1993) reported that 'few of the [public sector] organisations studied employed an explicit strategic-management framework'. They paid only very limited attention to the need for change management, and tended to focus on operational rather than strategic performance, with little use of performance measures and indicators to assess the achievement of longer-term or strategic, as opposed to operational, objectives. Moreover, in terms of increased member involvement in, and control over, strategic planning processes, chief officers were still considered, in general, to exert significantly more influence than members; thus, raising questions about the extent to which traditional 'professional' domination of policy making is being reduced (Young and Mills 1993).

A survey of performance systems (Palmer 1993: 32) suggests that, despite the growing emphasis on the need for more qualitative performance indicators, the measures most commonly collected by departments were quantitative. They related to costs, volume of service, utilization rates, time targets and productivity: 'indicators of quality of service, customers' satisfaction and the achievement of goals appear less often, if at all . . . Authorities, perhaps not surprisingly, concentrate on measuring what is easily measurable and this results in a bias towards measuring performance in terms of economy and efficiency, rather than effectiveness'. Palmer (1993: 36) concludes from her research that performance indicators are more often introduced within local authorities 'as an act of policy, or in compliance with external directives, rather than as a means of developing performance monitoring as part of the managerial culture.' As Jackson (1993) suggests, this tends to reduce the extent to which performance management systems can contribute towards organizational learning and improved service delivery, or even inform the strategic planning process.

Walsh (1992, 1995) also draws attention to the impact of market systems on the complexities of local authority strategic planning processes. Increasingly, in the context of market rather than hierarchical regulation of service delivery activities, strategy formulation will occur primarily within the 'purchaser' group of managers. They will assess consumer demands, make policies (embodying elected member values and strategies), develop new service provision and assess their performance against service specifications and measures of consumer satisfaction (Brooke 1989: 20–1; Audit Commission 1989a). Yet these managers are increasingly distanced from the service delivery process itself, and, as Walsh suggests, in the context of the planned extensions of CCT to various white-collar professional services, it is difficult to write formalized contract specifications in a form which allows for amendments to be made quickly and easily in response to changing political priorities or consumer demands.

The traditional 'departmentalism' of local authority structures and management systems – the division of local authority functions into rigorously differentiated departments based on professional specialisms – has always emphasized vertical rather than horizontal or lateral flows of information and communications (Haynes 1980). The latter tended to take place mainly at senior levels in the organization. As part of its advocacy of a corporate approach, the Bains Report urged the adoption of 'horizontal' liaison systems such as management teams and interdepartmental groups. These groups were to cut across departmental boundaries, with programme area teams grouped around the overall objectives of the organization, and project control groups to implement specific projects. Provision of such devices varies from council to council, ranging, for example, in the case of interdepartmental programme groups, from 43 per cent of the metropolitan districts to 80 per cent of the London boroughs in 1985 (Greenwood and Warner 1985). More recent suggestions for improving lateral communications include the designation of 'lead' officers or departments with a specific brief to develop operational and policy integration systems across the organization, together with the use of secondments, work attachments and horizontal career patterns 'to strengthen links across boundaries and to bring new/lateral/integrating thinking and perspectives' to the authority (Clarke 1996: 88).

Young and Mills (1993) and Young (1996) report increases in informal member and member/officer working groups and parties. In addition to the formal policy committee, providing overall direction for the authority and established by nearly all local authorities after Bains in 1974, new approaches are increasingly being adopted: councillor panels and working groups to explore specific policy areas and issues; equal opportunities committees; informal seminars for committees to review their working (Davies 1986). Closer working relations between officers and members are developing, with an increase in officers attending party group meetings. There are also increases in the contacts between chief executives and the council leaders (Young and Davies 1990), and in direct contacts between councillors and departmental officers (Stoker 1991).

The development of market systems also requires increased levels of 'horizontal' liaison between purchaser and provider functions. Increasingly, in the context of the 'mixed economy' and the 'enabling' council, such cooperation has to extend not just across internal departmental boundaries, but across organizational boundaries, as provider units become located increasingly in external private/voluntary sector organizations. Thus, 'officers will have a major preoccupation with inter-organisational relationships and the creation of networks to achieve the Council's strategic goals . . . the Chief Executive and Chief Officers will see an increasing role in looking outwards at their area as direct service provision by the authority declines . . . Members and Chief Officers will spend more time in developing convergent strategies with external agencies and in developing joint networks for service provision' (Brooke 1989: 21).

These developments can be seen as representing an apparent move from 'hierarchical' to 'market' through to the 'network' form of an almost 'boundaryless' organization (Peters 1992; Francis 1994; Walsh 1995). Aided by more sophisticated information technology, this organizational form is characterized by longer-term 'horizontal', cooperating and non-competitive relationships between parties, with an emphasis on the 'mutual adjustment' (Mintzberg 1989) and coordination of strategy. However, the limitations on the realization of such a model in practice tend to bear more heavily upon local authority organizations, with their more ambiguous purposes and functions, and public accountability requirements, than on private sector firms. Local authorities are publicly accountable organizations, required to justify and account for both the ends and the means of public spending and service provision. The use of more 'flexible' operating procedures may reduce the formal rigidity of the hierarchical, bureaucratic and departmental structures, but they are likely to form an addition to, rather than a replacement for, these traditional bureaucratic control mechanisms: 'the nonbureaucratic organisation exists in theory but, it is argued, does not provide practical alternatives for local government' (Davies 1986: 3.26). More fragmented market-based forms of service planning and delivery within an overall strategic framework are likely to be subjected to formalized, bureaucratic forms of coordinating mechanisms – including 'contract bureaucracy' – similar to those of the more traditional, in-house, hierarchical structure (Walsh 1992: 77).

Centralization and decentralization

Several authors have identified the traditional emphasis by local authorities on detailed, centralized, procedural and operational control at the expense of strategic overall direction (Audit Commission 1988, 1989a, 1990; Kay and Malone 1989; Stoker 1989; Campbell 1991). Thus, councillors have tended to focus on operational management issues and the production of services rather than strategic needs and consumer requirements, and committees on routine business rather than policy analysis or review. Central services have tended to focus on detailed central control of planning, resources and personnel, rather than on providing corporate direction. Assessing the limitations of this relatively centralized approach, Stoker argues that, in many authorities: 'control is exercised at too detailed a level at the expense of effective resource management and policy direction. Too often, detailed control has been a substitute for deciding what needs to be controlled. Detailed supervision can reflect a lack of willingness to develop staff to exercise management responsibility. The passing of issues up the hierarchy may reflect a lack of clarity about the authority's goals' (Stoker 1989: 33).

Since the 1980s there have been moves towards a more devolved or decentralized management style (Young 1996). High levels of detailed control over operational decision making have been replaced by 'more effective overall control' (Stoker 1989: 34). This involves the delegation of greater

operational responsibilities and more control over finances and other resources to managers at the lowest possible levels, within a framework of
clear organizational and departmental goals, clear service specifications and
performance indicators. Young and Mills reported that, within the three
service departments covered by their survey: 'decentralisation continues
steadily in housing services, with more than two-thirds of authorities now
operating a wholly – or partly – decentralised service . . . almost half of all
Social Services Departments are seeking further decentralisation in the context of a move towards specialisation [of service provision] . . . close to half
of the Local Education Authorities are seeking "maximum feasible decentralisation" to schools under Local Financial Management, which has seen
very large increases in the proportions of schools affected between 1990
and 1992' (Young and Mills 1993: 21–2). A 1988 survey reported an
increase from 12.4 to 26.2 per cent of local authorities who had adopted
devolved budgetary control to unit/centre managers in some or all departments, and some authorities have developed comprehensive cost centre
management systems throughout their organizations (Stoker et al. 1988).

Such trends towards decentralization also involve changes in the role of
central services. Managers operating with CCT have demanded both greater
operational freedom and better value for money from central services,
resulting in close scrutiny of both the functions and cost of this provision
(Kay and Malone 1989; Walsh 1991; Hender 1993). As Stoker (1989: 33)
points out, 'The aim [of devolved management] is not to remove control
over managers but rather to change the nature of the control exercised by
the administrative and political centre of the authority' – to move towards
control systems based on the standardization of outputs, using clearly
defined performance standards, rather than through detailed operational
controls. Correspondingly, the role of the centre should be to move from
an emphasis on centralized routine intervention towards 'more discrim-
inating strategic guidance' (Campbell 1991: 13), both in relation to its
controls over the performance of service departments and in relation to its
own service provider role.

These developments reflect the trends in the private sector towards divisionalized forms of organization. However, increased delegation to departmental and divisional heads and line managers has to be undertaken within
a regulatory framework of centralized monitoring and control of resource
allocation. Similarly, in relation to decentralized service delivery systems,
control of professional work activities through performance outcomes is
likely to be supplemented by operational rules and procedures issued by
the senior management of each department or division. These are designed
to ensure statutory compliance, uniformity and equity of service provision,
plus consistency of standards and practice. In addition, 'rationing' devices
are also likely to be employed to fit the available supply to the potentially
unlimited demand for service. The requirement for public accountability,

through the chief officer to the elected member committees, limits professional autonomy. Johnson (1972) identifies this as a 'state mediation' strategy for controlling practitioner activities. In general, as Mintzberg (1989: 172) points out, 'public service regulations on appointments and the like, as well as a host of other rules, preclude the degree of division manager autonomy available in the private sector . . . appearances and even trends notwithstanding, the diversified configuration is generally not suited to the public and not-for-profit sectors of society'.

It is therefore difficult to avoid the conclusion that decentralization or divisionalization in local authorities involves centralized service and resource utilization performance controls which operate as an 'overlay' over conventional operational bureaucratic controls. This may result in more rather than less bureaucratization. The continuing local public accountability requirements of local authorities can also inhibit the degree of decentralization within partner or co-working arrangements with other agencies. For example, in the context of a community care implementation exercise: 'one particularly striking feature was Health Service complaints about the slowness of local authority decision-making and impatience with the need to "consult politicians"' (Langan and Clarke 1994: 88). Thus, there is a temptation for local government to avoid the dangers of public censure by adopting control mechanisms which become so detailed and prescriptive that they seriously limit the operational decision-making autonomy of unit managers. Increases in their newly devolved *responsibilities* may not be aligned with increases in the levels of decision-making *authority* given to them for resource allocation and service delivery.

Some dilemmas with reform

This chapter has outlined the extensive changes which are occurring in local government. An increasing number of authorities have made, and are continuing to make, significant moves towards 'new' management models, although authorities continue to differ in the extent and nature of the changes which they have implemented. Overall, this 'new' model appears to represent moves from the bureaucratic structures traditionally associated with local authorities – emphasizing direct, detailed hierarchical and relatively centralized control systems – towards more flexible structures with relatively more decentralized control systems. The latter are based on specification of performance outcomes, within a framework of clearly specified organizational values, formalized strategic planning, and devolved management systems. Within the context of the 'enabling', 'competitive' and 'mixed economy' council and the purchaser/provider split, there is also more emphasis on the 'horizontal' regulation of activities. This operates through market/contractual relationships between purchasers and providers within semi-autonomous business units located in authorities as well as with other external agencies.

Yet, as discussed above, such changes may represent more of an *amendment* to, rather than a *replacement* of, traditional hierarchical forms of local government organization. Indeed, many private sector organizations are also frequently reluctant to reduce their reliance on relatively detailed and centralized control systems, especially when operating within rapidly changing/ hostile external environments. This is often for reasons relating to senior management fears of losing power and status, and the practical difficulties of maintaining control over decentralized management units (Mintzberg 1989; Robbins 1990; Hales 1993). Such problems are exacerbated within local government, subject to strong external political control systems, and required to operate within a national institutional framework. As noted earlier, it is also difficult to identify the ultimate outcome or 'product' of local authorities, since the criteria for assessing the effectiveness of local authorities remain essentially political. The extensive external political control of local authorities, legitimated by direct elections, and their statutory obligation to provide specific services require a critical degree of central coordination and control through senior management to the elected members. The latter are responsible – and directly accountable to the public – not only in terms of outcomes (however these may be defined), but also in terms of methods and processes: of 'means' as well as 'ends'. This suggests that local authorities may need to retain, albeit in amended and more flexible forms (including opportunities for involvement by more 'empowered' local communities and citizens in decision-making processes), many elements of the hierarchical bureaucratic organizational form to regulate the activities of both their own staff and external contractors.

There would, then, appear to be a potential tension: between forces encouraging centralized bureaucratization and those compelling local authorities to adopt more flexible, adaptive and post-bureaucratic procedures. Ultimately, there should be a contingent 'fit' between an organization and its environment. It is this that has led to the increasing popularity of contingency theory among local government theoreticians, and to a reaction among senior management against bureaucracy as an appropriate structure to ensure organizational effectiveness. To understand the application of the 'new managerialism' to local government, it is necessary to consider the nature of contingency theory in more detail. This will enable there to be the identification of an analytical framework for a more detailed study of the changes which are taking place.

2 Analysing organizations: theoretical perspectives on the 'new managerialism'

The structure of an organization may be defined as 'the tangible and regularly occurring features which help to shape its members' behaviour' (Child 1984: 4). Characterized by different degrees of complexity, formalism and centralization, structure reflects the pattern of roles and relationships within an organization, and represents the ways in which work is divided into specialist tasks which are then coordinated to ensure goal achievement (Lawrence and Lorsch 1967; Dawson 1986). However, there are great diversities in how organizations may be analysed. Four major schools may be identified, each of which has relevance for the analysis of local authorities as organizations: (a) the 'classical'; (b) 'post-Weberian'; (c) human relations; and (d) contingent. The first three are reviewed in order to provide a context within which the fourth may be understood. Contingency theory is then discussed in more detail, since it is used as the analytical framework for the remainder of this study.

The 'classical'

The 'classical' approach, with its emphasis on bureaucratic organizational forms, has often been seen as particularly relevant for the study of local government, given the latter's traditional association with bureaucracy. F. W. Taylor (1947), Weber (1947) and Fayol (1949) are usually considered to be the key theorists within the 'classical' school, each of whom is concerned with the imposition of 'organisational order and objective reason on institutional whim and personal irrationality' within the organizational design process (Lessem 1989: 183). Each, however, approached organizations from a different perspective. Taylor was an American industrial engineer, committed to improving productivity on the shopfloor through more efficient and 'rational' job design and reward systems. The German philosopher/sociologist Max Weber based his 'ideal type' bureaucracy on assumptions of legal-rationality, which, he considered, epitomized modern capitalism. Fayol, a French industrial engineer and administrator, produced a set of general principles which, he considered, governed the effective design and management of organizations. Yet, as Morgan (1986) points out, they all use the metaphor of the organization as a machine, involving the specification of an ideal blueprint of design for the most efficient means (formal structure) for achieving predetermined ends (organizational goals). As Weber states, 'Experience tends universally to show that the purely bureaucratic type of administration . . . is, from a purely technical point of view, capable of attaining the highest degree of efficiency . . . it is superior to any other form in precision, in stability, in the stringency of its discipline, and in its reliability' (Weber 1991: 124). The distinguishing features of a bureaucracy, as identified by Weber, reflect the 'traditional' local government management systems discussed in Chapter 1. Clearly defined roles are hierarchically structured, with subordinate incumbents accountable to superordinates. Positions are salaried, with a career structure providing opportunities for personal advancement up the hierarchy, while appointments are made on the basis of merit, preferably according to qualifications. Work activities are governed by prescribed systems of rules and procedures, which ensures formal equality of treatment for all those within the organization. These features are reflected in F.W. Taylor's principles of scientific management and Fayol's fourteen principles of administration. Individuals are regarded as depersonalized components of machines, as demonstrated in: Taylor's concept of 'economic man'; Weber's 'Dominance of a spirit of formalistic impersonality – without hatred or passion, and hence without affection or enthusiasm' (Weber 1991: 127); and Fayol's list of universal management roles 'to forecast and to plan, to organise, to command, to coordinate and to control' (Fayol 1949: 5–6).

These 'classical' authors continue to underpin many contemporary approaches to the analysis of public sector organizations. Recent examples include: Burns and Stalker's (1961) mechanistic management system; Handy's (1976) role culture; Deal and Kennedy's (1982) process culture; Hales's (1993) models of 'rationalized' and 'bureaucratic' organizations; Mintzberg's (1983) machine bureaucracy; and the machine metaphors of Watson (1986) and Morgan (1986). However, unlike the classical theorists, such authors identify the bureaucratic model as *but* one of several forms of organization design, rather than a universal prescription to be adopted by *all* organizations. This is because of the 'dysfunctions' of bureaucracy that are emphasized by the post-Weberian and human relations approaches.

The 'post-Weberians'

The works of Merton (1968), Gouldner (1954), Selznick (1966), Blau (1955) and Blau and Scott (1963) are concerned with the 'dysfunctions' of bureaucracies. Much of their work focused around the study of publicly funded organizations in the USA in the 1950s and 1960s, and their conclusions reflect many of the criticisms made by contemporary authors of both the 'traditional' and 'new' forms of local government management (Leach *et al.* 1994; Hood 1995a). Thus, Merton argues that features of bureaucratic structures result in behaviour which can frustrate the achievement of organizational goals. Employees are discouraged from being innovative even when such behaviour could improve goal achievement (for example, more effective service to customers). Rule-governing behaviour can be an end in itself, resulting in 'a displacement of goals . . . an instrumental value becomes a terminal value' (Merton 1968: 253). Failure to achieve organizational goals can result in yet more rules, and thus the situation deteriorates still further. Staff may manifest symptoms of the 'bureaucratic personality', with an 'almost compulsive adherence to institutional norms (in this case bureaucratic rules and regulations)' (Burrell and Morgan 1979: 423).

Alternatively, employees can engage in 'unofficial' or 'informal' forms of behaviour which exist alongside or which may break or bend formal rules and regulations. These can result in the more effective achievement of end goals – or be directed towards the realization of a particular employee grouping's own sectional interests, which may or may not be aligned with formal organizational goal achievement. Thus, Blau and Scott (1963: 35) emphasize that 'the formal structure is only one aspect of organisational social structure and that organizational members interact as whole persons and not merely in terms of the formal roles they occupy'. Blau's (1955) classic study of a public sector law enforcement agency illustrates how employees sought guidance from each other in their handling of cases, despite regulations explicitly forbidding such practices. Blau concludes that such 'informal' practices actually improve operational efficiency. Similarly, Selznick (1966) and Gouldner (1954) argue that the formal structures of rationally designed organizations are always subject to modification by 'informal' human behaviour. Gouldner, for example, argues that effective organizational functioning depends on the extent to which members feel that rules and procedures are legitimate. He identifies three forms of bureaucracy: (a) 'mock bureaucracy', where rules are imposed by an outside agency but which neither workers nor managers accept, such that 'joint violation and evasion of rules is buttressed by the informal sentiments of the participants'; (b) punishment-centred bureaucracy, when rules are initiated by either management or workers, and are 'enforced by punishment and support by informal sentiments of *either* workers or management'; and (c) representative bureaucracy, where rules are agreed by both groups, resulting in 'joint support buttressed by informal sentiments, mutual participation, initiation, and education of workers and management' (Gouldner 1954: 218–19).

As Burrell and Morgan suggest, the work of these theorists draws attention to the fact that the 'reality' of organizational life cannot be seen purely in terms of a machine or a system with a unitary goal. Instead, organizations are aggregates of individuals and groups working towards their various ends. Such a view moves towards a more pluralist perspective with an emphasis upon 'the plural nature of the interests, conflicts and sources of power that shape organizational life' (Morgan 1986: 185). This is reflected, in local government, in terms of interdepartmental professional rivalries, elected member/professional officer differences over questions of service design and delivery and, more latterly, conflicts of interest between purchaser and provider managers operating within quasi-market service delivery systems (Laffin and Young 1990; Leach *et al.* 1994; Walsh 1995).

Thus, power struggles and conflicts between organizational actors are seen as inevitable components of organizational life, and as an intrinsic part of the structure of an organization. However, these authors tend to differentiate clearly between *legitimate* sanctioned power relations (based on the formally defined authority vested in official role structures, exercised through officially prescribed means to achieve officially prescribed organizational ends), and *illegitimate* or 'political' power relationships (operating outside the official organizational structure, using illegitimate means to achieve ends which may be legitimate or illegitimate). In addition, the exercise of such political power tends to be analysed in terms of its functional or dysfunctional consequences for the effective and efficient operation of the organizational system: 'Politics has to do with power, not structure ... politics can be viewed as a form of organisational illness, working both against and for the system. On the one hand politics can undermine healthy processes, infiltrating them to destroy them. But on the other, it can also work to strengthen a system, acting like a fever to alert a system to a graver danger, even evoking the system's own protective and adaptive mechanisms' (Mintzberg 1989: 236).

The 'human relations' approach

In contrast to the 'organizations as machines' model, human relations theorists start from the assumption that individuals 'are people with complex needs that must be satisfied if they are to lead full and healthy lives and to perform effectively in the workplace' (Morgan 1986: 40). The seminal text *Management and the Worker* (Roethlisberger and Dickson 1939) emphasized the importance of informal structures, consisting of unofficial working relationships. They and later writers draw attention to the importance of psychological 'needs' if organizational goals are to be met. Thus, attention has to be given to the functioning of groups and teams within organizations and to the development of management styles which guide and support staff rather than organizing and controlling them (McGregor 1960; Likert 1961). Assumptions of 'self-actualization' focus upon employees' 'self-fulfilment' needs (Maslow 1943), which require organization structures that maximize opportunities for 'challenging' work, including employee involvement in decision making (Argyris 1964; Herzberg 1966). Many of these perspectives underpin the emphasis, within the new public sector managerialism, on empowering and developing teams and individuals within the new, more decentralized, local government structures discussed in the previous chapter.

Systems and contingency theories

In the context of their 'human relations' work, Roethlisberger and Dickson clearly perceived organizations as complex open systems of interrelated parts or subsystems, which interact both within organizations and with their external environments. In summarizing the various 'organization as systems' approaches adopted by many subsequent systems theorists (see, for example, Burns and Stalker 1961; Rice 1963; Katz and Kahn 1966), Burrell and Morgan (1979: 170) define the open systems model as 'a process of mutual influence and interaction between four functional imperatives or subsystems and the environment in which they are located.' These are: (a) the strategic control subsystem, operated by senior management (and elected members in the case of local government), with the purpose of maintaining equilibrium between the organization and its external environment, and determining the goals and direction of the organization to ensure its survival; (b) the operational or productive subsystem, consisting of staff operational roles, which transforms 'raw' inputs into outputs of products or services for customers or clients; (c) the human subsystem, which refers to the needs of individuals occupying functional positions within the organization; and (d) the managerial subsystem, responsible for the function of internal control and coordination of the organization. Contingency theory uses systems concepts of organization in an attempt to identify the 'best fit' or most effective structure for its own particular situation or set of circumstances. Moreover, given that within the contingency approach, different functional specialisms or parts of the organization may well interact with different environments or use different operational processes, it is clear that this differentiation will require varying structures for effective operation of each of these different functional subunits. Integrative mechanisms are then required, to coordinate these functional activities towards achieving overall strategic goals (Lawrence and Lorsch 1967). Thus, different types of organizational structures are required for different situations, both for the various subunits within the organization – different functional departments – and for the organization as a whole. This theory underpins the debate outlined in the previous chapter about the extent to which the management structures of public sector organizations should and do differ from those of the private sector, and about the wisdom of attempting to impose one particular service design and delivery structure – such as market systems – across all local authority service functions, regardless of their different characteristics.

Hales (1993: 152–3) identifies five sets of variables which are most commonly seen by contingency theorists as influencing the structural form of an organization: (a) the size (usually in relation to numbers of employees) and age of an organization; (b) the technology, in terms of (i) the level of sophistication of the technical system and the extent to which it controls work methods, and (ii) the nature of the 'transformation process' (turning inputs into outputs), including the degree of uniformity of inputs and predictability of methods; (c) the environment, such as markets, economy, political and legal systems, and the nature of the external control system (i.e. elected members in the case of local authorities); (d) the organization's goals; and (e) the organization's employees, such as their characteristics in terms of motivation, skills, knowledge and attitudes. All of these factors are taken into account and used by the protagonists in the continuing debate about the extent, and significance, of differences between private and public sector organizations.

In criticizing what they perceive to be over-deterministic elements within these contingency variables, authors such as Child (1972) and Dawson (1986) stress the need to take into account the role played by actors in exercising choice over the contingency factors to which they choose to respond or which they choose to use: 'The "objective facts" of the context do not have an automatic effect on internal operations. They will be noticed and interpreted by individuals, all of whom have their own particular interests to safeguard and their own perceptions of the appropriate strategies and tactics that should be followed ... People not only create the "links" that exist between contingent factors and structure, but they are also creators of the contingency factors themselves' (Dawson 1986: 128). Thus, managers can choose to enter or leave a particular market; they can attempt to create demand for their products and to control and change (through using various techniques such as mergers, joint ventures or lobbying governments about legislation) their competitive environments. Managers' scope for choice may be constrained by particular contingency factors, but such constraints will not necessarily determine their choices for action. Similarly, within the institutional constraints governing the role and function of local government, individual local authorities' elected members and chief officers are able to exercise a degree of choice over the particular service strategies and management systems to be adopted within their particular authorities.

An early example of the use of open systems/contingency approaches to identify particular forms of organization design is the well known study by

Burns and Stalker (1961). They identify a continuum along which organizations can be located, ranging from 'mechanistic' to 'organic'. The mechanistic or bureaucratic system has clearly defined roles of responsibility and task allocation, with hierarchical systems of control and coordination, and there is strict adherence to rules and procedures. The organic system involves fluid definitions of roles and responsibilities, centred on expertise rather than hierarchical positions, with extensive horizontal and interdepartmental information flows, and maximum flexibility of structure to encourage innovation and problem solving by individuals. Bureaucratic structures are seen as appropriate for organizations operating in environments with high degrees of stability and certainty, and where employees have low expectations of discretion and autonomy. Conversely, organic structures are more appropriate for organizations operating within complex and uncertain environments with highly qualified, trained and 'discretionary' staff.

The 1970s and 1980s saw the proliferation of typologies, located towards one or other end of this mechanistic–organic continuum, including the 'traditional' versus the 'new' models of local government management outlined earlier. Private sector typologies, which reflected and informed this 'traditional'/'new' distinction, include: Handy's (1976) 'role' as opposed to 'task' cultures; the 'old model assumptions' compared with the 'new model assumptions' (Kanter 1984); the role (classic) organization in contrast to the entrepreneurial organization (Macrae 1982), or type A and type Z organizations (Ouchi 1981), focusing upon the need for American firms to move from inflexible, hierarchical forms to the adoption of certain features of Japanese companies; and modernist and postmodernist organizations (Clegg 1990). In differentiating between these latter two models, which reflect the ending of the post-war boom in Western economies in the 1970s, Clegg (1990: 181) sees the postmodernist structural form as 'a more organic, less differentiated enclave of organisations than those dominated by the bureaucratic designs of modernity ... Where modernist organisation was rigid, postmodern organisation is flexible. Where modernist consumption was premised on mass forms, postmodernist consumption is premised on niches ... Where modernist organisation and jobs were highly differentiated, demarcated and deskilled, postmodernist organisation and jobs are highly de-differentiated, de-demarcated and multi-skilled.'

Arguably, one of the most influential of these structural typologies – on both private and public sector organizations – was developed by Peters and Waterman (1982) in their seminal book *In Search of Excellence*. Appendix 2 illustrates the application, word for word, of some of these 'excellence' attributes to the 'new management' approach adopted by one particular local authority in the 1980s. Peters and Waterman advocated the replacement of traditional rational/bureaucratic forms of structure by a more flexible, decentralized and task-orientated (essentially organic) approach, which they claimed to be associated with successful performance in a number of 'excellent' companies. Subsequent texts by Peters (Peters and Austin 1985; Peters 1987) emphasize the importance of leadership and culture, customer responsiveness and an organizational orientation towards continuous improvement, innovation and change in order to ensure success within a rapidly changing environment. In the 1990s Peters continues the theme of going 'beyond hierarchies' towards organic forms of 'de-integrating' network structures which transcend both intra- and inter-organizational boundaries found within traditional bureaucratic approaches: 'Most of yesterday's highly integrated giants are working overtime at splitting into more manageable, more energetic units – i.e., de-integrating. Then they are turning round and re-integrating – not by new acquisitions, but via alliances with all sorts of partners of all shapes and sizes' (Peters 1992: 303). Clegg (1990: 181), too, emphasizes the development within his postmodernist organization of 'more complex and fragmentary relational forms, such as subcontracting and networking'.

Organizational forms will undoubtedly continue to differ according to contingent situations and the choices made by their senior managers (Baker 1992; Francis 1994). However, growing numbers of both public and private sector organizations are adopting, albeit in partial forms, many of the features associated with these more flexible 'post-bureaucratic' structures. Clearly, the generic 'new' public management model outlined in Chapter 1 parallels closely these private sector initiatives, with particular variants of the 'new' approach identified by Leach et al. (1994) and Ferlie et al. (1996) placing different emphases on particular aspects of these organizational design features. Indeed, within some local authorities, it can be argued that the adoption of some 'post-bureaucratic' elements – such as the de-integration or contracting out of operational activities – has been developed to a greater extent than in many private sector organizations.

Mintzberg's analytical framework

Mintzberg (1983, 1989) uses the open systems approach to identify five key systems of organizations (both private and public sector), together with subsystems and design parameters. These combine in various ways, resulting in five *configurations* of organization design found within particular situational or contingency contexts. He focuses initially on the two fundamental requirements of all organizational structures: 'the division of labour into distinct tasks, and the achievement of coordination among those tasks' (Mintzberg 1983: 3). Five key mechanisms are used by different types of organizations, and at different levels within organizations, to coordinate work. The simplest is that of (a) *mutual adjustment*, where control of the work rests with the 'doers' (as in very small organizations), or among highly skilled and differentiated specialist professional teams in larger organizations such as local authorities, where the complex nature of the task requires mutual sharing and adaptation. Once organizations grow larger, the mechanism of (b) *direct supervision* tends to be used, where 'one person takes responsibility for the work of others, issuing instructions to them, and monitoring their actions' (Mintzberg 1983: 4). The remaining three methods rely on impersonal mechanisms of *standardization*. Where the nature of work processes can be highly pre-specified or programmed (as in manual assembly line or refuse collection tasks and in routine clerical/administrative functions such as council tax collection), coordination is achieved through (c) *standardization of the work process itself*, by determining to a high degree *how* the work is to be performed. Coordination through (d) *standardization of outputs* focuses not on the how but the *what* of the work process – on the performance outcomes or results of work activities, such as particular profit or output targets. When neither the work process nor work outputs can be standardized, coordination is achieved by standardizing staff competences – by (e) *standardizing the skills and knowledge* required for effective job performance by, for example, the many highly trained and skilled professional staff employed by local authorities. Most organizations will use a combination of all five, with particular concentrations of particular coordinating methods used in particular parts of the organization, in relation to particular forms of work, and also in terms of decisions made about the nature of the control and decision-making systems considered appropriate for a particular organization.

Conceptualizing organizations as configurations of systems, Mintzberg identifies six basic organizational systems or parts (see Figure 2.1). Applying this model to local government, the *strategic apex* is composed of the chief executive and chief officers, who as the senior management team have overall responsibility for running the organization, including the formulation of strategy in the context of carrying out the policies of those in control – the elected members. Given that the nature of this involves a high degree of discretion, coordination is likely to focus around mutual adjustment. The *middle line* – of managers – links the strategic apex to the operating core, thus building up an organizational hierarchy, which may be tall, as in the case of the traditional local government bureaucracy, or flatter, as in other 'new' organizational forms. All five forms of coordinating mechanisms may be found in the middle line, although senior managers' work is likely to be less detailed and more discretionary than that of their junior colleagues. The *operating core* consists of those employees who are responsible for actually delivering services; coordination through one of the three standardization mechanisms is likely to dominate here.

In larger and more complex organizations, such as local authorities, a *technostructure* will be developed, with staff located outside the middle line hierarchy. This consists of such functions as finance, information technology and personnel, where specialist staff are responsible for developing

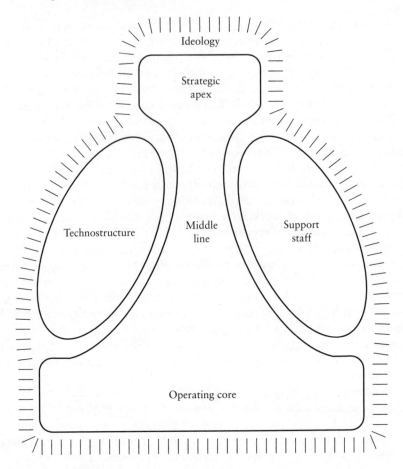

Figure 2.1 Six basic parts of the organization.
Source: H. Mintzberg (1989) *Mintzberg on Management*. New York: The Free Press, 99.

systems to plan and control the work of others. Outside the middle line there may also be a *support structure*, where staff are responsible for providing 'routine' administrative, technical and other 'maintenance' services for line managers and core operating staff. Later, in 1989, Mintzberg added a sixth system – organization *ideology* or culture – which reflects the increasing importance attached to this concept during the 'new' management models of the 1980s and 1990s. He defines organization culture as the 'traditions and beliefs of an organization' (Mintzberg 1989: 98), and stresses the key role played by the 'rich system of values and beliefs' which can also provide an additional *coordination* mechanism.

These parts or systems, in conjunction with their coordinating mechanisms, combine to form five organizational configurations or types of structure:

the machine bureaucracy, the adhocracy, the divisionalized form, the professional bureaucracy and the simple structure. The coordinating mechanisms of the *machine bureaucracy* focus on standardization of work processes. Hence, the key part of the organization is the technostructure, responsible for designing the standardization of work systems. This configuration tends to characterize larger, mature organizations with simple and stable environments and is commonly found in mass production, mass service and public sector organizations. It reflects closely the traditional municipal bureaucracies – along with elements of the professional bureaucracy – which are seen as characterizing local government management in the pre-1980s era. The *adhocracy* represents the opposing configuration, with its emphasis upon 'expertise, organic structure, project teams, task forces, decentralization of power, matrix structure, sophisticated technical systems, automation' (Mintzberg 1989: 209). Coordinating mechanisms of this configuration focus on mutual adjustment, and characterize young industries operating within complex and dynamic environments requiring frequent product changes, such as those found in creative, media and high technology organizations. Although some of the rhetoric of the 'new managerialism' advocates a move towards adhocratic structures for local authorities, the requirements for public accountability through a strategic control tend to preclude the adoption of such a structure in local government.

The *divisionalized* form and the *professional bureaucracy* both represent some dilution of the formal structures of the machine bureaucracy. The former consists of market-based divisions, loosely coupled together under a central headquarters, where divisional managers run their businesses in a semi-autonomous fashion, subject to coordinating mechanisms which focus on the standardization of outputs. The diversified organization form is characteristic of large and mature organizations, and increasingly of public sector organizations, such as local authorities, with diversified product/services markets. It reflects some of the elements of the 'new' local government managerialism in relation to the development of more fluid and flexible, decentralized, local authority structures, with semi-autonomous business units which are expected to develop innovative patterns of service design and delivery – albeit subject to the overall strategic and operational controls exercised by the local authority strategic core. The key part of the *professional bureaucracy* is the operating core, consisting of highly skilled professionals carrying out complex forms of work, with coordinating mechanisms based upon the standardization of skills and knowledge. It is this configuration which, along with elements of the *machine bureaucracy* outlined above, has traditionally characterized local government. The *simple structure* uses direct supervision as its main coordinating mechanism, with the key part of the organization being the strategic apex, reflecting the domination of the chief executive, who exercises strong personal control over activities. This form is characteristic of smaller and young entrepreneurial organizations and of some autonomous departments or divisions within larger organizations – possibly, for example, of some, relatively self-contained units within local government, such as sports and residential/community centres.

Mintzberg's contingency analysis of organizational structures is useful because it provides a clear and systematic ordering framework for identifying (a) the structural features of local authorities and (b) the key features of managerial role prescriptions associated with these different structural forms. Essentially, his five organizational configurations prescribe the different management roles required within them. This organization restructuring, and moves from one configuration to another, will lead to the restructuring of managerial roles as well as to changes in their styles and behaviour.

The nature of managerial work

Mintzberg (1973: 7) claims that the work of the classic management theorists such as Fayol, which focused on the objectives of managerial work, tended to produce 'abstract generalities, devoid of the hard data of empirical research'. This, he argues, generated little knowledge or understanding of the complex reality of managerial work – what activities are undertaken by managers, and why. He uses his own intensive observation of managers' activities plus detailed analysis of their diaries to identify three sets of role behaviour: (a) *interpersonal*; (b) *informational*; and (c) *decision-making*. These provide a useful framework for studying the changing forms of management behaviour required when local authorities attempt to implement new organizational prescriptions (see Figure 2.2).

Mintzberg (1989: 15) defines a manager as 'that person in charge of an organization or one of its subunits'. All managers are vested with formal

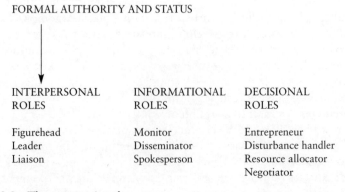

FORMAL AUTHORITY AND STATUS

INTERPERSONAL ROLES	INFORMATIONAL ROLES	DECISIONAL ROLES
Figurehead	Monitor	Entrepreneur
Leader	Disseminator	Disturbance handler
Liaison	Spokesperson	Resource allocator
		Negotiator

Figure 2.2 The manager's roles.
Source: H. Mintzberg (1989) *Mintzberg on Management*. New York: The Free Press, 16.

authority over an organizational unit. Thus, managers fulfil three *interpersonal* roles – *figurehead*, *leader* and *liaison* – derived directly from their formal authority and status. Through these, the manager 'emerges as the nerve center of his or her organizational unit' (p. 17). Within this context, they carry out the three *informational* roles: *monitor*, *disseminator* and *spokesperson*. Information is then used as the basic input into activities associated with managers' *decision-making roles*: *entrepreneur*, *disturbance handler*, *resource allocator* and *negotiator*. These are now described in relation to broader prescriptions of organizational restructuring in local authorities.

Interpersonal roles

The literature describes several significant changes in relation to the manager's *leader* role which may arise when organizations, public or private, undertake organizational restructuring towards the new models outlined above. The leader role refers essentially to the manager's responsibility 'for the work of the people of an organizational unit' (Mintzberg 1989: 16). The development of devolved management systems, and the greater emphasis on the roles of the middle manager as a 'change agent', can lead to an increase in the extent of the accountability, or what Dopson and Stewart (1990a) describe as the 'visibility' of middle managers. This may be reinforced by the use of specific performance targets which make very visible these managers' degree of performance success or failure. The rise of contract management in local authorities, derived largely from compulsory competitive tendering legislation, can also involve a greater degree of 'identification of individual "local" managers' (Stoker 1989: 34), with clear individual accountability for performance achievement against preset performance criteria. Given that managers' own performance will depend, at least in part, on the productivity of their subordinates, the 'managing people' function is taking on increasing importance (Clarke 1996). Moreover, a key feature of the move from 'personnel' to 'human resource management' puts greater emphasis on the responsibility of line managers, rather than personnel specialists, for people management activities (Hutchinson and Wood 1995).

The importance of the *leader* role of the manager, together with the associated concept of entrepreneurialism, has dominated popular management texts of the 1980s (Peters and Waterman 1982; Kanter 1984; Peters 1987). Within the tightly defined structure of the traditional hierarchical bureaucracy, associated with local government management, the power and the authority of the manager is clearly defined. There is also an emphasis on conformity by both managers and subordinates to rules and procedures, as well as on the processes rather than the substance of decision making.

This equates with the 'management' role identified by Zaleznik (1977), and with the 'transactional' leadership style identified by Bass and Avolio (1990). The exercise of any degree of innovative behaviour is limited by formal role constraints and the 'role' culture pervading bureaucratic structures (Handy 1976).

However, the move towards the more organic and loosely structured 'task' orientated organizations associated with the 'new' public management approach requires a more proactive managerial style, corresponding to Zaleznik's (1977) 'leadership' model, and Bass and Avolio's (1990) 'transformational' leadership style. Here, the manager's authority is expected to be based less upon formal role prescriptions and more upon personal expertise and attributes requiring innovative approaches to problem solving. He or she is expected to inspire subordinates through the projection of personal enthusiasm and commitment: 'Every manager must motivate and encourage his or her subordinates, somehow reconciling their individual needs with the goals of the organization' (Mintzberg 1989: 16). They are encouraged to adopt 'empowerment' strategies which create an environment in which new ways are valued and people are encouraged to experiment and take risks. However, local authority middle managers' perceptions of the impact of this 'leadership' model upon their own behaviour can be less positive.

First, 'empowerment' strategies can lead them to feel 'by-passed' (Schlesinger and Oshry 1984). Such strategies can, through their allocation of increased autonomy to their staff, cause them to feel insecure about the continuing need for their own job (Collard and Dale 1989; Collard 1992). They may also be reluctant to delegate when they are held responsible, through performance measures, for achieving targets. Second, many managers appear to prefer 'directive' to 'consultative' management/leadership styles. As Buchanan (1992: 148) points out in a study of semi-autonomous groups: 'Some managers found it "painful" to relinquish their traditional directive management style and moved to other parts of the company.' Scase and Goffee (1989) also found that even in loosely structured organizations, where consultative management styles would be expected to predominate, just over 50 per cent of the middle managers actually preferred this style, while in bureaucratic organizations this figure was only 36 per cent. The reasons for this appear to relate to the generally 'directive' role models pursued by senior managers, and to managers' own 'doubts about their ability to manage through face-to-face negotiation and to exercise more personal forms of leadership' (Scase and Goffee 1989: 76). These concerns reflect the well documented anxieties that many managers display, not only towards consultative leadership styles, but also towards the ambiguous role and vague job descriptions which often characterize more loosely structured organizations (Ellis and Child 1977; Scase and Goffee 1989; Huczynski and Buchanan 1991).

Mintzberg's second interpersonal role, the *liaison* role, refers to contacts outside the vertical chain of command. He found that managers spent as much time with colleagues outside their work units as they did with their own subordinates. Moves from formalized hierarchies to the more flexible open structures associated with the 'new' public sector managerialism can involve an increase in the volume of lateral communications, described as 'networking' by Mueller (1991) and as 'horizontal management' by Barham and Rassam (1989: 109): 'Managers in the future will have to manage an increased and more diverse range of lateral relationships, including those with managers from different functional areas, other business units, project teams, team members, customers, suppliers, joint venture partners, etc.' This increase in lateral communication activities reflects the need for managers to acquire greater knowledge across an increased range of specialist areas, both within and outside their organizations. Unable to rely on formal status and authority in many of these encounters, managers require negotiating skills similar to those needed for effective consultative leadership styles (Kanter 1984). Freed, to an extent, from the traditional organizational communication barriers (where an individual's access to information is specifically defined and constrained by hierarchical position), the manager needs to exercise a high degree of initiative to operate effectively within an informal communication network which can be highly political: 'Easy and unlimited access to information is not always welcome; it challenges authority, undermines power structures and opens to view the daily corporate disasters, most of which are usually kept under wraps' (Barham and Rassam 1989: 108). Moreover, within a context of an increase in interdisciplinary and cross-functional project work associated with moves towards matrix or 'network' forms of organization, managers are increasingly involved in liaison with staff from other disciplines as well as from other organizations (Watkins *et al.* 1992; Wheatley 1992).

The literature has little to say directly about the *figurehead* role – the performance of 'duties of a ceremonial nature', both inside and outside the organization, such as officiating at, say, a retirement party, or attending a public function (Mintzberg 1989: 16). However, given the changes in the extent of public sector middle management leader roles, it can be argued that middle managers may be taking on more responsibility for this, once seen as the preserve of senior managers.

Information roles

Through contacts developed within the liaison role, managers collect, process and distribute a large volume of information, much of which takes oral rather than written form, 'often as gossip, hearsay and speculation' (Mintzberg 1989: 18). Numerous popular management texts – in relation to developments in both the private and public sectors – point to the increasing significance of the information role of the manager, due to a number of developments. First, the pace of change requires them to be more sensitive to the potential effects of political, social, economic and, more recently, ecological/environmental developments (Wilson and Rosenfeld 1990). Second, the moves from hierarchical control to employee involvement require managers to disseminate a much wider range of information about general strategic, as well as operational, issues. Third, the developments in information technology are changing the nature of their roles. Surveying fifteen studies assessing the impact of new technology on managerial roles, Dopson and Stewart (1990a) identify essentially two opinions. On the one hand, computers may replace many middle managers as information gatherers and disseminators: 'the computer provides most of the information flow to top management that was once provided by middle management and can accomplish this task with greater speed, accuracy and selectivity' (Dopson and Stewart 1990a: 5). Hence, the middle management role may disappear altogether. On the other hand, information technology could 'release managers from their traditional coordinating functions to take on new challenges' (p. 8). Freed from the burden of spending time obtaining information, managers can focus on more strategic, longer-term planning issues.

Decisional roles

As Mintzberg points out, managers' informational roles are not an end in themselves; rather, information is the basic input to decision making. 'The manager plays the major role in his or her unit's decision-making system. As its formal authority, only the manager can commit the unit to important new courses of action . . . only the manager has full and current information to make the set of decisions that determine the unit's strategy' (Mintzberg 1989: 19). Within the *entrepreneurial* role, 'the manager seeks to improve his or her unit, to adapt it to changing conditions' (p. 19). The popular management literature of the 1990s places considerable emphasis on bottom-up entrepreneurship as an important aspect of managers' work (Fulop 1991). For example, Peters (1987) urges managers to 'learn to love change', and Kanter (1984: 212) sees middle managers as key change agents in an organization, going beyond the established definitions of their jobs to focus on: '*change*, a disruption of existing activities, a redirection of organisational energies that may result in new strategies, products, market opportunities, work methods, technical processes or structures . . . beyond what it takes to do the routine job, to maintain already established strategies and processes'.

Such transformations in required behaviour are usually accompanied by changes in other aspects of Mintzberg's decisional roles. Thus, it is argued that the role of *resource allocator* is undergoing several significant changes. First, the development of semi-autonomous work groups within local authorities demands extensive delegation, requiring managers to adopt more consultative leadership styles. Second, within the context of moves towards more decentralized decision-making systems and towards control systems focused on standardization of outputs or performance outcomes, organizations are introducing devolved management systems. As Barham and Rassam (1989) and Dopson and Stewart (1988, 1990a) suggest, middle line managers are acquiring new responsibilities for 'staff' functions such as finance and human resource management which had previously been the province of staff specialists: 'Now . . . section managers are responsible for production, are custodians of the technology and are involved in commercial deals, not passively but actively. In short, they manage the total of the business aspects which were functional activities' (ICI executive, Dopson and Stewart 1988: 44). Conversely, specialist managers are requiring increased knowledge and understanding of other functional areas in the organization, including a thorough understanding of the organization's business as well as a good knowledge of marketing and finance.

While some managers, in both the private and public sectors, appear to welcome the broadening of their job roles and the greater freedom to take a wider range of decisions without necessarily involving functional specialists (Dopson and Stewart 1988), others may regret the dilution or removal of some task elements which they had enjoyed. Feelings of isolation and problems with maintaining an adequate level of professional/technical expertise have also been reported among specialist managers who have been moved from centralized functional departments to posts located within decentralized business units based on production/service delivery functions (Hutchinson and Wood 1995). New responsibilities for functions such as human resource management – including responsibilities for implementing formal performance appraisal systems, and for ensuring the provision of suitable training and development programmes – require additional managerial skills and time. Yet many managers have to reconcile these demands with a requirement to achieve financial and other quantitative performance targets against which their performance will be predominantly assessed and rewarded (Kinnie 1991; Purcell 1992).

Devolved decision making involves the allocation of responsibility to middle and front-line managers, who become accountable for achieving results against product/service delivery and resource utilization targets (Henley *et al.* 1992). However, the term 'to devolve' simply means to transfer or to pass over, and it is important to distinguish between the devolution of *responsibility* for various functions to middle managers, and the delegation or decentralization of decision making *authority*. The latter may or may not form part of the devolved management process (Horngren and Sundem 1993). Thus, for example, with regard to devolved budgetary management, managers may be held responsible for, and their performance assessed against, financial and service/product delivery targets. However, they may lack the authority to exercise control over key budget elements such as staffing, or using underspends in one area to finance additional expenditure in another (Solomons 1965). Hence, control systems, especially in periods of organizational retrenchment, may become tighter and more centralized, threatening a diminution in the levels of operational decision-making autonomy allocated to managers under a more decentralized system (Hales 1993). The manager's degree of freedom to manage within the framework of performance outcome targets and criteria can become constrained by increased levels of action planning and control over work processes as well as over outputs (Cameron *et al.* 1987; Robbins 1990; Smith 1990).

Mintzberg's two other decision-making roles include those of *disturbance handler*, when managers have to deal with unforeseen or unexpected pressures, and *negotiator*, when the manager spends time in discussions with colleagues outside his or her immediate work unit. Both of these are likely to assume more significance for middle managers as local authorities adopt new 'parallel' forms of structure, including profit centres, business units and project teams, where managers are likely to become increasingly involved in 'horizontal management'. The transactions required between these teams and units require managers to negotiate with the members of other work units and, through the development of 'boundaryless' organizations (Francis 1994), with members of other organizations.

Thus, it is clear that the changes in organizational design in local authorities require significant changes in middle manager behaviour across all three of Mintzberg's managerial role sets: the *interpersonal, informational* and *decisional*. However, as his contingency model of management suggests, the precise nature of these changes will vary according to: particular types of organizations, including public/private sector differences; the location of a particular manager's role within an organization; and managers' own personal preferences. A key component of the 'new' more decentralized local authority organizations involves giving middle managers a greater degree of discretion over how they carry out their responsibilities. This requires, in turn, greater reliance on 'self- or mutual regulation, intrinsic rewards and an achievement ethic . . . rewards that emphasise the intrinsic satisfaction of individual autonomy, team work and task accomplishment' (Hales 1993: 158). As expectancy theorists such as Vroom (1964) suggest, managers will differ in the extent to which they perceive such rewards as being available from their restructured roles, the extent to which they seek to realize such rewards from their work and the degree of work satisfaction they derive from such rewards.

This chapter, then, has reviewed some theoretical approaches to the study of organizations and managerial roles – in both the private and public sectors. Within this context, it has focused on contingency theory as a perspective according to which organizational change can be analysed. Mintzberg's model of organizations and managerial roles has been discussed, since obviously changes in the former will impact upon the latter. Contingency theory provides an appropriate framework for understanding the nature of change within local government and how this is affecting managerial roles. Clearly, the 'new managerialism' – if it is to be successfully implemented – requires fundamental changes in the ways in which managers execute their duties and achieve their goals. There are, then, a number of required *role prescriptions* associated with this 'new' approach. It is now necessary to determine how managers are *supposed* or *ought* to behave according to these prescriptions associated with the doctrines of the 'new managerialism' in local government.

3 Changing managerial roles in local government: the new prescriptions

Towards the 'new managerialism'

The shift from 'traditional' to 'new' forms of local government structure requires significant changes in the prescribed roles and behaviour of middle managers if the aims of these 'new' management systems are to be realized. This involves a fundamental redefinition of managerial roles, frequently described as a move from 'professionalism' to 'managerialism' and/or from 'administration' to 'management' (Flynn 1993). In terms of the 'professional' aspects of local authority management, middle managers within the traditional local government structures and systems are seen as operating with a largely 'professional' orientation within specialist departments responsible for service provision, such as social services, education and planning. Flynn describes such an approach as involving three key features: (a) professionals are managed by other professionals, who are largely autonomous from management structures imposed from outside the profession; (b) service provision is governed by standards and codes of 'professional practice'; (c) professionals – not their clients – have expert knowledge as to how to solve problems. In other words, professional services are provided *to* people, not *with* them (Walsh 1989).

It is, of course, important to emphasize that this professional ideal was never as fully realized in local government as it was, perhaps, in the 'traditional' professions such as law and medicine. Because of requirements of public accountability – through departmental chief officers to committees of elected councillors – most local government professionals tend to exercise what Rowbottom (1974) describes as 'delegated discretion' rather than professional autonomy. Nevertheless, professional staff have tended to seek to maximize their areas of autonomy – to varying degrees of success, depending in part on the nature of their historical development and their relative status (Johnson 1972; Ackroyd 1996).

Conflicts can exist between professionals' 'cosmopolitan' orientations – to national professional codes of standards, values and practices – and the more 'local' orientations – to the interests/objectives of their employing organization – of their managers (Gouldner 1957). Under 'traditional' local government management systems, the managerial (as opposed to the professional supervision and regulation) functions of the departmental 'professional' middle managers tended to involve largely 'administrative' activities. Managerial roles involved essentially 'administering systems which are in a steady state' within a departmental framework of tight budgetary and procedural controls (Flynn 1993: 191). Managers had little or no control over, or responsibility for, the management of finance and other resources, since these were centrally controlled by finance, personnel and other departments (Campbell 1991). This old-style municipal administration operated essentially within 'an organisation obsessed with budgets and procedures and forgetting about the users', and tended to be dominated by rigid adherence to professional standards and prescriptions, with little regard for community/consumer needs and involvement in service planning and delivery (Flynn 1993: 191–2).

During the 1980s and 1990s, local authorities were encouraged to move away from this traditional system based on 'administration', towards the new 'managerialist' approach associated with the new public management models. This 'managerialism' was based on the view that 'managers have "the right to manage", which means that they should be in control of the organisations which they run, and that they should be very proactive . . . It is this view of managers as controllers which underlies many of the managerial reforms in the public sector' (Flynn 1993: 191; Farnham and Giles 1996). In the context of moves towards divisionalized forms of structure and the development of semi-autonomous 'provider' business units, managers are expected to acquire responsibilities for new functional areas such as finance, personnel and other resource management. They are required to become proactive and outward- rather than inward-looking, providing responsive services which meet 'purchaser' and end-user/local community needs/demands (Stewart 1988b; Stoker 1989; Kerley 1994).

Professional orientations, within the context of more formalized strategic planning systems, are required to move towards a more 'local' focus, corresponding to Johnson's (1972) 'patronage' control strategy or Reed's (1996) 'organizational professionals', where employing organizations exercise control over professionals' work activities. Powerful clients – local authority purchasers – define service objectives and, increasingly, the scope and nature of professional service delivery. Within performance management systems, both middle managers and core professional staff are required to accept 'calls for greater accountability to politicians and managers' (Stoker 1989:

64). Moreover, 'professional expertise, traditionally associated with the delivery of services, will no longer be an adequate substitute for managerial competence. Professional staff will more and more seek to augment their specialist knowledge by management training' (LGMB 1993b: 13; Watkins *et al.* 1992). Similarly, the role of middle managers is expected to focus less on professional supervision, and more on the new 'managerialist' aspects of their roles. Chief officers' roles will tend to move towards that of the 'engaged professional advocate': 'Instead of the earlier advocate stance of Olympian detachment and assumed indifference to local politics, the contemporary professional advocate adopts a stance of engagement in and concern for local political processes, and will generally work comfortably enough with a council whose political persuasion strongly favours the development of the particular service' (Laffin and Young 1990: 111). Essentially, this new managerialist model operates on the assumption that differences between local government and the private sector are disappearing in the sense that managing, say, a social services department is basically the same as running a company.

The formally prescribed changes required in managerial behaviour according to the new managerialism model are now analysed. It is important to stress that the emphasis is on behaviour that middle managers are *supposed* or *ought* to be adopting. The literature on local government provides little evidence about the extent to which *real* behavioural changes are actually taking place on the part of these managers. The distinction between prescribed and real behaviour change is important because, as Ferlie *et al.*'s (1996) 'transformational change' suggests, adaptations in *actual* behaviour and attitudes as well as the *prescribed* 'surface' changes in structures, systems and roles are required if the 'new management' model is to be seen as representing real or 'transformational', as opposed to merely 'rhetorical', change within local government management systems.

Interpersonal roles

The figurehead role, 'the performance of duties of a ceremonial nature' (Mintzberg 1973: 150), has always been prominent in local authorities. Thus, 67 per cent of chief executives consider that representation of the authority's interests on formal occasions constitutes an essential aspect of their role (Norton 1991). Clarke (1988: 8) also mentions the importance of the 'ritual function in the external environment' of chief officers, and the growth in public relations activities associated with the more 'responsive' local authority is likely to increase the significance of these activities on the part of senior managers (Franklin 1988). Within the context of increased decentralization of decision-making powers to lower level managers, and the growing importance of customer relations, it can be argued that middle managers will also be required to assume more responsibility than was hitherto the case for these ceremonial duties.

The changes prescribed for middle managers' leadership roles under the 'new management' approaches arise from the increased devolution of responsibilities to these managers. It is argued that they are becoming increasingly 'visible' in terms of demonstrating results. They are required to be more accountable for performance against preset targets, and the broadening of their roles as *managers* gives them added responsibilities in such matters as personnel and finance. In general, the concept of leadership in local government is relatively new. Local authorities' tradition of 'administration' rather than 'management' tended to emphasize a largely administrative role for middle managers, of essentially responding to the demands of senior managers. A number of writers now emphasize the importance of the leadership role for first line managers (LGTB 1984), and for all managerial staff (Buckland and Joshua 1992; Clarke and Stewart 1990; Hadley and Young 1990; Issac-Henry and Painter 1991; LGMB 1991, 1993b), as well as for chief executives (Norton 1991) and senior officers (LGTB 1984, 1988a; Jackson and Robson 1989). The concept of this new leader role associated with the new managerialist approaches tends to reflect private sector developments towards more 'transformational' leadership styles (Storey 1992). Thus, Clarke and Stewart (1990: 26) stress: 'there will be a premium on leadership . . . at all levels in the organisation . . . The ability to inspire and motivate staff to innovate and develop service and to be their own agents for change, as well as to understand and marry the needs and interests of service users with those of the organisation and its personnel are essential.' They identify the need for managers to develop both the *task* (setting performance standards, and clarifying the basic values underpinning the authority's policies and approaches to service delivery) and the *people* components of the leadership role: that is, motivating staff and evaluating their performance, with an emphasis on communication, staff development and providing a 'role model of personal standards for staff to follow.' Similarly, the LGMB (1993b) stresses the importance of both 'leadership' and 'people management/relationship' skills for managers throughout the organization, and defines these as follows:

Leadership skills – the ability to demonstrate leadership – both 'Individual' Leadership and 'Team' Leadership, to inspire, guide, motivate individuals and teams. 'Strategic Leadership' in setting and maintaining organisational direction and Leadership of 'Change' to maintain momentum and enthusiasm in change efforts – Well developed people management/relationship skills – Skills to relate to, motivate, develop, appraise, empower and release potential of staff. Ability to develop and lead a team. The personal flexibility to act as both a team member or team leader. Ability and willingness to delegate – An ability and enthusiasm to manage diverse workforces with proven commitment to positive action and equality.

(LGMB 1993b: 23–5)

Hadley and Young (1990: 140) describe the transformational-style 'synergic' leadership approach adopted by East Sussex for managers throughout the authority, especially at lower levels, involving 'the underlying notion of creating conditions in which increased scope for the growth and development of the worker and team manager carries the final responsibility for the performance of his (her) team. In this sense, his (her) role in ensuring at least the minimum required standards of performance is more negotiable within the team than the standards themselves and his stance has to be directive.' However, the extent to which these ideas are being implemented by local authorities, and the degree of any real change in middle managerial behaviour, remains uncertain.

The local government literature prescribes increased levels of activity in the liaison roles of middle managers because of moves from 'vertical' hierarchical to more 'horizontal' market and/or 'network' forms of organization. Thus, managers are exhorted to 'develop the abilities to build and maintain complex relationships with a wide variety of key people'. (LGMB 1993b: 23). In the context of developing a more flexible 'learning organization', Clarke and Stewart (1988: 12) emphasize the need to 'actively encourage horizontal as much as vertical communication and activity' on the part of managers. When accompanied by devolved management systems, which encourage middle managerial innovation and a 'willingness to challenge traditional thinking', such initiatives increasingly include cross-organizational and inter-organizational activities such as participation in working parties, secondments, involvement with professional associations, etc. (LGTB 1988a). Middle managerial roles are increasingly seen as involving work within a context of interdepartmental and interdisciplinary groups and project teams. This often requires more understanding and knowledge of additional specialist areas, more contacts with managers from different functional areas, and 'intelligence and information systems which cross professional boundaries'. (LGTB 1988a: 64; Watkins *et al.* 1992).

In the context of the 'enabling', 'competitive' and 'mixed economy' council, differentiation on the basis of professional specialisms is being supplemented by a greater degree of functional differentiation: 'between purchaser and provider, customer and contractor, strategic and operational, the generalist managers and the professional' (LGMB 1993b: 11). This involves middle managers in increased liaison activity between such functions, including contacts with voluntary/private/other public sector agencies located outside as well as within the local authority as well as with a wider range of customers and local community groups. The liaison role of the middle manager is seen as crucial in ensuring effective implementation of

market/networking forms of organization, since 'inter-organisational partnerships will founder if middle management do not share a sense of commitment to joint working' (Brooke 1989: 55). In the context of a 'new,
outward-directed' local authority managerial style, there is an increasing
need for building and maintaining external relationships. As Hadley and
Young (1990: 11–12) state, 'Management involves community leadership
and the creation and maintenance of networks within the authority's social
and economic environment. Management will help give voice to public grievance and suggestion, and enhance the ability of citizens to acquire leverage
not only in their dealing with the authority itself, but with other public
service providers operating in the locality.' The purpose of these liaison
activities is to gather, process, exchange and disseminate information which,
in turn, is used to support the manager's decision-making role.

Informational roles

The prescribed enhancement of the leader role, in conjunction with an increased use of strategic approaches and performance management systems,
suggests increases in 'vertical' information and communication flows, especially with the growing use of information technology. Within the context
of examining the potentially radical impact of computerized technology on
these information systems and, ultimately, on organizational structures,
Tapscott and Caston (1993) suggest that information flows have three
main functions: (a) to improve work group performance; (b) to ensure
effective organizational integration; and (c) to enhance inter-organizational
coordination. These critical shifts in the use of IT enable organizations 'to
have a high-performance team structure, to function as integrated businesses
despite high business unit autonomy, and to reach out and develop new relationships with external organisations – to become an "extended enterprise"'
(Tapscott and Caston 1993: 14). A survey by the Society of Information
Technology Managers (1991) suggests growing investment in more sophisticated IT systems by local authorities. These are increasing authorities'
capacity for achieving integration of various information systems across
the organization and, although to a lesser extent, with other agencies: 'most
authorities now have a considerable infrastructure of terminals and personal
computers in their offices which could be used for electronic communication, and facilitate access by one part of the authority to information held
in another ... Authorities now need to work more closely with health
authorities, housing associations, voluntary associations and private companies. They need to examine the information systems and facilities which
are available to them for communicating and exchanging information with
these agencies' (LGMB 1993c).

The emphasis on core values and policies emanating from the centre, and on strong leadership at all levels of the local authority, requires effective dissemination of these through middle managers to front-line staff. These managers are required to make use of various improved communication systems, including the use of e-mail, newsletters, staff presentations, briefing sessions, training programmes, meetings etc., to 'sell the changes to their work-teams'. The 'well managed' authorities in one study all emphasized the need for 'a commitment to informing, developing and motivating staff, to create the climate of identity and motivation necessary to deal with the pressure of change' (Leach *et al.* 1993: 20). Opportunities for feedback are required to ensure realization of the 'caring, sharing' employer image, and to encourage commitment to change among lower level managers and staff. The advent of strategic planning and devolved management systems also requires the dissemination of business plans, performance targets and re- source allocation models which govern middle manager decisions about service planning and delivery. Thus, in Stevenage, 'Managers are expected to monitor and review constantly the way in which their services are pro- vided to ensure that service delivery and service development are progres- sing according to plan and that the quality of service, as laid down in service specifications, is achieved. The development of the Council's information technology system has made possible the generation, dissemination and use of key information to underpin these processes' (LGMB 1993d: 44). In addition, purchaser managers will be expected to obtain operational informa- tion about service delivery issues, such as customer satisfaction, in order to contribute to the strategy formulation process.

The purchaser/provider split has also added to middle managers' liaison and information roles. Figure 3.1 illustrates the complexities of these in market/network service delivery systems. Thus, purchasing managers, hier- archically accountable to senior management in the strategic planning pro- cess, are required to liaise with referral agents (for example, in social services, with the NHS, education authorities, the police, housing agencies, etc.) and with the general public, as well as with service providers, to draw up service specifications and to monitor their delivery. Provider managers, also hier- archically accountable to senior management, must be responsible to pur- chasers for delivering services according to agreed specifications. This involves information exchanges with consumers/users, the processing of referrals from other agencies, and contacts with the general public.

As an LGMB (1993c: 19) publication points out, a more open 'informa- tion' culture has to be developed within authorities, to ensure that managers and their staff recognize the value of information, and become committed to using it effectively. However, a number of barriers can militate against this.

First, the use of computerized technology can pose problems for some managers whose attitude towards IT can vary between those of 'luddites' and 'enthusiasts'. Assessing the impact of IT systems, Davis-Smith (1987/8:

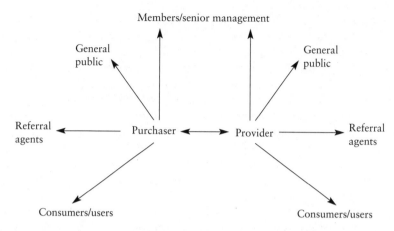

Figure 3.1   Purchaser/provider networks.
Source: Adapted from E. Scrivens (1991) 'Is there a role for marketing in the public sector?', *Public Money and Management*, Summer, 21.

unnumbered pages) states 'The role of middle managers may change quite significantly because of the way in which information-handling develops.' She contrasts the potentially positive aspects, involving opportunities for more challenging and satisfying work, with the more negative aspects (from the manager's point of view) where IT can be used 'to impose greater control and tighter checks on employees' outputs . . . loss of job security and prospects . . . fears of deskilling, loss of job satisfaction and an erosion of status and power.'

Second, in both market and the more traditional hierarchical and departmentalized forms of organization, the creation of an 'information' culture requires significant attitude changes towards seeing information as 'corporate property' rather than as the jealously guarded property of particular individuals or departments (LGTB 1990a). Information can be an important source of power and individuals may resist what they perceive as a threatening loss of control over access to 'their' information, resulting in 'authoritarian barriers to lateral or systemic thinking' (Hood 1991: 14–15). The purchaser/provider split can also form a barrier, inhibiting free information exchange, with the ever-present risk of the 'contract bureaucracy' (Walsh 1992). As Hulme (1994: 56) illustrates, contract regulation, especially under conditions of uncertainty and only limited competition (quasi-markets), can result in 'selfish' behaviour involving the withholding of information, rather than 'collaborative behaviour' where both parties agree to share information. 'Opportunistic' forms of behaviour – 'the guileful pursuit of self-interest' (Levačić 1993: 45) – can arise, where one party can take advantage of differential access to information or to market power to exploit or mislead the other, or to misrepresent intentions. This is particularly likely to emerge where quasi-market transactions are subject to high levels of certainty (as with many white-collar/professional services) – where powerful and large corporate purchasers can manipulate providers.

Third, professional staff can be reluctant to share information. 'To many professionals, "information is power" and "hoarding information" is one of their less worthy characteristics' (Watkins *et al.* 1992: 87). Such tendencies can restrict the information provided to multidisciplinary groups within which, increasingly, they and their managers are likely to be working.

Fourth, organizational 'political' pressures and managerial desires to maintain power and status, combined with technical deficiencies in information systems design and IT applications, can also inhibit internal information flows up and down the organization. Despite various initiatives undertaken by some authorities to identify employee views about the effectiveness of their communication systems, Skelcher (1992) found that many employees were dissatisfied with the quality and quantity of downward communication. They felt they had to rely too much on the informal 'grapevine' rather than the preferred source of meetings and discussions directly with their managers. Similarly, the majority of the respondents in an LGMB (1994a) employee attitude survey were a little more likely to feel that they received at best limited information (53 per cent) than they were to feel fully (75 per cent) or fairly well informed (37 per cent). More senior officers and/or managerial staff tended to be the most critical. Over 60 per cent felt that too little information was provided on the reasons behind major decisions and decisions taken by councillors, rising to over 70 per cent on 'plans for the future'.

Opportunities for upward communication also appear to be limited in many authorities; Skelcher (1992: 8, 11) suggests that 'employees often experience communication as a one-way process – downwards', with inadequate channels for conveying their views about service delivery and other issues upwards; 'when there is an opportunity to express opinions and ideas they seem to disappear into a vacuum since no feedback is given on what has subsequently happened.' Just over two-thirds of the LGMB (1994a) survey respondents expressed similar views. In addition, Skelcher found that many employees felt that their managers were poor at communicating information about the goals of work units and how these related to the overall organization strategy.

Thus, while many publications stress the importance of improved vertical and horizontal information/communication flows, it appears that progress may be limited within many authorities. Contributory factors are likely to involve the attitudinal/power/status problems mentioned above, together with the tensions arising from market regulation of service provision, insufficient training provision for enabling managers to function effectively within an 'information culture' and technical problems arising from inappropriate communication/information design. Essentially, however, managers themselves, within the new 'information culture', are increasingly required to accept responsibility for managing their own information, developing an understanding of the IT facilities available and becoming more competent in using facilities such as personal computers, 'which are fast becoming standard in the offices of all local authorities' (LGMB 1993c: 20).

Decision-making roles

Managers' interpersonal and informational role activities are not ends in themselves; they form the basis on which managers make and implement decisions about their work unit strategy and action (Mintzberg 1989). Corresponding to changes in the interpersonal and information roles outlined above, there is a shift in many local authorities towards devolving operational decision-making powers to middle managers. Devolved management systems involve the allocation of (usually operational) decision-making responsibility and/or authority to line managers who become accountable for resource management. Additional *responsibility* is not always aligned with increased *authority*; for example, managers may be held responsible for managing their budgets, but they may lack the authority to control budget elements such as staffing without seeking approval from senior managers. The devolution of budgetary *authority* involves at least a degree of organizational decentralization which occurs when 'the authority to make specified decisions is passed down to units and people at lower levels in the organization's hierarchy' (Child 1984: 146).

Local authorities are increasingly adopting devolved management systems, although the extent to which this involves the devolution of authority as well as responsibility is not always clear (Stoker *et al.* 1988; Young and Mills 1993; Leach *et al.* 1994). For example, in Berkshire, middle managers have been empowered to make more operational decisions concerning their line units, including the deployment of financial, personnel and other resources. They have become accountable for their performance against various performance criteria within a framework of clear organisational policies (Geeson and Haward 1990).

The aim of devolved management is to enable middle managers to improve the efficiency of their resource utilization, and to achieve more flexible and creative service provision which is more responsive to local community needs and demands: 'their energies can be focused upon getting on with the job rather than being diverted by elaborate bureaucratic rituals or protracted lobbying and negotiations with senior management for the resources they want but do not have' (Hoggett and Bramley 1989: 10). Moreover, given that managers tend to value opportunities for independent thought and action (Stewart 1982; Scase and Goffee 1989), budgetary devolution is also intended to enhance motivation and job satisfaction as well as to strengthen organizational commitment.

The introduction of decentralized resource management systems requires changes within organizations' financial and other management control mechanisms. Traditional forms of 'detailed control', exercised through the direct supervision and standardization of work processes of bureaucracies associated with pre-1980s local government administration, are required to give way to 'more effective overall control'. Here, the emphasis is on managers themselves taking greater responsibility for controlling their own, and their colleagues', performance (Stewart 1988a; Stoker 1989; Lowndes 1992).

In practice, however, many local authorities are reluctant to reduce their reliance on detailed and centralized control systems for reasons associated with senior managers' fears of losing power as well as because of public accountability requirements. Increased managerial autonomy over operational decision-making is continually under threat from local authorities' internal procedural rules and regulations; from the possible centralization of the purchasing role in market approaches to service delivery; and from tight and detailed specification of work processes within contracts and service level agreements which specify the work to be undertaken by providers. Such tendencies are likely to be exacerbated in local government by the public accountability requirements for controls over 'both means and ends ... to explain and justify actions taken' (Stewart and Ranson 1988: 4); the high political sensitivity of certain operational areas; the uncertainty of the relationship between the process of providing and the actual outcomes of services such as in child care; and external threats such as central government expenditure cuts (Flynn 1993). Echoing these concerns, Stoker et al. (1988: 64) and Hoggett and Bramley (1989) query the extent to which, apart from education, devolved resource management is likely to include the delegation of authority as well as responsibility below chief officer level, to middle managers. 'Given the problems and difficulties of breaking from traditional, hierarchical, detailed and centralised systems of control, there are good grounds for being cautious about whether the growth in decentralised resource management systems represents a significant shift towards a new style of management and organisation within local government' (Stoker et al. 1988: 64).

Four key elements can be identified within the devolution process which have the potential for either enhancing or constraining middle management autonomy. First, there is the extent to which it involves the alignment of managerial *authority* with management *responsibility*. Public sector middle managers in Dopson and Stewart's (1990) study tended to feel that they were given 'responsibility' rather than 'power' under the new management system. Second, financial control systems can operate to enhance managers' decision-making powers, through the use of mechanisms focused on controlling budget totals, or to constrain these powers through systems focused on controlling budget details (Audit Commission 1989a). Key issues here include the extent to which detailed and complex rules dilute the manager's authority to vire between budget heads and to use savings achieved on one expenditure head to increase spending on another. External controls imposed by central government legislation can also constrain managers' freedom to deploy resources – especially in the context of generating new business and becoming more 'entrepreneurial'. The mechanisms required to regulate contractual relations between purchaser and provider managers can 'easily become proceduralised and bureaucratised with variation orders for any change, and a plethora of work orders and invoices' (Walsh 1992: 77).

Third, managers require easy access to *specialist* staff (such as finance and personnel) and to efficient information systems to maximize their control and management of their resources. As outlined above, information systems may be inadequate, and specialist staff may find it difficult to make the transition to their new roles of supporting the line managers' business operations. They may experience role conflict in attempting to reconcile two potentially conflicting demands: ensuring adherence of line managers to corporate standards, policies and procedures, while, at the same time, trying to be responsive to the latter's business needs (Rawlinson and Tanner 1990). Fourth, managers require training, which is not always forthcoming, in new financial, personnel and contract management skills if they are to exercise their new devolved responsibilities efficiently and without undue strain (Watkins *et al.* 1992).

Towards entrepreneurial management

Reflecting private sector developments, the entrepreneurial role of managers – 'perceiving the changed circumstances and formulating the organisation's response to them; developing a vision' – is seen as the cornerstone of a successful transition to more effective local authority management systems (Thompson 1992: 39). Similarly, the LGMB (1993b: 24) emphasizes the importance of managers developing 'Change management skills – the ability to identify opportunities, initiate or respond to change, maintain momentum, and monitor progress in change efforts. Have a positive attitude towards change, and obtain the commitment of others to change efforts. A capacity to cope with ambiguity, uncertainty and change, and view problems as opportunities or challenges.' Managers are expected to be 'entrepreneurial in the sense of constantly looking for opportunities to innovate and find new ways of working to improve the effectiveness of the organisation' (Clarke and Stewart 1988: 31). Issac-Henry and Painter's survey of seventeen authorities provides several examples of a deliberate adoption of this approach. For example, Gloucestershire County Council attaches considerable importance to developing the entrepreneurial role of *all* managers, involving a 'bias for action' through the devolution of decision-making responsibilities and 'innovativeness; cultivating a climate where new ideas are actively encouraged and embraced' (Issac-Henry and Painter 1991: 74). In a similar vein,

Tower Hamlets' decentralized neighbourhood office structure has attempted to create an environment with 'opportunities for individuals to take initiatives and experiment with new ways of working and service delivery ... Entrepreneurial and active officers have opportunities to create new agendas, schemes and projects – to become the sort of "champions" Peters and Waterman want to nurture in the private sector' (Lowndes and Stoker 1992a: 145).

Harrow and Willcocks (1990) suggest that there are limits on the extent to which the less bureaucratic and more flexible organizational structures, necessary for the full exercise of managerial innovative and risk-taking powers, can be adopted by local authorities. The regulatory frameworks necessary for ensuring public accountability and equity of treatment of clients 'cut across the opportunism and risk at the heart of entrepreneurial activity', and continue to limit the extent to which local authority managers can experiment, risk-take and innovate (Harrow and Willcocks 1990: 296). These authors suggest that the adoption of more cautious 'low risk small win' rather than 'high risk big win' change strategies are more suited to public sector institutions 'if the goals remain what they are commonly held to be, namely greater efficiency, better management and better service' (p. 301). Basically, the scope of local authority middle managers' innovative activities is likely to be restricted to incremental, as opposed to radical, innovations within a framework of clear corporate policies and rigorous control systems.

Entrepreneurial management also requires adequate resourcing if it is to prove effective. Lowndes and Stoker (1992a: 145) describe the 'marketplace' approach adopted by Tower Hamlets; 'where resources and policy instruments are given to the most successful entrepreneurs.' However, certain departments, such as nurseries, had a 'cinderella' status which inhibited the allocation of additional resources to their officers; moreover, officers differed in the extent to which they possessed the commitment and entrepreneurial skills necessary for generating new ideas, and gaining the resources and policy authorizations needed to implement them. Most importantly, local authorities – unlike the private sector – are dependent on increasingly limited public funding and spending constraints. They are subject to legislative constraints on external trading which restrict the income they can generate by exploiting new market opportunities. In addition, the purchaser/provider split, with precisely defined service specifications, may inhibit provider managers' scope for introducing innovations. The agreement of the purchaser managers will be required. Purchaser managers, separated from the 'coalface' of service provision, may lack first-hand knowledge of customer needs/demands, thus reducing their awareness of the need for change (Cochrane 1994; Langan and Clarke 1994). Nevertheless, it can be argued that, within these constraints, changes in middle management roles in many local authorities reflect a more entrepreneurial approach. This is well represented in the case study of change in the structure and management system of East Sussex Social Services Department (Hadley and Young 1990) and provides an interesting example of the tensions which can arise from the introduction of devolved and 'entrepreneurial' roles for middle managers.

The first stage in this department focused on the development of strong centrally driven policies to 'gain control of the organization' and to introduce key structural changes. Managers were required to compete for all management posts in the new structure. This often meant a painful transition to 'non-managerial' positions for those who failed to secure a new management post. A clear system of delegation and accountability was introduced for the managers of units, including, at a later stage, devolved budgets. Operational instructions included clear prescriptions about the particular kinds of work, policies and programmes of services to be provided for each client group. Management control and information systems were established, involving measures to assess the performance of each work unit. The concentration on financial and other quantitative measurements was often criticized for implicitly ignoring what many managers perceived as the more important qualitative 'outcomes' of their service provision. While some managers felt 'hemmed in' by these information demands and performance targets, others appreciated the chance to evaluate and justify their achievements. Lastly, there was 'less visible, but even more important, the creation of a managerial culture emphasising commitment to the goals of the organisation and loyalty to the director' (Hadley and Young 1990: 199). A residential sector strike in the early 1980s was seen by the director as providing 'the ultimate test of the loyalty of his managers as well as an example of how conflict and crisis can present opportunities for accelerating change' (p. 203). Structural changes also included new area-based teams combining different professional skills, and extensive programmes of training and related project work to establish the new culture. The strong central leadership by the director raised mixed feelings. Some managers felt inhibited by his style from expressing doubts or criticisms about senior management policies, and disliked the atmosphere of 'yesness' which tended to prevail in meetings; others felt 'the experience has been ... positively liberating both in terms of one's personal approach to one's work and in terms of enabling a whole multitude of initiatives' (p. 203).

These developments clearly represent moves towards both closer central direction *and* increased local discretion. Once the central management policies and controls had been consolidated, the second phase of increasing devolution to the front-line managers and staff extended local discretion, where 'within the policy guidelines laid down by the authority, front-line teams could increasingly take over responsibility for the shaping of integrated and responsible services suited to their different localities' (Hadley and Young 1990: 205). Many examples are provided in the case study of innovative and more responsive methods of service delivery arising from the increased devolution of authority. A previous emphasis on control through centralized systems was 'replaced by an emphasis on trust'. It could be argued, however, that the term 'replaced' should read 'complemented by', given the nature of the central policy, procedural, performance and operational control 'guidelines' listed above. For example, restrictions within the devolved budgeting system meant that virement between services could only be made up to £7000 before seeking authority from senior management (p. 127). The particular pressures on middle managers are aptly illustrated by the following quotation from an area manager:

> The departmental management team fear the organisation will get out of control. In reality, the opposite is the case for people tend to be conservative. After four or five years in a culture in which you are jumped on for getting out of line it is difficult to get people to take risks. Ken Young (the director) goes on about giving away power but this has meant it was OK as long as you did what he wanted. There was a stage where we had to turn that centrally driven culture around. Patch teams were sceptical about the 'opportunity' to plan. They said we had already decided. It is a slow business getting them to change.
>
> (Hadley and Young 1990: 206)

However, this study suggests that the development of devolved resource management and 'entrepreneurial' management is constrained by a number of factors. While many middle managers will, under devolution, experience increased levels of responsibility and accountability – particularly for resource management – these may well not be accompanied by similar increases in the level of their decision-making authority (Flynn 1994). Diversified organizations such as many local authorities, subject to strong visible external political controls, tend to adopt only limited forms of decentralization below divisional/senior departmental management. While control systems may move towards an emphasis on performance measurement against financial and service delivery criteria, such systems will also tend to be supplemented by additional operational rules and procedures. Overall, devolved management, in conjunction with the purchaser/provider split, can intensify the tension of 'pulls' which exist between parts of the organization competing to acquire greater degrees of power and influence. As Campbell (1991) suggests, middle management desires for greater autonomy, potentially available from devolution, can conflict with senior management desires to increase levels of centralized control, especially over resource management, in a hostile environment of increasingly rigorous external (central government) funding and regulatory controls. The purchaser/provider split also appears to be generating a new set of 'horizontal' tensions between purchaser managers' desires to maximize their control over service specification and design (and to minimize costs), and providers' desires to maximize *their* control over the service delivery process (and to maximize the generation of surpluses). To reduce such tensions, additional control systems are likely to be required, given the 'quasi-market' nature of many local authority markets and the absence of true market mechanisms for resolving these conflicts: 'the use of market mechanisms does not remove the need for control, but rather requires the development of system management concerned with the behaviour of the new market structure' (Stewart and Walsh 1992: 30).

The scope and nature of these tensions are likely to vary across service areas which differ across a range of organizational dimensions. These include: the nature of the product/service and the work process; the nature of the customer base and the market (fully competitive to essentially non-competitive, 'arm's length' service provision); the degree of political sensitivity of a particular service; and the extent to which service objectives are unambiguous, measurable and susceptible to predetermination of the desired outcome, and, hence, amenable to the discipline of contracts or service level agreements (Stewart and Walsh 1992; Walsh 1992, 1995; Flynn 1993, 1994). In general, 'The greater the uncertainty and the more complex the interactions (with customers/the public), the more difficult it is to develop the use of contracts in the management of an activity or in relations with the public. Where political salience is high and the activity cannot be pre-determined, organisational control will be tight, leading to centralisation unless political control can itself be decentralised' (Stewart 1992: 17–18).

For example, following an investigation into suspected 'irregularities', and losses incurred on certain contracts undertaken by a district council's direct works department, the council treasurer and policy committee decided to exercise more direct control and tighter monitoring of this department's activities, plus the 'undevolution' of the department's finance section back to central finance. Thus, following a meeting of the policy committee, a statement, published in full in the local paper, was issued by this council, including several measures for achieving these increased levels of more centralized control, such as:

> in respect of the building division . . . tenders for larger contracts only being permitted with the approval of the city treasurer and the deputy chief executive after a full financial appraisal . . . the department shall not enter into any new activity, or re-enter any activity now terminated without the approval of policy committee and a financial appraisal . . . the assistant director (finance) be transferred together with his finance section to the city treasurer and deputy chief executive's department . . . all tenders by WSD [the department] of over £5000 . . . shall be checked by the city treasurer and deputy chief executive for financial prudence prior to submission.

(Napier 1994)

In addition, market regulation of services within the context of continuing public expenditure restrictions is likely to involve management styles which emphasize 'price and volume control, rather than quality and service development' (Flynn 1994: 223). Thus, rather than a move to the 'commitment' strategies, and away from the 'control' strategies associated with the 'new' management, emphasis is likely to be made on the latter. This is illustrated in Table 3.1, which summarizes the two approaches as applied to the public sector/local government by Flynn (1994: 222–3).

Clearly, strategic choices exercised by particular local authorities can move them towards one or the other of these two approaches. Moreover,

Table 3.1 Management styles within market systems

Commitment	*Control*
Consumer-based delivery, rights to service standards or control of manner of delivery, emphasis on individual preferences and joint consumer/provider control over service design and delivery, first-hand consumer power/influence	Purchaser-based delivery, strict rationing of services with few rights exercisable without detailed control by authority employees, purchasers determine volume, shape and standards of service provision, second-hand consumer power/influence
Service design/delivery based on relationship between consumers and providers rather than providers/ purchasers – consumer led	Service design/delivery based on contractual relationships between purchasers and providers rather than providers and consumers – purchaser led
Provider worker/manager empowerment to enable direct responsiveness to consumers, commitment and trust strategies with people helped to grow into their jobs	Detailed control of work processes through scientific management and contractual regulation with little provider worker/manager empowerment, people located in strictly defined parts of the labour process
Control through quality and service development, workers and users enhance the value of services together	Control through price and volume, purchasers design services and instruct workers on methods
Growth of quality and innovation	*Control* of quality and innovation
Overall provider emphasis on providing high quality services subject to resources available, losses on some activities at some time is less important than service quality	Overall provider emphasis on making as much money as possible, service quality considered but management focus is on keeping costs down and revenue up

Source: N. Flynn (1994) 'Control, commitment and contracts', in J. Clarke, A. Cochrane and E. McLaughlin (eds) *Managing Social Policy*. London: Sage, 222–3.

much will depend on the extent of the cooperation achieved between purchaser/provider managers. A high degree of 'collaborative' rather than 'selfish' behaviour is required to ensure effective operation of market-based service delivery systems which are genuinely flexible and responsive to consumer needs (Hulme 1994). However, Flynn (1994: 224) considers that 'only when the pressure to reduce or contain spending is eased will it be possible to operate markets in a way which emphasises quality and service user control'.

Emerging tensions

These tensions and limits on middle management autonomy raise a number of important issues in relation to the changing nature of managerial roles. As the Audit Commission (1989a) suggests, the absence of authority for managers to use, for example, the revenue generated by achieving savings in one area to offset overspending in another, or to use at least some of the surpluses or 'profits' for new projects, can reduce the impact of these incentives which encourage managers to improve resource utilization and service delivery effectiveness. Such constraints can operate to frustrate managers' attempts to make more creative and innovative decisions about resource deployment and service delivery. Especially when combined with expenditure cutbacks, they can make managers sceptical about cultural rhetoric urging them to adopt more entrepreneurial and risk-taking management styles, which in reality they do not feel empowered to achieve (Preston 1991). Practices such as *ad hoc* mid-year withdrawals by senior management from managers' budgets, and/ or unexpected increases in staffing costs outside managers' control, can inhibit managers' attempts to plan and monitor budget spend effectively. They can also increase the risk of managers exceeding the budgetary targets for which they are held accountable, for reasons seen to be largely outside their control, which can then encourage them in manipulating and/or questioning the validity of performance appraisal systems (Moizer 1991).

Managers can also become sceptical about the utility of performance measurements systems because of the problems of identifying appropriate performance measurements. Drawing upon the 1990 LGTB/LACSAB survey, Spence (1990) reported that most senior managers considered that they had been able to develop appropriate objectives and targets even in service sectors, such as social services, where outputs were not easily measurable. However, much depends upon what are agreed as 'appropriate' measures; quantitative output criteria are obviously relatively straightforward to identify, but they may not reflect the final 'outcome' of the service in terms of meeting overall client needs. As an East Sussex team manager indicated, 'The minimum I have to achieve is very much financially based. My residential homes must have a certain level of occupancy ... But that says nothing about the *quality* of care' (Hadley and Young 1990: 123). A recent survey

(Palmer 1993) demonstrated the heavy reliance of many authorities on value-for-money and other quantitative, rather than more qualitative and 'outcome'-based, measures. Clearly, to be meaningful, performance measures should vary according to the nature of the service. Brignall (1993: 30) argues for recognition of the value of 'managerial intuition and judgement' as well as more 'formal "rational" information system' approaches to performance measurement in difficult-to-measure areas of work such as social services.

Similarly, in the context of the purchaser/provider split, Flynn (1994) and Cochrane (1994) suggest that, increasingly, local authorities are becoming divided into two main groups. The core of purchaser managers enjoy relatively high levels of job permanence and status. As key implementers of, and contributors to, the authority's strategic planning process, they are responsible for drawing up service specifications in the context of these local strategies. The jobs of provider managers – even those employed directly by an authority – will be less secure or permanent, and probably of lower status given their more remote connections with the strategic planning process, and their dependence for work on the decisions made by purchasers. Moreover, increasingly detailed service specifications are likely to limit the scope of their authority over service delivery processes. Such tensions are also unlikely to promote good relationships between the two functions. Much depends here on the nature of the systems developed by the authority to control these relationships, and also on managers' willingness and/or ability to develop appropriate behavioural skills.

The acquisition of devolved responsibilities and 'entrepreneurial' roles requires managers to develop new decision-making skills. As the LGMB (1993b: 23) suggests, managers with devolved management responsibilities in the new market systems need to develop not only business and commercial skills, but sound decision-making and problem-solving skills: 'The willingness and ability to make informed and timely decisions, both individually and as part of a team. To act decisively when necessary. To access and use information to inform decisions. To exhibit superior judgement in decisions.' Essentially, under devolution, middle managers are expected to sort out problems themselves (the disturbance-handler role) rather than pass them up the hierarchy to more senior managers. Moreover, their new responsibilities for resource management also mean that, while help and support should be available from specialist staff, they are expected to take the initiative in early identification of potential problem areas, and take the responsibility for at least suggesting solutions, even if authorization for implementation is required. They also need to appreciate the importance of cooperative behaviour required to develop effective relationships between purchasers and providers, with other agencies and community groups/consumers, with senior management, with specialist staff and with their own staff. They need to acquire negotiating skills necessary to gain the support of all parties involved in service provision: 'the ability to create win–win situations' (LGMB 1993a: 23).

The importance attached to these negotiating competences is illustrated in a recent publication which focused solely on 'influence and influencing' as a day-to-day aspect of the management role (Clarke and Stewart 1994). The authors identify five different forms of 'influencing', including: *'cooperation*, where the emphasis is on shared aims and resources; *bargaining*, with the emphasis on negotiation; *opposition*, only to be used sparingly where an organisation opposes something another wishes to do; *persuasion*, where argument and assertion are important; and *facilitation*, where resources are used to help another organisation secure its aims' (executive summary). Each of these influencing methods can be used by middle managers as appropriate in different contexts. Within the organization these will include: contributing to strategy formulation; implementing change management; team-building; negotiating performance/resource utilization targets with both superiors and subordinates; and working in multidisciplinary, cross-functional and interdepartmental groups and project teams. Clarke and Stewart (1994) suggest that effective deployment by managers of all five forms of 'influencing' behaviour depends on several key factors: acquisition by managers of the appropriate skills and competences; provision of training by the authority to help managers acquire these competences; the effective mobilization by managers of resources such as information, knowledge and money; and the design of 'appropriate' structures and processes within the authority, and between the authority and other agencies, to enable and facilitate the exercise of 'influencing' forms of behaviour. These are likely to bring about fundamental changes in the organizational identities as well as the work roles of middle managers. These, in turn, are likely to affect levels of job satisfaction.

Job satisfaction

This normally refers to intrinsic rewards such as opportunities for self-respect and status, independent thought and action, and personal growth and development, and extrinsic rewards such as security, pay and promotion prospects obtained from work (Maslow 1943; Herzberg 1966). A recent LGMB (1994a) survey provides information about levels of 'work satisfaction' among middle managers. In terms of the factors considered to be 'most important', 'interesting work' was rated top (by 78 per cent), followed by: 'feeling you have accomplished something worthwhile' (70 per cent); good pay (67 per cent); security (58 per cent); good pension (41 per cent); long-term career prospects (33 per cent). Overall, 63 per cent of the senior/principal officers (roughly representative of middle managers) were 'very/fairly satisfied' with their jobs. In terms of the survey's job satisfaction factors, which equate broadly with intrinsic rewards, 86 per cent reported that they were very/fairly satisfied with the 'interesting' nature of their work, while 73 per cent felt they had 'accomplished something worthwhile'. In relation to the extrinsic rewards obtainable from work, over 60 per cent were very/fairly satisfied with pay and pension levels, but this fell to only 24 per cent with promotion opportunities, 40 per cent with longer-term career prospects and 35 per cent with job security. Some 52 per cent felt they had 'too much work' to do.

The extent to which high levels of intrinsic work satisfaction and low levels of satisfaction with job security and career/promotion opportunities have been affected by the changes outlined above is uncertain, given the scarcity of studies concerned specifically with changes in local authority middle managers' work satisfaction levels. In terms of changes in intrinsic work satisfaction, a recent large-scale survey (although not focused specifically on local government or middle managers) found that levels among public sector managers had declined slightly between 1980 and 1990 in relation to opportunities for personal growth and development, and scope for feelings of self-esteem. There was a small increase in the level of satisfaction about opportunities for independent thought and action (Mansfield and Poole 1991). Focusing specifically on middle managers (in both private and public sectors), Dopson and Stewart (1990b: 37–8) summarize their views about the impact of role change on work satisfaction levels as follows: 'the broader changes had created a more challenging environment in which to work. Most of the public sector managers . . . enjoyed their work more because they were more accountable; jobs were also viewed as more interesting, both because of the increased responsibility and because of the new management systems that had clarified objectives.'

They did, however, find evidence to suggest a less positive attitude to organizational and management changes amongst the public sector managers (in comparison with their private sector counterparts). This arose largely from the political constraints and the associated requirements for public accountability, specific to the public sector, which inhibited the degree of middle managerial freedom to innovate and exercise authority. 'There was a feeling that managers were given the responsibility, but not the power, to meet specified targets' (Dopson and Stewart 1990b: 39). Equally demoralizing for middle managers, decentralization can involve inadequate specification of suitable financial control and performance review systems, and of clear policy and procedural guidance, which can leave devolved managers floundering and unclear about the extent of their authority – described as an 'environment of chaos' by one-third of Lowndes and Stoker's decentralized local authority staff. Moreover, the satisfactions gained from public sector organizational changes can be diluted by stress arising from increased workloads, reduced resourcing and demoralized staff.

Local authority managers can be enthusiastic about the new opportunit-ies for more autonomy and creativity in their work, the greater contact with the public and the more informal and less 'bureaucratic' management styles. Yet such rewards can be limited through inadequate training provision, inad-equate financial/management information systems and feelings of stress from 'the gap between the demands placed on them and the lack of resources and time to meet them . . . poor management, specifically a lack of support and supervision in a context of constant change and the absence of any sense of strategic direction' (Lowndes and Stoker 1992b: 146). Similarly, Leach *et al.* (1993: 16), in examining change management practices in six-teen 'well managed' local authorities, reported that, in most cases, overall levels of job motivation remained high, but that 'In all cases, middle man-agers felt that they faced higher expectations, increasing pressures, longer hours and the need to develop a range of skills relatively quickly.'

Such pressures can also coincide with the requirements placed on middle managers to become more accountable for their performance against more rigorous and tightly defined standards, arising out of the adoption of form-alized performance review systems. These can provide useful feedback on managers' performance, including identification of their development/train-ing needs, and more opportunities for recognition for good performance (Dopson and Stewart 1990a, b; Hadley and Young 1990; Spence 1990; Spencer and Welchman 1991). Yet over half the managerial grade officers in the LGMB (1994a) survey considered that good performance was 'not recognized' in their authorities. Moreover, resource constraints, increased workloads and the pressures of continual change can operate to dilute such benefits, along with the constraints on middle managerial decision-making autonomy and risk-taking.

In terms of extrinsic rewards such as pay, job security and career/pro-motion opportunities, Mansfield and Poole (1991) identified a significant increase in public sector managerial dissatisfaction with pay and security. The highest level of dissatisfaction expressed in both 1980 and 1990 was with promotion opportunities. Various central government initiatives – par-ticularly CCT legislation – and trends towards flatter hierarchies and more flexible (numerical and functional) human resource management strategies would certainly appear to pose a threat to the job security, 'stability' and 'safety' traditionally enjoyed by local authority staff and managers (Stoker 1989; Farnham 1993). For example, the extensive reorganization and 'delayer-ing' undertaken in one local authority – in response to financial constraints and the need to produce better quality and more flexible services – meant that 'all 9,500 employees have had to apply for posts at or around their current level. So far, the top three levels have been appointed. The spotlight is now on the lower managerial tiers where job cuts will be heaviest . . . NALGO, the white collar public service workers' union . . . expects 500 of its 3,000 members at the council to lose their jobs' (Tighe 1992: 14). As noted earlier, increasing numbers of staff, including middle managers, are faced with the prospect that the role of the local authority as a direct service provider and as a direct employer of staff is diminishing. In the context of the 'enabling' and 'competitive' council, 'staff' are no longer employed directly by the local authority, while those remaining are likely to be anxious about their futures. While most jobs to date which have disappeared are located within manual work categories (LGMB 1994b), the forthcoming extension of CCT to hitherto largely untouched white-collar professional services is increasingly threatening the job security of middle managers, especially those employed within the provider rather than the purchaser functions.

The Local Government Joint Watch Statistics (LGMB 1994b) do not publish information about changes in staff numbers according to staff grades. Moreover, middle managers are not recognized or identified as a category within the national grading structure. However, within the senior officer (SO) and principal officer (PO) grades, where many middle managers are probably located, information provided by Nulty (1994) suggests that there has been an increase between 1987 and 1994 in the full-time equivalent staff numbers represented within these grades. The distribution of staff within the six main grade categories has changed, with a decline in the proportion of staff in the lower grades, and an increase in the proportions of staff in the SO and PO categories. This is possibly due to an increase in junior/middle managerial appointments required to 'handle the contracting processes and to supervise contracts' within the CCT services (LGMB 1992a: 2), and to the growth in some white-collar service sectors such as finance (due to the Community Charge) and social services. It may be that the main threat to middle managerial jobs, through the forthcoming extension of CCT to professional services, is yet to come.

There are likely to be significant differences between individual managers' expressed levels of work satisfaction in relation to differences in their particular organizational and job contingencies as well as in their own personal circumstances and values. In relation to private/public sector differences, Dopson and Stewart (1990b: 38) found that: 'Overall . . . managers in the public sector appeared to be less enthusiastic than their counterparts in the private sector about both the possibility and the desirability of change.' They suggest that the more cautious and less positive attitude to change found among public sector middle managers may arise from the expectations with which they entered the public sector; expectations of security and organizational and role stability, with orientations towards the 'administrative', and 'professional' role identities associated with the more 'traditional' public sector ethos. For these managers, changes towards more entrepreneurial and proactive, and less stable and structured, roles – with less emphasis on professional expertise and more on the new 'managerialism' – may require more extensive and more difficult role reorientation and redefinition than for their private sector colleagues.

Implementing change

Much, of course, depends on the way in which changes in management systems and role prescriptions are planned, introduced and managed. Thus, Leach *et al.* (1993: 16) found 'a key difference (in motivation levels) between authorities where middle managers felt supported and valued by their authority and those where they did not. In the latter cases, further pressures/ demands could result in a process of demotivation.' Dopson and Stewart also emphasize the importance of ensuring that the reasons for change are both fully explained and seen as legitimate by staff. One of the factors contributing to the less positive attitudes towards change expressed by public sector managers can relate to feelings that change is owing, at least in part, to unnecessary (party) political pressures, rather than to more compelling and legitimate reasons, such as the competitive threats which might be posed by a private sector organization. Interestingly, Walsh (1991, 1995) found that the changes necessary for introducing CCT – including staff cuts – were achieved relatively smoothly in most authorities. CCT legislation – however unwelcome – was seen as basically unavoidable, and the need for changes in staffing levels, work practices etc. was seen by trade unions as necessary if local authority works departments were to retain duties in the face of competitive threats from private sector contractors. Training provision is also necessary to help managers to adopt new roles. As suggested throughout this chapter, the extensive changes in interpersonal, informational and decisional roles all require extensive training and support to help managers to develop the necessary new competences. Yet a number of senior/principal officer responses to the LGMB (1994a) survey suggest that many authorities may be deficient in key change management areas. For example, about three-quarters of respondents stated that they received too little information about plans for the future, as well as about the reasons behind major decisions. Further, only 41 per cent felt that they received *sufficient* training for their jobs.

   In terms of likely future developments within local authorities, these officers expressed rather pessimistic views about the probable effects on their work experiences, especially in relation to their levels of job satisfaction, the amount of training they expected to receive, their career prospects, workloads, job security and general morale. No reasons are given for these pessimistic responses, but organization and management changes within local authorities are taking place largely within a hostile external environment of continuing resource constraints, tighter central government service delivery prescriptions and expanding public demands for better quality services. Despite the election of a Labour government, these trends are likely to intensify the factors which offset the rewards of more interesting, challenging and stimulating work which can arise from the 'new' management systems. Managers are likely to become increasingly accountable for results achieved within an organizational context of more rigorous controls over both work processes and outcomes, with reduced levels of job security and promotion opportunities, increased workloads, reduced resource levels and increasingly pressurized and demoralized staff.

This chapter, then, has outlined the changes currently taking place in local authority management role prescriptions. These equate with moves from a traditional emphasis on professionalism/administration to that of 'management'. In the context of shifts to divisionalized and decentralized forms of structure – together with the purchaser/provider split – middle managers are likely to acquire devolved decision-making responsibilities in areas such as finance and personnel and to be accountable for achieving more rigorously defined performance standards, relating to both resource utilisation and service delivery targets. They are expected to adopt more proactive leadership styles, with an emphasis on motivating their staff to achieve higher performance levels, and on facilitating opportunities for staff training and development. They are also expected to be more entrepreneurial, actively searching for ways to improve resource utilization and service efficiency and to achieve greater degrees of responsiveness to customers' needs.

Both purchaser and provider managers are becoming involved more extensively in liaison and information processing/exchange activities. This is taking place both vertically – with subordinates as well as with senior management/elected members – and horizontally, in the context of purchaser/provider relationships. In addition, there is an increasing level of collaborative cross-functional project work with staff and managers from other departments within their own authorities, as well as from other public, private and voluntary organizations. While their work may become more interesting and challenging, it may also become more demanding. Managers are being required to acquire new skills and to achieve results within a context of increased workloads, resource constraints and lower levels of job security.

As Mintzberg's contingency model suggests, the precise nature of the changes in middle managerial role behaviour under the 'new' local government management approach will be affected by the extent to which local authorities have actually introduced new forms of structures, systems and prescribed management roles. Such changes are likely to operate differently between various service/functional departments. Moreover, even within local authorities that are well advanced in the adoption of 'new' management systems, several constraints are likely to limit the extent to which managers' behaviour changes accord to new formal role prescriptions. Such constraints will operate at behavioural and structural levels, especially in relation to devolved management systems, internal markets, information and communication systems, and the nature of a local authority's change management strategy.

However, while the evidence suggests that a growing number of local authorities are adopting new forms of structure and managerial role prescriptions, there is a scarcity of empirical studies focusing on middle managers' own reported experiences of these 'new' systems; on the extent to which *real* behavioural changes are taking place according to the 'new managerialism'. The rest of this study focuses upon the opinions of managers about the impact of these changes on their *behaviour*. Based on the analysis of a local authority – used as a critical case – the remaining chapters describe the implementation of structural changes and the 'new managerial' role prescriptions, and explore the impact of these on managers' behaviour.

4   A study of change: Barset County Council

This chapter identifies the key changes in management structures introduced by one particular local authority's elected members and corporate management team since 1984/5, when a new Conservative leadership embarked on a programme of organizational and managerial reform which 'has had ramifications throughout the county council, and has set BCC [Barset County Council] in the vanguard of local change'. (The source of this quotation is withheld to protect the authority's identity. For similar reasons, all the names of the individuals mentioned in this and subsequent chapters are changed.)

Barset County Council

At the time of the research, BCC was one of the largest English county councils. With over 90 elected members, the authority had a gross annual budget of over £1 billion, and employed approximately 30,000 full-time equivalent staff – larger, as a publicity document pointed out, than many national and international companies such as the Beecham Group and Burmah Oil. It serves a mixed rural and urban area, which contains historic sites of significant national importance, with some distinctive local economic and geographical characteristics. These have helped to provide the authority with a strong sense of local identity and tradition going back over centuries. The Conservatives (including some notable local political dynasties) controlled BCC from its inception following the 1888 Local Government Act until the local government elections of 1993. Reflecting national trends, they then lost control for the first time in the authority's history, and it became a 'hung' council. Until the mid-1980s, as a consequence of its relatively stable political and social environment, the authority's own assessment of its position was that it was 'rather insular and out of touch', and that its 'gentlemanly' and rather 'ossified' traditional organization was not really equipped to address the challenges posed to local government functioning since the late 1970s (policy document 1992). The processes whereby BCC transformed its traditional municipal organization into what became known nationally in the early 1990s as a 'flagship' or exemplary model of a 'new public management' authority are outlined below, using Hinings and Greenwood's (1988) contingency model of the factors which influence the processes of organizational change.

They identify two analytical categories of factors which have the capacity to *pressurize* an organization towards change or stability. These consist of *contextual* factors (such as fiscal and other external environmental, ideational and institutional pressures) and *strategic choice* factors (including the particular underpinning ideas and beliefs about the authority's mission and value-set). A third category consists of *enabling* factors, which can assist or impede the scale of changes achieved within the authority. These involve the degree of concentration of power within the authority (dispersed, concentrated or intermediate), the extent of transformational rather than transactional leadership and the leadership's capability to manage. Hinings and Greenwood use this framework to identify the forces which precipitated the authorities in their sample to move away from the traditional heterogeneous professional bureaucracy and towards an alternative corporate organization form. Essentially, these factors consist of high levels of external pressures, a strong value commitment to change on the part of the organizational 'elite' (senior elected members and management) and at least one 'enabling' factor – moves towards transformational leadership and/or the existence of significant expertise in corporate planning and change management (Hinings and Greenwood 1988: 140–1). Fiscal pressures were largely high or medium in strength, while environment or task and organizational size were low in significance.

Forces for change

An analysis of the factors precipitating the internal changes in structures and management systems within BCC during the 1980s suggests a close similarity with Hinings and Greenwood's model. For Barset, as for other authorities, the institutional/ideational and fiscal pressures for change during the 1980s were extremely high. These can be summarized under three main categories: first, to improve the three Es of economy, efficiency and effectiveness, exacerbated by central government constraints on local authority spending; second, to establish market conditions for service provision, through subjecting certain services to compulsory competitive tendering, and introducing internal markets with a clear distinction between the providers and purchasers of services (the 'enabling', 'competitive' and 'mixed economy' council); third, requirements to create more 'customer' orientated systems for planning and delivering services (Elcock 1993). Emanating from a variety of ideational sources, such as central government, the Audit Commission, the Local Government Management Board and popular management texts by Peters and Waterman (1982) and others, these pressures precipitated moves within BCC towards a private sector style 'business-like' approach to service delivery, including an emphasis on more coherent strategic planning and performance review systems, and on greater responsiveness to the 'customer'. A video and booklet produced in the early 1990s outlined clearly the 'vast range of pressures for change' experienced by the Authority during the 1980s, which resulted in the replacement of a 'traditional' local government management model by a 'strategic management' approach. This was well described in an internally prepared publicity document:

> The world of local government in the '80s has seen enormous change. The election of a Conservative Government in the late '70s had radical implications for everyone, but perhaps more for local government than for any other business sector. The difficulties facing the economy during this period combined with the Government's new philosophy regarding its role in controlling local government finance resulted in an avalanche of legislation affecting the structure and function of local government ... This took place against a background of rising public expectations over the services to be delivered and the way in which they are delivered, producing more sophisticated and demanding customers. A vast range of pressures for change were experienced which had to be addressed by local authorities, including:
>
> - pressures for development, versus environmental concerns and population change
> - growing awareness of social issues, particularly child abuse
> - continuing concern about educational standards
> - fears about the workforce's ability to respond to the changes of a changing economic environment
> - the opportunities and threats [presented by unique local developments – information withheld to protect confidentiality]
> - the increasing demand for local services to be seen to be provided in an economic and effective manner, and to be capable of competing on equal terms with the private sector
>
> It is widely accepted that the 'traditional' ways of managing local authorities are no longer acceptable on their own ... BCC has recognised the shortcomings of its historical approach to service delivery, and has used the lessons of strategic management to tackle the challenge presented by a changing world.
>
> (BCC publicity document)

This clearly expressed need for a move away from the 'traditional' local government management systems to a 'strategic management' approach draws attention to the presence within BCC of the second of Greenwood and Hining's key change factors precipitating 'reorientation' from one organizational form to another: namely, the emergence during the 1980s of a political leadership and key senior managers who were strongly committed to change. In the mid–late 1970s, following the 1974 local government re-organization, several new (ruling group) Conservative members were elected, who held different ideas from the members of the 'old guard' about the management styles and structures which should operate in the county.

Basically, the pre-reorganization members tended to accept the 'traditional' local authority design archetype of an essentially federated structure. This consisted of the heterogeneous professional bureaucracy, where the influence of the service department professional chief officers was extremely strong, dominating service development policies. Although BCC's Policy and Resources Committee possessed the capacity for strong corporate control (all policy decisions made by service committees had to receive approval from this central committee), the policy decisions of departmental chief officers, supported by the more traditional elected members, tended to prevail, resulting in a lack of coherent overall corporate policy. The corporate planning structure introduced during the 1970s had little impact on chief officers' domination of service planning: there was little or no overall corporate planning or control of service provision.

From the late 1970s, three key Conservative ruling group members, with strong views about the need to 'repoliticize' the control of the council (considered to be too heavily officer-dominated), sought to regain political control and introduce 'genuine' (councillor-led) corporate control over service planning and delivery. Efforts by these members to achieve this change by setting up reviews and plans for restructuring of individual departments (beginning with Highways) met with resistance from both officers and the more traditionally orientated (and less 'political') members. They achieved only limited change, but they helped to create the conditions necessary for achieving subsequent and more wide-reaching county-wide changes. One of these members acting as a key change agent (Cllr Harvey) was elected as council leader in the mid-1980s, following a previously unsuccessful attempt.

Significant factors influencing the outcome of this crucial council leader election probably included the national developments noted above (the election of the Conservative national government in 1979 with its programme of public sector reform) which enhanced the legitimacy of Cllr Harvey's change programme, plus dissatisfaction with the performance of the previous (traditional Conservative establishment) council leader. Harvey was an 'outsider' (rather than a member of the Barset Conservative Party establishment), and, in terms of the impact of his election on the direction of change within Barset, one commentator considered that 'there is a sense in which

Harvey's victory in 1984 replicated Mrs Thatcher's victory nationally in 1975. Each was an outsider bent on radical change, and each had the good fortune to face an establishment leader whose popularity was on the wane.'

Harvey subsequently embarked on an intensified and accelerated programme of structural change which embodied the three key 'new management' principles outlined above: improvement in the 3 Es; the introduction of a 'mixed' economy of service provision; and an emphasis on greater responsiveness to local customer/community requirements. Indeed, BCC, in its annual reports during this period, drew attention to the way in which Barset had actually pioneered some of these new approaches, which were subsequently adopted by the government as a basis for preparing legislation. Harvey focused on the need to replace the traditional, professionally dominated, federated structure described above with a more unitary or genuinely corporate structure. This involved a 'cabinet' style structure of senior members to determine policy, with the Chief Executive acting as line manager to departmental chief officers, and the introduction of clear command structures to achieve stronger corporate control and strategic management of the council. Such initiatives included a redefinition and clarification of professional chief officers' roles, equating broadly with a move in emphasis from Laffin and Young's (1986) professional advocate role (involving strong professional domination of policy) towards the role of the 'enabler'. This stresses chief officers' 'capacity to implement policy change specified by the members, on behalf of the members ... The members look to them to grasp and carry out their politically-determined policies' (internal document).

Following the (mid-1980s) recommendations of an external consultancy report, Harvey identified the need for a new Chief Executive (the previous executive retired), who 'would become the Authority's chief strategic planner. He or she would lead the management team and be responsible for the overall planning and budgeting process, the development of manpower policies and reviews of the Authority's organisation and management' (article written by the new Chief Executive 1990). As Harvey himself put it, he sought a Chief Executive 'with the clout to tell chief officers what to do', and who would play 'a vital role' in taking change forward. The role of the new Chief Executive – Salisbury – equates with Hinings and Greenwood's (1988) third key reorientation impetus – the need for the existence of 'capability' for change management within the organization.

Salisbury adopted from the outset what Hinings and Greenwood (1988) describe as a 'transformational' leadership style (clear definitions and restatements of overall values underpinning elements of organizational form), focusing not just on changing structures but also on changing processes. Beginning with a seminal paper delivered to the Policy and Resources Committee in September 1986 on the importance of 'changing the culture', he continued this process with the identification of three key underpinning principles: devolution, management not administration, closeness to the customer. These, with various amplifications and additions (particularly about the need for a permanent change orientation throughout the organization) provided a coherent and restated set of values underpinning the changes up to, and including, the period of this research (mid-1992 to early/mid-1993). Other 'new wave' chief officers, mostly on short-term contracts, were also appointed during the mid-1980s. The impact of the 'new management' style adopted by one such chief officer (in Social Services) on his staff was so marked that his name 'Butlerism' passed into common usage as a synonym for the (initially) heavily contested 'new public management' changes imposed on the department. Also seen by staff as symbolic was his non-social work background (relatively unusual for a Social Services Director), which they interpreted as a measure of senior management/elected member determination to weaken the power and influence of professional staff over service policies and delivery.

The focus of both the new council leader (elected in 1992) and the Chief Executive (Salisbury continued in post) was to continue with these policies, with particular emphases on developing the role of members, improving the monitoring and policy direction of direct services 'without backtracking from the principle of devolution', continuing to reshape the organization towards a mixed economy of service provision, and recognizing the 'value' of staff by minimizing as much as possible any adverse impact of change on their work (BCC newsletter).

Changes in structure and management systems

In accordance with this management philosophy, Barset implemented a number of changes in its structure and management systems. An emphasis was placed upon corporate values which highlighted the importance of managerial accountability and a 'performance culture', and the need to achieve more numerical and functional flexibility to improve efficiency. BCC was also among the first local authorities to break away from nationally determined pay and grading systems. A locally determined pay and benefits system was introduced in 1990 for white-collar staff across all departments (excluding teachers/lecturers and uniformed services), with a new grading system, involving fewer and broader overlapping grades, facilitating the development of more flexible job descriptions. Corporate guidelines over job descriptions clearly identified the requirement for these to focus on job objectives and 'key performance indicators', and to achieve greater flexibility: 'in a rapidly changing environment, you may need your employees to be more flexible . . . the job description is only a guide, and may vary in detail over time' (Management handbook).

The increased use of short-term contracts, especially for senior officers, and the increase in part-time staff numbers between the mid-1980s and 1993 also enhanced numerical flexibility. Between March 1983 and March

1993, the number of part-time males increased by 41.5 per cent and part-time females by 1.4 per cent. Organizational restructuring and moves towards a 'mixed economy' of service provision (including the externalization of some services such as computing) involved the disappearance of some positions and the requirement for staff to apply for new posts. While BCC has emphasized the need to minimize redundancies and to redeploy staff wherever possible, such trends suggest a reduction in traditional local government job security, and a BCC Report commented on the increased levels of stress for staff at risk from job losses, and/or under pressure to maintain service provision levels, often with 'diminished resources and less support'.

The new pay system also included a performance-related element, which meant that staff progressed up incremental scales only if they achieved the necessary performance standards. The staff development and performance review system, in operation for white-collar staff, involved the setting of annual individual performance targets. These linked into departmental business plans against which performance was assessed for both pay purposes and identification of training and development needs. In addition, the performance ethos and focus on the outputs, rather than the processes, of job tasks was strengthened by the introduction of the purchaser/provider split.

These trends suggest a move towards increased authority and control for managers (greater authority to make operational decisions about resource deployment and service delivery), and decreased levels of specialization as senior professionals took on more responsibilities for resource management functions. Although *individual* managers continued to function on a specialized professional basis, they were increasingly involved in much more broadly defined interdisciplinary, multiskilled and functionally flexible *group* working. This cut across traditional inflexible professional and department boundaries, both within BCC and between BCC and other organizations.

These changes reflected complementary changes in training and general organizational acculturation systems. During the late 1980s and early 1990s, a wide-ranging and intensive programme of cultural change was instigated, with the repeated dissemination throughout the organization of core corporate values. These were supplemented by principles involving a 'ready, fire, aim' approach to decision making, a focus on strong transformational leadership styles at all organization levels and the need to adopt an entrepreneurial attitude towards change. In addition, management training and development initiatives, as well as service-based training schemes, were introduced. These included competency-based management development programmes, and the establishment of a corporate training board to fund and plan a number of management development initiatives. The 1992/3 'learning themes' included a focus on managing change and uncertainty, managing finance, quality management and customer care, leadership, equal opportunities and health and safety. Concerns were also expressed about the difficulties of maintaining a 'cross-cutting sense of (corporate) identity' in a situation when the extension of CCT to professional services could lead to an increasingly fragmented county council. As the Deputy Chief Executive stated: 'We are in law a single entity, and as long as we have these unifying responsibilities, there are going to be issues of cohesion and continuity across the Authority – of identity. We need to make the best use of resources, and not just see the Local Authority as a series of services linked purely legally. Also, people in BCC like to work together – sharing corporate values, members' directions and objectives and priorities are forces for combination AND fragmentation, but the balance at the moment is tipping towards fragmentation because of the imminent impact of CCT for white-collar services.'

Professional commitment to 'good practice' was expected to be expressed from within a firm framework of BCC's own (ultimately politically derived) explicit strategies about service delivery policies and priorities. There was also an emphasis on the need for middle managers to develop and maintain managerial, as well as professional, competences and expertise. BCC developed a number of prescriptions about the nature of the role behaviour expected from *managers* at all levels and within all departments in the organization, and middle managers were required to play a key part in implementing the 'new' management model. Barset's introduction of devolved management was designed to maximize lower level managers' accountability for, and control over, the resources (people, property, money and information) necessary for providing effective and responsive service delivery, within a firm framework of performance monitoring and review systems. In the context of acting as change agents, they were expected to use their devolved powers to become 'outward-looking; future-orientated; proactive; opportunistic; entrepreneurial'. They were urged to: 'stick their necks out, take risks, have vision in order to carry the process of change forward with conviction. This cannot be simply at the Chief Executive level. This style must run right down through the organisation – managers throughout the organisation must be willing to stand up and be counted, to make progress, to take risks' (internal document). This was in a context of enabling the provision of more flexible service provision, tailored more precisely towards meeting the needs and demands of more sophisticated consumers.

Within BCC there was an emphasis on the importance of managers throughout the organization adopting a transformational style of leadership – 'a strong leadership, which gives an organisation a sense of style' – in pursuit of the core corporate values. In terms of people management, reference was made to the need for all managers to focus on 'enabling' rather than 'disabling' their staff, and to 'give people room' to develop their abilities and energies to the full (internal document). Managers were expected to demonstrate commitment towards developing and training their staff, and a key element of BCC policies was to 'train and motivate managers to achieve the effective operation of their departmental appraisal scheme.' This included: the setting of training priorities for managers' work-sections; considering the most appropriate way of 'enabling the individual to learn'; focusing on the importance of managerial support, feedback sessions and appraisal interviews to maximize the value of training; and ensuring integration of learning into the individual's work behaviour (management handbook). The handbook also emphasized the importance of managers 'involving employees in work issues, a process which often generates greater employee satisfaction and can result in improved motivation and performance.'

Managers' leadership styles were seen as vital for ensuring commitment to change objectives throughout the organization, for providing a clear sense of direction under the pressures for change and for ensuring effective performance of three key sets of activities – the 'must do' activities (statutory responsibilities), the 'need to do' activities (meeting consumer demands) and the 'want to do' activities (pursuing member policies). Staff were encouraged to develop questioning attitudes about themselves and their work, and change was to be achieved 'with' staff, rather than being imposed 'on' them. The Chief Executive also considered that this development of the leadership role gave 'the opportunity to many of our managers to become *leaders* for the first time, and serves as a motivating factor throughout the organisation.'

BCC's emphasis on the importance of developing 'lateral linkages' on an intra- and inter-organizational basis focused attention on the importance of managers' information roles. This was to be at the level of improving work group performance, improving intra-organizational integration and developing more effective liaison with external agencies and consumer/community groups. Thus, the management handbook stressed the need for managers to become extensively involved in communication activities with their staff: 'you must ensure you get the information you need, and then pass on the relevant pieces to enable staff to fulfil their role . . . Communicating is a core part of the manager's job.' At the organizational level, managers were urged to share elements of good practice, 'actively' to seek opportunities to work with staff from other departments on joint ventures and to liaise with other departments and external agencies that were likely to be affected by changes in work practices.

All the changes in both decisional and interpersonal roles suggested that managers' involvement in, and responsibilities for, information exchange and processing activities would increase: between purchasers and providers (both within and outside BCC); between managers and external consumers/local community groups; and between managers and their service planning and delivery counterparts in other BCC departments and external agencies. In recognition of these developments, the BCC management handbook emphasized the increasing importance attached to information. This was seen as 'a key resource in all aspects of the Authority's services . . . Devolution of accountability has brought with it increased demands for information, and places greater responsibility on departments and managers to plan, develop and maintain information systems to meet their needs.' Similarly,

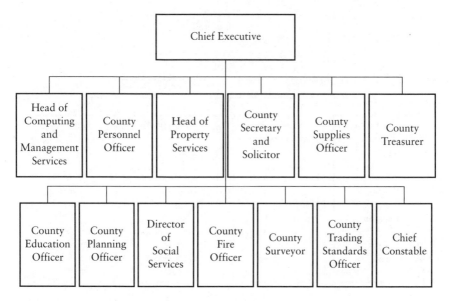

Figure 4.1 Barset County Council departmental structure, 1984/5.

BCC's Corporate Communications (formerly Public Relations) Section stressed its objective of enabling BCC to become a more 'open' organization, and to break down intra- and inter-organizational boundaries. It emphasized that: 'Communication has become the responsibility of all of us. We can't sit back and say it's down to the Public Relations unit, or anyone else. We have all got a part to play – it's the responsibility of everyone.'

Restructuring services

The grouping of service delivery activities into units and departments within local authorities has traditionally been undertaken on the basis of professional expertise. This resulted in a structure of highly differentiated service or operational departments: education, social services etc. Changes since the 1974 reorganization have led to extensive restructuring by many authorities. This has included trends towards a smaller number of larger departments or directorates, some decentralization of central services functions to service departments and some decentralization within service departments of service provision and decision-making power (Young and Mills 1993). Almost all authorities have a designated management team at the strategic apex.

BCC's structure broadly followed the traditional model in 1984/5, with seven service departments and seven corporate service departments, including the Chief Executive's department – fourteen in all (see Figure 4.1). These were organized around conventional service provision specialisms.

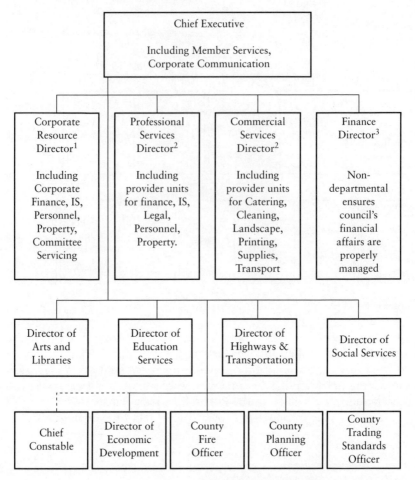

Figure 4.2 Barset County Council departmental structure, 1993.
Notes: [1] Denotes the corporate purchaser functions. [2] Denotes the corporate provider functions (including the Commercial Services Department). [3] Denotes the Finance Director's corporate function, which is neither a purchaser nor a provider function.

Considerable change took place in overall departmental structure during the 1984/5 to 1992/3 period. There was a move 'away from a structure based on traditional professional and functional divisions with its associated hierarchies. This had impeded management control, communication and, most importantly, good customer service' (internal document). The number of direct services departments increased from seven to nine (additions were Arts and Libraries and Economic Development). In early 1993, reorganization of the corporate resource departments took place on the basis of separating the providers of corporate services from the purchasers of corporate services functions. Each of these two functions had its own

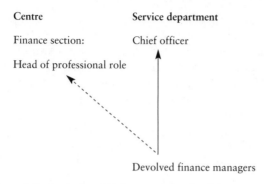

Centre   Service department

Finance section: Chief officer

Head of professional role

Devolved finance managers

Figure 4.3 'Dotted line' relationship between devolved finance managers, Central Finance and Service departments.

director, with a subsequent reduction in the number of chief officers posts which headed up the existing corporate departments (see Figure 4.2).

Another key change for corporate services involved the devolution of most Personnel, Finance and IT staff to service departments' establishments. Here, in a quasi-matrix form, the staff were vertically accountable through their own specialist line managers to the departmental chief officer, and horizontally accountable to their line manager 'customer' at all organizational levels for providing services (see Figure 4.3).

In the context of the authority's move towards the 'mixed economy' or market form of service provision, most service departments were reorganized into purchaser and provider functions. The purchaser responsibilities were to assess consumer need/demand, define service specifications, purchase these from a range of possible providers (BCC or independent sector) and monitor service delivery against policies and specifications. The provider (or contractor) role held responsibility for providing the specified service for the purchaser at an agreed price. *External providers* were non-BCC public, voluntary or private organizations, including some previous BCC sections (e.g. part of the IT department) which had been 'floated off' to the private sector. *Internal business units* (IBUs) were set up, which operated with a properly managed trading account, with income and expenditure recorded as a surplus or deficit. They can trade competitively outside BCC and/or operate in an area which has become subject to CCT legislation. *In-house contractors* operate like IBUs, but in areas currently subject to CCT legislation. *Internal provider units* operate on a similar basis to the IBUs, but do not, as yet, conform to the IBU trading account requirements.

During the period of establishing purchaser/provider contractual relations and accredited IBUs, BCC developed a number of policies designed to ensure smooth and effective operation of the system, and to avoid unproductive competition between provider units. These policies indicated that: 'staff destined for future Purchaser and Provider roles will need to co-operate in many ways, particularly with cost information, interim support and work specification' (internal newsletter). In addition, policy was 'to assume' that a 'substantial' proportion of each IBU's activities would be for *internal* BCC customers, and that each department would develop its own operating policies, especially with regard to decisions about which activities should be provided in-house (subject to legislative requirements). Given these constraints, only a few units' activities – largely within the Commercial Services Department – could be equated with private sector commercial organizations in terms of operating under more or less free market conditions. Social Services, Finance and Highways departments (although there were differences between operating functions) operated more on a regulated 'quasi-market' basis. Moreover, for all departments, government regulations, which restricted trading activities outside BCC and forbade 'profit' generation, hindered operating freedom. Furthermore, purchaser managers were required to follow the county's policy to 'support staff in competing for work they currently do as part of the County Council, and therefore Purchasers have particular obligations towards IBUs' (*Working Together* newsletter). Ultimately, the intention in 1993/4 was to extend the purchaser and provider split across the entire authority, which would 'in the long run mean fewer separate departments with a consequent effect on the senior management structure.' Over 100 years of traditional municipal organization, involving strong service departmental 'baronies', would have been overturned. Proposals were subsequently held in abeyance for reconsideration, following the change of political control in 1993 and the national Local Government Review.

An additional feature of the reorganization during the 1984/5 to 1992/3 period included a focus on reducing the tiers of management to achieve a flatter structure: 'A flat structure removes unnecessary tiers of managers, and places responsibility and accountability for work with those who actually do it. This increases job satisfaction, effectiveness and reduces management costs' (internal newsletter). These changes in the design of departmental structures were accompanied by significant changes in the authority's planning and control systems.

Strategic planning

There were abortive attempts by many local authorities at corporate planning in the immediate post-1974 local government reorganization, when the concept of strategy and performance review vanished under the sheer weight of detailed policy objectives and action plans for every conceivable activity (Haynes 1980). Most local authorities relied essentially on the annual, incremental budgeting process for planning their service delivery (Elcock *et al.* 1989). This process tended to be dominated by senior (professional) managers (chief officers) competing for resources, in the interest of maximizing resource allocation to their own departments, with strong tendencies towards adoption of Laffin and Young's (1990) 'professional advocate' role by these chief officers. Programme planning of service provision – identification of client/community needs and categories, and design of programme to meet these demands – was carried out largely on a departmental basis and tended to be dominated by specific professional interests. Control systems were based on tight centralized control of inputs – finance, personnel etc. – and of work processes, to a greater or lesser degree depending on the nature of the task and the strength of service managers and staff opposition to such intrusions on their professional autonomy. Little or no attention was paid to outcomes, so that, overall, 'control is exercised at too detailed a level at the expense of effective resource management and policy direction' (Stoker 1989: 33).

During the 1980s and into the 1990s these practices began to change in a growing number of authorities in response to the pressures for change. Local authorities focused more on the use of formal strategic planning systems designed to 'concentrate resources and management attention on a few critical thrusts which cohesively integrate the entity's major goals' (Caulfield and Schultz 1989: 8). Many authorities adopted core mission or value statements, and there was slightly more uneven progress towards the adoption of strategic planning systems (Young and Mills 1993). Authorities also manifested a new commitment to quality service standards, and to increasing their responsiveness to customer/local community needs. Control systems were moving towards a focus on performance outcomes.

Changes made by BCC during the 1984/5 to 1992/3 period in its planning and control systems correspond very closely to these new approaches. In common with most local authorities, BCC in the early 1980s lacked a coherent strategic planning system and relied on the annual, largely incremental, budgeting process. This operated until the mid-1980s, with the following problems, outlined in an internal document:

- a lack of clear and focused objectives;
- an absence of processes for establishing priorities and making choices;
- a tendency for departments to act independently and parochially and to 'fight their own corner';
- policies being driven by historical factors and budgetary constraints rather than customer demands;
- lack of clarity in the roles of councillors and officers, and poor communications between councillors and staff;
- an absence of information about what customers really want.

It [BCC] failed to plan to any extent. Rather, it indulged in annual incremental budgeting compounded by a pre occupation with economy, and perhaps with efficiency, but not with effectiveness.

(Internal document)

As a consequence of these problems, Barset decided in 1986/7 to introduce a formal medium-term planning process, which was fully in place by 1990 across the organization. This was designed to provide a mechanism for 'making difficult choices, in a heavily constrained financial environment . . . where the demands are almost infinite whilst the resources are very clearly finite . . . [which] is the means of making spending decisions in a systematic, informed and efficient way' (internal document). Particular emphasis was made on focusing on organizational 'capability' to ensure strategy implementation. There was an emphasis on 'pragmatism' through a focus on critical policy, service and activity areas rather than an attempt to cover everything, which 'overwhelms the decision-makers with information'. There was specific recognition of the need to change processes, behaviour and attitudes at all levels in the organization.

The changes involved drawing up a mission statement and three-year medium-term strategic plans for all services. These were translated into annual operational business plans – thus integrating the strategic plan with the annual budget – for each department, with performance targets and indicators against which managers' performance was measured. From these, and also serving as a mechanism for enabling bottom-up input to be made into the planning process, were derived individual managers' own performance targets. Value-for-money and policy reviews were undertaken for all service areas on a regular basis. Increasingly sophisticated approaches to defining strategy were adopted, including: a projection of future key issues commissioned from an external management consultant; increased involvement by other agencies (the 'enabling council') and consumer groups in the planning process; and the use of several market research studies to identify consumer views about priorities for service development and the quality of service provided. Citizens' Charters were also introduced, together with formal complaints systems for all major services. As the Chief Executive explained, his 'getting closer to the customer' involved a movement away from 'the professional knows best' approach to an emphasis on strengthening 'the practices already employed by many staff; giving people more choice; treating them with respect as individuals; involving them; being sensitive to customer preferences.'

The adoption of a 'policy-led' approach to strategy formulation also emphasized the need for a move away from professional officer-dominated policy-making processes. This approach emphasized that strategy formulation was very clearly the preserve of elected *members* who, in an inevitably politically value-based decisional environment, were ultimately responsible for determining strategy. 'Producing a policy led budget is more of a political than a technical matter . . . There is no "correct" answer to any policy issue – identifying priorities and deciding what is most important is ultimately a matter of opinion and values . . . Officers with their expertise can advise Members . . . Policy cannot be the sole preserve of officers' (article by BCC corporate planning officers). Chief officers were also required to accept budget and manpower cutbacks in direct contrast to the previous situation, where 'the traditional symbols of success have been bigger budgets, more people and more services.' It was made clear that, essentially, 'professionals advocating their service need to place it in the context of the wide range of demands made on the County Council' (internal document). The new formal channel for enabling lower level managers and staff to contribute towards strategy formulation was achieved through staff performance reviews and target-setting systems, which both derived from and contributed to departmental business plans and, through these, to overall policies. Managers were, through the dissemination of the new 'entrepreneurial' organization culture, positively encouraged to be proactive in developing imaginative ideas for enhancing service effectiveness.

In general, control systems moved towards an emphasis on performance outcomes and measurement: 'Managing performance has not been one of BCC's strengths in the past and a great deal of effort is currently being committed to improve this situation' (internal document). Control systems became more decentralized, but within the context of an increasingly strengthened role for the centre in setting policy and monitoring service delivery. Both performance-based and proceduralized control over decentralized resource management was enhanced by the installation of more sophisticated and 'user-friendly' computerized financial management control systems. These were also designed to give control over budgetary monitoring processes to the user managers, while providing a standardized framework for monitoring their resource deployment.

Barset's new strategic planning process included increased provision for the coordination of strategy at the upper levels through seminars and workshops held for members and senior officers throughout the budgeting process, as well as through various policy review and performance review groups. The performance appraisal system also provided vertical integration between senior management and operational levels in the authority. It provided a vehicle for communicating strategic objectives down the departmental hierarchies, to be used in setting staff performance targets, and then for channelling information about performance against these targets back up to senior levels. Increased emphasis was placed on the need for strengthening the role of the centre in monitoring service delivery performance. The use of lateral linkages or connections was also required between the managers at operational levels, both between and within departments and between BCC and other agencies. Thus, departments were expected to 'create an environment' where managers would 'look positively for opportunities to work with staff from other departments' on joint initiatives, and to ensure the avoidance of duplication or conflict in the development of new ventures – especially within the context of the devolved management system (management handbook).

The new purchaser/provider split also provided an integration mechanism through the requirement for the individuals occupying these roles to liaise

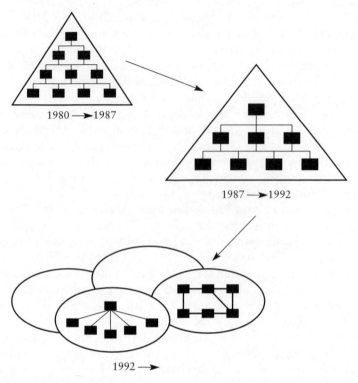

Figure 4.4 Barset County Council's move from hierarchical to decentralized to market/network structural forms.
Source: Barset County Council corporate planning review.

on the drawing up of service level agreements and on the day-to-day amendment of these once they were in operation. The requirements, due partly to legislation and partly to corporate/departmental policies, to involve consumer and pressure groups more extensively in service design, delivery and monitoring also extended liaison operations across organizational boundaries. The *Working Together* programme, with its newsletters and seminars, represented a recognition by BCC of the need to ensure integration of key values and practices across the organization, especially within the context of increasingly semi-autonomous business units operating within the devolved management system. The county also adopted an open systems strategy, with a rapid growth in the use of UNIX and personal computer technology to allow easier exchange of information across departments and, in some cases, with other organisations. All of these initiatives combined to reduce strong professional separatism and departmentalism associated with traditional local authority structures. Figure 4.4 describes the shift in emphasis during the 1980s from a tall hierarchical structure, to flatter hierarchies, to a 'semi-cluster' or 'network' form of organization (Tiernan *et al.* 1994) in the 1990s.

Devolution

Barset's operational decision-making systems in the mid-1980s corresponded broadly with the highly centralized control systems which characterized traditional local authority structures up to this period. Despite the geographical dispersal of some central departmental staff – in Finance, Personnel and IT – to service departments, the authority to deploy resources (within allocated budget and manpower levels) remained largely with these central departments. They exercised detailed control over departmental resource management, with little or no *formal* authority devolved to chief officers or lower level managers. There was a consequent lack of clear managerial accountability, and the associated dangers of 'inflexibility, where the roles became ends in themselves' (Chief Executive), control over outcomes (effectiveness) and clear managerial accountability for results. Thus, in explaining the need for change, the Chief Executive stated:

> The authority is seeking to end the stranglehold of central departments and departmental head offices on local initiatives and responsibility as this has frustrated staff and confused accountabilities. Devolution allows them greater discretion to run services, using their professional judgement and experience, so as to satisfy customer expectations. Front-line managers are being given more scope for action where there is no over-riding reason for greater central control. In BCC, devolution is taken to mean a management style which allows those managers nearest the point of delivery the maximum control of the functions which impinge on them and the service required to enable them to operate, within a specific organisational framework where accountabilities and limits of authority are clearly understood.
>
> *(Working Together* newsletter)

Thus, in relation to budgetary devolution, spending power is allocated to each service department, and monitored centrally. Then, the devolution of '*Responsibility* for control over a given service budget rests with the Head (Chief Officer) of the Service Department ... *Authority* to spend is then cascaded down within the service department to local budget managers – i.e. those front line service providers who, from their understanding of local needs, are best placed to determine spending decisions. The loop is completed by holding managers accountable for their actions and performance' (internal document). At operational level, this process ensures that professional judgements about service delivery are made within a firm management framework.

• From only 50 budget-holders in the pre-devolution mid-1980s, the authority had moved to a total of over 2,500 budget-holders in 1993. In line with Audit Commission (1989a) recommendations for effective devolved resource management, BCC attached considerable importance to providing managers with the specialist support services, training and management/ financial information necessary for carrying out effectively their devolved resource management responsibilities. Sophisticated and 'user-friendly' financial management information systems, with local input and access, were introduced across the authority to enable managers to control and monitor their budget spend. In addition, computerized data systems, such as client record systems for Social Services, were developed. Emphasis was placed on ensuring close collaboration between specialist IT staff and line managers in designing the computer operating systems so that they met as closely as possible the business needs of line manager 'customers'. Similar relationships were also expected to operate between personnel and finance staff and their line manager 'customers'.

Devolution of control over resource deployment to chief officer level meant that staff establishments were no longer subject to detailed central control. However, with staff forming such a large proportion of departmental budgets, central monitoring of staff practices continued to take place. When overall funding became tight, or when there was a need to redeploy redundant staff, central control was exercised over departmental recruitment to new or existing posts and/or establishment totals. The levels at which changes in planned spend by departments required committee approval were also raised. Most of the Finance and other central departmental staff (Personnel and IT) were devolved to service department establishments. Here, their roles involved a combination of providing support to meet the business needs of service line managers and monitoring departmental practices to ensure that these met corporate, departmental and statutory standards.

The pre-devolution 'traditional detailed financial regulations' were initially replaced by an emphasis on 'freeing up the rules, with procedures designed to give managers more control over their resource management. However, following unexpected overspend problems in 1990 and adverse comments on control systems by external auditors, a programme was devised to provide 'the appropriate financial controls for a devolved environment.' These included a financial management handbook, which set out the corporate standards, the key controls which had to be operated and more detailed procedures relating to financial activity for each department, plus detailed guides for budget managers. Limits to delegated powers in the management of devolved budgets were outlined in relation to managers' authority over varying their budgets, making transfers within and between budget headings and incurring expenditure on headings not included within their budgets. A similar personnel management handbook was also introduced. As the Deputy Chief Executive explained, the 'specified organizational framework' within which devolution occurred was only clearly specified after devolution had been introduced, rather than being installed before.

In conclusion, it is evident that BCC made extensive changes in its internal structure and management systems between 1984/5 and 1992/3 in ways that reflected very closely the 'new' local government management model outlined in Chapter 1. They were precipitated by a combination of external and internal organizational factors. These included central government policy initiatives and legislation, rising consumer expectations and the coming to power of a new 'change-orientated' political ruling group in 1984, followed by the selection of a new Chief Executive. The traditional emphasis on the maximization of relatively centralized and hierarchical control over resource management and work *processes* moved towards an emphasis on control over *outputs* and *outcomes*. There was clear managerial accountability for achieving results measured against resource utilization and service delivery targets, including adherence to more rigorously specified service quality criteria, within a clearly specified corporate culture of BCC core values and beliefs. These control systems operated within a devolved management framework in line with a new strategic planning system designed to maximize elected member (rather than professional officer) control over policy decisions. These policies formed the basis of the annual business plans drawn up for each department, which included resource utilization and service delivery targets to be met by all managers and staff. The traditional emphasis on vertical and hierarchical regulation or organizational activities moved towards an emphasis on horizontal market regulation and coordination – through the introduction of the internal market system with the purchaser/provider split – and towards the 'network' or 'boundaryless' form of organization.

Such structural changes required new prescriptions for middle managerial roles, operating in two key areas. First, there was an emphasis, within the strategic management approach, on ensuring that the management of professional service delivery was geared specifically towards the BCC elected member-based, 'local', policy objectives rather than to more 'cosmopolitan' professional orientations. Second, there was an emphasis on the requirements for service managers to acquire and develop managerial, as well as professional, skills. They were required to be accountable for achieving clearly specified performance targets, and to act as change agents. They were expected to adopt inspiring and motivating styles of leadership and, in the context of BCC's new staff development and appraisal system, to encourage staff to perform up to and beyond their capabilities. Particularly within BCC's network form of organization, they were required to become involved in interdisciplinary, flexible work groups. They had to be proficient in negotiation necessary for working effectively within the purchaser/provider split, and for liaising with personnel from other BCC departments as well as from other external agencies.

However, the key issue is the extent to which BCC's organizational restructuring and new middle managerial role prescriptions: (a) were fully understood and internalized by middle managers; and (b) resulted in the manifestation of actual *behavioural change*. Thus, changes in formal management systems and role prescriptions changes may or may not be manifested in the *actual behaviour* adopted by more junior managers. If little change occurs at this level, moves towards new forms of organization are largely cosmetic. Genuine 'transformational' change (Ferlie *et al.* 1996) will not be achieved. It is therefore essential, when attempting to assess the impact of changes within BCC, to consider the views of these managers about the extent to which formal BCC change prescriptions resulted in the implementation of new forms of management behaviour.

5 Changing leadership and managerial roles

Chapter 4 identified the structural changes which had been introduced within Barset County Council since the mid-1980s, and concluded that the management systems in place by 1992/3 corresponded very closely with the 'new' local government management model. This and the following chapters analyse BCC middle managers' perceptions of these changes, and the extent to which 'official' reforms instigated by lay members and senior management have permeated their behaviour. Mintzberg's model is adopted to analyse these perceptions. It begins by examining moves from 'manager' to 'leader' roles as experienced by these individuals, and then analyses changes in their 'informational' roles. The functions of the four departments from which these managers were selected are outlined in Appendix 1.

Leadership roles

Senior management at Barset County Council placed great emphasis on the role of the 'leader' as opposed to the 'manager'. Indeed, this was one of the key planks of the cultural change programme. Documents emphasized that managers throughout the organization should exercise leadership to enthuse their staff by setting clear policy directions, and to encourage them to adopt the new 'entrepreneurial, outward looking, future orientated, risk taking, high visibility' organizational values. In addition, they were urged to be 'enabling, not disabling', to involve their staff in decisions about work issues and to develop their skills and competencies through ensuring training and development opportunities. BCC's manager/leader distinction

Table 5.1 Distinction made by managers between 'manager' and 'leader' roles

| | Selected departments | | | | |
	Social Services	Highways	Finance	Commercial Services	Total
Difference identified	12	7	9	9	37
Not sure	–	3	3	–	6
No difference	–	2	–	3	5
	12	12	12	12	48

corresponded closely to the differences between Bass and Avolio's concepts of transactional and transformational leadership styles, with the latter focusing on the three key aspects of: (a) charismatic and inspirational styles; (b) individualized consideration of each individual's own abilities and orientations; and (c) the provision of intellectual stimulation and challenging work for staff. Given the importance attached to this, managers were asked if they saw a difference between the role of a manager and the role of a leader and, if so, to specify the differences. As Table 5.1 demonstrates, the majority of them claimed that the two roles were different: 19 of the 48 were able to provide a definition of both the leader and the manager roles; 16 defined the leader role, but were unable to define the manager role; two could define neither, although they considered that the roles were different.

The respondents tended to equate 'management' with the more reactive role of 'just maintaining the status quo', with a concentration upon largely administrative tasks. 'Management' involved a reliance on the formal authority represented within the manager's hierarchical role position, and this authority was used to monitor closely the work of staff and to 'issue orders' in a rather autocratic fashion, rather than attempting to work with them, or 'let go' and allow them more freedom to manage themselves. As two of them explained:

> I think the difference between a manager and a leader is: the manager manages the status quo. A leader creates the new status quo – it's about change, and directing people towards change, and encouraging them towards change.
>
> (Commercial Services provider manager)

> A manager – life as a manager in the old administrative days, when all they did was sit in a box in the corner of a room in a little office, and dealt with all the paperwork. A manager is someone who takes what is coming down the line – I will process that, manage this – and off we go and just do it, do the same things, and keep them going, while I think what they [BCC] are looking for is someone up there, to set an

example, and set the direction, you know, to lead the troops over the top. A leader is very much more proactive. Setting direction, setting targets, motivating people, making sure that people actually enjoy their work, that they've got a future career path, have got somewhere to go.

(Finance manager, Education Department)

In contrast, the responses of the 35 managers who provided definitions of the 'leader' role focused largely on the 'charismatic and inspirational' aspects of transformational leadership. They tended to emphasize the leadership facets associated with personal charisma, such as 'earning the respect' of their staff through 'leading by example', setting a clear sense of direction (especially when engaged in change management) and 'taking staff with you' by 'inspiring', 'enthusing' and 'motivating' them. The adoption of 'participative' and 'consultative' leadership styles was seen as important here. Many emphasized the importance of direct personal contact with their staff, in the sense of being 'visible' to them through 'managing by walking about' and talking to them. As one of them suggested:

A manager ensures that a job is done, but a leader actually shows that as well – he shows by example, and being there. He pushes the boundaries a bit . . . I used to find it embarrassing to be a leader, but I don't now – the actually showing by example and being different. Being in front, being watched. And I've thought up a lot of little things to do that, make that more obvious. You say to people, because of the new procedures: 'We have to be much more respectful of the public we deal with.' So I do it with them, in front of them, that sort of thing. And I show myself making mistakes and apologizing for them. That sort of thing, in front of them, in case conferences when I chair them.

(Social Service purchaser manager)

They were also asked to identify any changes which had occurred since the mid-1980s in their leadership behaviour. Overall, 31 of them reported that their leadership styles had changed in the direction suggested by the county's 'transformational leader' prescriptions (see Table 5.2).

When asked about changes in their own leadership styles, many focused upon the importance of 'enabling' and 'empowering' their staff, as well as on the need to adopt strong inspirational and charismatic leadership. They attempted to: encourage each staff member to identify the skills and knowledge areas where he or she required development/training; set more challenging tasks and targets for their staff, based on each individual's own particular abilities, strengths and weaknesses; and provide training and other development opportunities according to individuals' own specific needs. The staff development and performance review (SDPR) system was seen by many of them as a vehicle for encouraging them to undertake this in a more formalized and structured way:

Table 5.2 Managers' adoption of BCC's transformational leadership style

	Selected departments				
	Social Services	Highways	Finance	Commercial Services	Total
Shift towards BCC's leadership style					
Yes	8	9	7	7	31
No change	1	2	2	5	10
Not sure	2	1	2	–	5
No subordinates at time of interview	1	–	1	–	2
	12	12	12	12	48

I see the SDPR as a means of developing individuals. Some of the team members have got far greater potential than others, of course. And one way of actually trying to develop that potential is by setting targets that are going to be a challenge to them, whereas in the past they would just have been expected to get on and do their daily work and achieve the annual programme. I set targets which try and develop the individual, so that they have to stretch themselves to achieve them.

(Highways provider manager)

There's more opportunity now to give people work other than their normal core work – to help develop them as individuals and future managers. I feel I have the responsibility to try and develop the people I have working for me. I've involved a lot more people in developing this computer system, that wouldn't traditionally have been involved in the past. I think it will develop these individuals – their characters, their strengths.

(Commercial Services provider manager)

Many managers also emphasized the importance of stimulating and motivating staff by delegating responsibility for decision-making and task achievement to them, within a framework of broad guidelines or targets, leaving staff free to manage the 'how' and the 'day-to-day' aspects of their work, thereby ensuring staff 'ownership' of their work:

I like very much to give people clear guidelines of what I expect, and allow them to go away and achieve that within that, knowing they've got the support to report back if they feel it's not working. That way they can actually feel ownership of something. I think my skills are better placed at the strategic level. I've done the task bit myself; I've no wish to interfere. Like the information systems thing – it was my customer services manager who actually did the project. She defined it, what we wanted, went away and did it – and did a very good job ... The whole point really is to progress people on and develop their skills.

(Commercial Services provider manager)

As well as trying to focus on individual development needs on a one-to-one basis, many reported various efforts to develop their own work units as *teams*. Responses here ranged from delegating particular decisions to their teams to involving them, through participative and consultative leadership styles, in decisions which had to be made:

With certain elements of the job – like the client will write in with a comment about something, but I won't make a decision and tell staff, 'this is what we're doing from now on.' I would circulate the letter or memo or whatever and ask for people's comments to get them thinking about what they're actually doing ... it can ease pressures on me, because if I've been asked how we would solve a problem, and I find out what their views are, it saves me having to sit back and think about it. And it actually gets them involved, keeps them involved, and then it's a two-way exchange of information. I can bat ideas off of them, and they can similarly throw ideas at me.

(Highways provider manager)

I will make the decision at the end of the day and I think people understand that, but I will do it through people. For instance, we've got a budget ... and I've got this, this morning. It was agreed yesterday by the Committee – the business plan targets – what we've got to do. I am actually going to give my locality managers the budget sheets on Monday, and give them that and say: 'What I'd like the four of you to do is go away and agree how you are going to apportion these targets between the four of you, and then come back to me.' It saves me the work and it's good experience for them.

(Social Services purchaser manager)

Within the context of culture change in the authority and the development of various strategies by senior management to achieve more effective and open communication systems, managers were encouraged to discuss with their staff and feed back up, increasing volumes of information about changes affecting both their own departments and the county as a whole. Many emphasized the importance of ensuring that staff were fully aware of, and understood the reasons for, the structural and cultural changes under way within the authority. Methods adopted for achieving this included: 'management by walking about'; 'setting an example' to staff by their own behaviour of what was expected in the 'inspirational' and 'charismatic' style described above; holding team meetings more often.

I'm doing it [holding team meetings] more formally now. Every four
weeks we have a team meeting, where I – I've really been pushing the
customer service idea, and it's been difficult for some of them, and
every four weeks we have a meeting where people can just moan –
'we're getting fed up with the job', and moan about the customers.
Remember, they're not allowed to be rude to the customers, no matter
how idiotically they behave. When they come on, you know, 'I've
cocked the machine up', we've got to be sort of polite and help them
through it, and it does wear on them, and they've got to have a
screaming point, so we have once a month or so, where they can come
in and really . . .

> (Finance manager, Highways Department)

There's so many changes going on, the impact on morale is quite high
– the uncertainty, the fears about externalization, internal business
units – people are quite worried so I see it as important to enhance the
communication process . . . I've attended some of those *Working Together* seminars, and I've made quite an effort to feed the information
back to my team and help people to see what's going on.

> (Social Services provider manager)

Many managers across all departments reported departmental policy initiatives requiring regular team meetings and briefing sessions at every level
to improve communication flows up and down the organization. While
this represented an extension or formalization of practices which had already
existed to some extent, it also represented a significant change in style for
some managers:

Communication with staff is very important – it's a key part of management, making sure that people know what is going on. I was criticized
for not having regular team meetings as frequently as others – my comments in the performance review, you know, were 'not communicating
with staff as frequently as thought desirable', and I have them quite
frequently now.

> (Highways provider manager)

But what of those in the 'no change' and 'not sure' categories of responses
about changes in their leadership styles? Most of these reported that either
they had always tended to adopt the 'transformational' style of leadership
or they adopted a 'contingency' approach to leadership, changing their personal style according to staff needs and changes in the operating environment.

All of the managers mentioned various constraints on the extent to which
they were able to pursue the 'transformational' leadership style. There
were limits on the extent to which they felt able to innovate or take risks
within the still relatively 'risk-averse' culture of local government. In addition, some felt inhibited in being able or willing to 'let go' in the sense of

encouraging their subordinates to take risks or make mistakes, and delegating responsibility to them for task achievements: 'they're *my* targets that they're doing, and I need to keep a close watch on their progress.' Moreover, as Bass and Avolio (1990) note, empowerment strategies require resources for training and development. Some managers identified problems with finding the funds or time to enable staff to pursue development opportunities. Lack of time was also cited by some as a problem which prevented them from devoting as much attention as they felt they should to inspirational and motivation activities.

In addition, some of them raised the issue of competence among their staff in terms of their abilities and willingness to be developed and 'stretched'. For example, a Commercial Services manager explained that some of his staff (particularly longer serving members) were less willing than others to accept the need for greater flexibility in their work practices: 'some of them still haven't quite got round to the idea that if a customer rings up to order something, it has got to be done then and there – it can't wait till somebody else comes back from lunch.' A related point was that some saw a contradiction between the requirement for them to be directive and inspirational, while at the same time being required to pursue participative and consultative strategies. As one explained:

> In some ways I've had to become more directive, more autocratic almost . . . It's linked in with the Barset changes because, at the end of the day, when we looked at what actually needed to be done to get the team into some sort of healthy shape to actually be able to cope with the demands on the purchaser/provider split, clearly, there were some people in the team who were less than enthusiastic about all of that. At the end of the day they had to be dragged kicking and screaming whether they liked it or not because we *have* to respond – there's no choice any more, and there's a limit to the time you can spend consulting and cajoling.
>
> (Social Services provider manager)

Ten managers (five in Social Services) commented, sometimes negatively, on the rather 'macho' nature of the leadership style advocated by BCC senior management, and the Chief Executive in particular. Social Services managers mentioned 'Butlerism', a reference to the name of the previous departmental director, who was perceived as using a strongly directive and 'macho' style. This approach was felt, however, to be in retreat under the current director, who was seen as using a softer, more sensitive approach. These perceptions arose partly from the fact that the new director, unlike his predecessor, came from a social work background, and was thus seen as being more receptive to concerns raised about the impact of changes on professional practices and values. His less autocratic approach was also seen as deriving from his own personal preferred method of exercising leadership.

Some mentioned the problems attendant upon combining performance-related pay (PRP) and staff development needs within one system. These included the reluctance of some staff to 'take risks' or be set challenging targets (in case they should fail), or to be honest about their development needs, in case this should be seen as a 'weakness' for pay award purposes. Some of them expressed appreciation of the way in which the PRP system reinforced the message of the new 'performance culture' and clarified the objectives towards which they should be working. Others regretted the way in which it focused on the notion of a 'reward' for work well done, rather than on the intrinsic pride taken in a job well done for its own sake. It was considered that such pride could actually be undermined when staff received a lower pay award than they felt they deserved.

They were asked about the leadership style of their own line managers. The responses suggested that just over half the respondents saw their line managers as operating a leadership style which tended towards the transformational model. They were given a substantial amount of freedom in determining their methods of working, within the framework of performance targets and business plans, and with advice or guidance provided by their line managers when needed:

> He's great to work for. He's very much people orientated, and really wants people to take – really be responsible for their sections, which is good, and he encourages you to do this . . . This place is always alive and buzzing – he never stands still for a minute. He's faster than his own shadow, and it kind of galvanizes you into action. I suppose it makes me work longer hours and at times I think perhaps I ought to give more priority to my family life . . . but at the end of the day, it's good fun. It's that type of atmosphere.
> (Commercial Services provider manager)

Of the remainder, a few respondents felt that their line managers were either too *laissez-faire*, in that insufficient support and guidance were provided, and access was poor, or too autocratic and/or controlling. These respondents felt subjected to undesirably close levels of supervision, which inhibited their freedom to develop new ways of working. This often made them feel that their levels of expertise were undervalued, and that they were not trusted to produce results on their own:

> I don't think I've ever worked with one [a boss] who is so controlling. I don't like to use the word autocratic, but it's bordering on that. And he's like that with everybody, so it's not I'm singled out because he's worried about *me* – it's just his style. Checking and double checking on everything – it's frustrating and occasionally it's infuriating. I don't know how he's got the time for it – I really don't.
> (Social Services provider manager)

Overall, the managers' responses about the leadership styles which they had adopted suggested that there was some progression, in accordance with the county's own prescriptions, towards the transformational leadership model. This appeared to be occurring particularly in the case of the development of charismatic and inspirational leadership styles.

Ceremonial roles

There are various *ceremonial* leader roles, often of an interpersonal nature, which do not involve significant information-processing or decision-making activities. They are largely symbolic, reflecting the formal authority associated with the manager's particular position within the organizational hierarchy (Mintzberg 1973). Within their work units, managers officiate at various ceremonies – such as celebrations to mark the occasion of a staff member's promotion, departure or marriage. Outside the work unit, they are involved in various official events, opening, for example, a new by-pass or youth club with which their work units have been involved, or, perhaps, attending a formal lunch with local politicians or other community representatives. Given the extent of the organizational 'de-layering' and reduction in the importance of rigid hierarchical role definitions associated with the more flexible and open management systems, it appears likely that middle managers will become more involved in this role, especially with regard to activities outside their work units. However, most of the BCC managers reported no change in the extent to which their activities within this role had changed since the mid-1980s (see Table 5.3).

All of them reported participation in small quasi-formal events with their staff, such as leaving/retirement ceremonies, the presentation of engagement presents and the like. This was seen as a normal part of the leader role, and no change was reported here. However, in connection with formal, social or ceremonial duties outside their own sections, most reported that this role, both currently and in the past, constituted a very insignificant and infrequent

Table 5.3   Changes in managers' ceremonial role performance

	Selected departments				
	Social Services	*Highways*	*Finance*	*Commercial Services*	*Total*
No change	9	9	11	7	36
Increased	3	2	1	2	8
Decreased	–	1	–	3	4
	12	12	12	12	48

aspect of their work. The relatively few examples provided included attendance at official opening ceremonies for new buildings or new services, occasional attendance at dinners or lunches with local suppliers, contractors, local groups and other public sector officials, and putting in a 'presence' at the beginning of various internal events, such as a special training day. Most of them explained that, while they might occasionally deputize for their line managers, this role tended still to remain within the provenance of more senior staff. Finance managers explained that because their function was seen as essentially a support activity, they rarely became involved in the formal occasions connected with service provision events of one sort or another. Those managers who had experienced some kind of increase felt it was important in terms of promoting their own departments within an increasingly competitive environment. One Social Services manager felt that there was a fairly careful selection of people who attended formal occasions, which often involved contact with elected members:

> There's more of it. I suppose just the fact that my responsibilities have grown, and there's a sort of elitist thing about that. In some situations we like to have the person who is actually doing the job, so the person within the resource gets to meet a well known bigwig, but there is still a sort of guardedness about our employers (councillors), and so Area Directors are very nervous about who meets Lady Treadwell, or who meets whoever else, and we're almost vetted to see whether we would be socially acceptable. And I clearly am now. They used to be very nervous of me and I used to get to see nobody. It was quite clear that I wasn't trusted ... then I had to do it and they realized I didn't do anything too disastrous!
>
> (Social Services provider manager)

Overall, however, it appeared from the managers' responses that little change had taken place in their ceremonial role behaviour. Yet it is important to note that most reported a significant increase – outside the purely formal ceremonial role – in their contacts, involvement and information exchanges with a range of individuals and groups both within and outside BCC.

Liaison and informational roles

In terms of their *liaison* and *informational* roles, managers are involved in the acquisition of information from various sources, and then processing, using and transmitting this information to others (see Figure 5.1).

The analysis of an organization's information and communication systems can take place across a number of different dimensions, each of which will influence the nature of the manager's informal role behaviour (Townley 1989). For example, information can take written or spoken forms, and

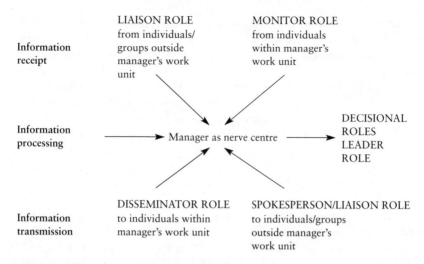

Figure 5.1   The informational role of the manager.
Source: Adapted from H. Mintzberg (1989) *Mintzberg on Management*. New York:
The Free Press, 16–21.

information flows can take place on a one-way or two-way basis between sender and recipient. The distinction is also commonly made between *formal* and *informal* systems of communication and information flows. *Formally*, a manager's job description prescribes the exchange of information on specific issues, to be made in a particular format, with designated individuals holding particular positions both inside and outside the organization. Under *informal* systems, the manager makes his or her own decisions, outside the formal network, about whom to contact about what, and about what format should be used for receiving, processing and transmitting such information. On a broader basis, this distinction can be subsumed within the conceptual model of relatively *closed* or *open* information systems. Relatively *closed* systems tend to focus primarily on prescribed vertical channels of communication and information flows. The emphasis is on flows from senior management to middle managers, rather than from the bottom up, with limits on horizontal flows within and between departments at middle and lower levels in the organizational hierarchy.

'Traditional' local government structures and management systems tended towards this 'closed' end of the continuum. Traditional departmentalism – the division of local authorities into rigorously differentiated departments and sections based on professional specialisms – combined with relatively little devolution of authority and responsibilities to managers at the lower levels of hierarchies, operated to restrict both horizontal and vertical bottom-up information (Haynes 1980). Both the volume of information circulated and the scope of managers' access to it were limited. There were tendencies for information to be used as a weapon in individual and departmental struggles for power, and 'to be treated by departments and even sections of departments as if it were their property' (LGTB 1990a: 14). More *open* systems focus on the importance of free information exchanges both horizontally and vertically, throughout the organization. Flatter hierarchies and devolved management systems involve managers in a wider range of responsibilities for the work of their 'empowered' teams of staff, located within semi-autonomous and self-motivated business units working towards fulfilling the organization's overall objectives. Here, managers and team members require full and open access 'to the information and tools required for functioning and collaborating within the team in a broader context' (Tapscott and Caston 1993: 12).

BCC senior management had adopted a strategy of encouraging managers to develop and maintain both formal and informal links between sections and departments as well as between BCC and other organizations. They had pursued a policy of facilitating such contacts and of achieving more open communication and information flows, both vertically and horizontally within the authority.

Managers' responses indicated that most of them were becoming more actively involved in developing and maintaining more contacts (outside their own work unit) with a wider range of individuals both inside and outside BCC. They were becoming more extensively involved in receiving, processing and transmitting a growing volume of information. Forty-four of the 48 respondents considered that their involvement, overall, in liaison and information processing activities had increased since the mid-1980s; 39 of them considered that BCC had become, in general, a more 'open' organization in terms of overall increases in the volumes of information circulating, and in terms of more open and accessible communication systems.

The individuals and groups (outside their own work units) with whom they reported increased involvement in the exercise of their liaison roles can be grouped into four categories. These involve: (a) contacts between purchasers/customers and contractors/providers of services; (b) liaison with BCC staff and with external agencies involving inter-disciplinary cross-functional collaboration; (c) working with individuals concerned with mutual exchanges of managerial, professional and personal information; and (d) working with senior management (and subordinates). The functions of these information exchanges can be analysed at three levels, using Tapscott and Caston's model: at *work unit* level to monitor and improve performance; at the *organizational* level to ensure the integration and coordination between increasingly semi-autonomous business units; and at the *inter-enterprise* level, to develop inter-agency cooperation in service planning and provision. The complex horizontal and vertical information exchange systems with which each manager operated at each of these levels are illustrated diagrammatically in Figure 5.2.

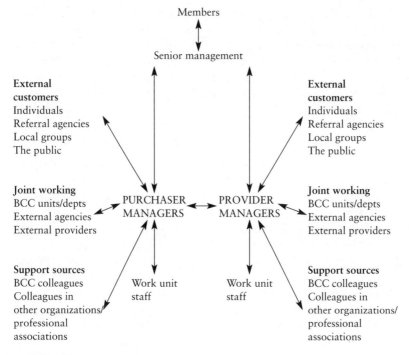

Figure 5.2 Managers' purchaser/provider networks.

Purchaser/provider roles

Information processing with regard to customer and purchaser/provider relationships operated at the level of ensuring improved team performance in terms of meeting customer/purchaser needs, and ensuring integration between various sections of the organization. Several of our respondents attributed the increase in their involvement in liaison activities partly to the introduction of the purchaser/provider split:

> There's growth in it [liaison activity] in as much as we now have a client [purchaser] side and the D & C [design and construction] side. Before, basically, we did everything – it was all Highways Engineering in days gone by, and someone was told to do a project and they designed it, and they went out and supervised it, and then they went out and did the next one. Now, we have the client role, and therefore we have to act as a client and therefore we have to liaise with the people who are actually doing the work [the provider] – we want to make sure they're spending our money in the right way. In days gone by we *were* the people doing the work.
>
> (Highways purchaser manager)

In addition, the purchaser/provider split provided a mechanism for integrating policy planning and resource allocation at departmental levels. Purchaser managers contributed towards departmental business plans and policies through feeding up suggestions for improvements and modifications to services on the basis of their contacts with external and internal providers, end-users and various local interest/community groups. The following quotation from a social services manager illustrates the complexities of provider managers' multiple customer identities within this market system, and the complicated nature of the information exchanges required between them:

> I think we tend to see that we've got three lots of customers. We've got the pure purchaser of the service which is the department, through the policy-makers and the area commissioners [of services] and all those people, and even the politicians – we tend to block them all together as one. Now obviously they are representing the interests of the end-user of the service – the clients. But obviously, these are a customer in their own right as well. Then we've got the third block which are the external agencies which is the district councils. Now, I guess in terms of how the councils are represented, it tends to be through the [departmental] purchasers, but, having said that, we work so closely with them [the councils] that I tend to represent their view. I might say, well this is the viewpoint of Twelvetrees District Council at this point, as we need to bear it in mind. So, yes. In a way they all interlink. I think the staff have got the idea that we've got three lots of customers, but at the end of the day, it's the person with the disability and their carer who are the people who are hopefully going to benefit.
>
> (Social Services provider manager)

As a consequence of the purchaser/provider split, and BCC's customer care policies, 43 out of the 48 managers reported significantly increased levels of involvement with a wider range of customer groups, both inside and outside BCC. The purposes of these information exchanges centred on each of Walsh's (1989) four customer care dimensions: service quality, access, choice of service and user-group/community participation in policy decisions. For example, some social service managers were involved with user and voluntary groups who participated in drawing up community care plans for their areas. The move towards improved service quality, access and choice involved Highways managers in increasingly extensive contacts with individual members of the public, chambers of commerce, parish councils etc., as well as with national and local interest groups focusing on, for example, environmental and nature conservancy concerns.

Purchaser and provider managers made a number of comments about the impact of the internal market on their information processing roles, which differed according to their function (purchaser or provider) and their departmental location. In the context of Williamson's (1975, 1985) transaction

costs analysis – which explores the advantages and disadvantages for organizational effectiveness of hierarchical and market forms of service delivery
– their comments illustrated clearly the pressures that market arrangements
can exert on managerial behaviour in the two key areas of (a) *bounded
rationality* and (b) *opportunism*.

Bounded rationality

This concept refers to the extent to which individuals' ability to make
(assumed) rational decisions is limited by their capacity to acquire/receive
and process information (Douma and Schreuder 1991). This is likely to be
the case under conditions of high degrees of uncertainty about the precise
nature of the service to be required by consumers, and where such services
are complex in nature. It will be difficult to write 'tight' contracts which
prescribe action to be taken by providers for all conceivable contingencies.
Attempts to do so are likely to result in the problems of 'contract bureaucracy', and will also restrict purchasers' and providers' abilities to respond
quickly to changing demands or circumstances (Nichols 1995).

Focusing first on the Highways and Social Services departments, some
(mainly purchaser) managers considered that the purchaser/provider division had improved the efficiency and effectiveness of their information-
processing and decision-making activities. Reflecting the potential advantages
of market systems outlined earlier, these respondents felt that the market
system had clarified responsibilities for service planning and delivery, compelling them to think more carefully about what they were doing, and
why, and providing opportunities for cost savings:

> The lines of communication are a lot clearer, the functions are a lot
> clearer, and, hopefully, they are more efficient because we have a
> client [purchaser] who is in charge saying: 'That's what we want
> done'. At the moment we're saying to D & C [the design and con-
> struction section]: 'Go and do that' – before very long, it will be going
> to D & C: 'Give us a price', and we'll say to Joe Bloggs consultants:
> 'Give us a price', and we'll get the best job and the cheapest job – not
> necessarily the same thing of course ... The advantages certainly
> outweigh the disadvantages.
>
> (Highways purchaser manager)

Similarly, some Social Services purchaser managers considered that functions were clearer, quality assurance mechanisms more effective, and cost
savings improved:

> I flag up the aggregation of needs, as it were, and then we have a
> meeting with all three of us – that's Service Development [contracts
> management], Service Provision and myself to work out what the service

level agreement needs to be . . . It's better now in that you are able to say what you want for the money – we have a decision that we will go to in-house first and if they can't provide we will go out, but if the in-house ones are going to be incredibly expensive and still no better, than I might choose a cheaper one outside – if it's going to be as good . . . A major part of my job is quality assurance and . . . it really needs to be at arm's length, you know – they are very angry people, some of our clients, and it's important to have someone else besides the social worker to pick up and listen – you can actually monitor the service that you're getting on a much more open basis.

(Social Services purchaser manager)

Yet most managers (some purchasers and almost all providers) within these two departments, while acknowledging these *potential* benefits of the market system, considered that, in practice, these benefits were being realized either not at all or to only a limited extent. Opinions differed between the two departments and between the two functions: Social Services managers presented more negative views than Highways managers, and providers were more negative than purchasers.

These more negative managers emphasized the adverse impact of the purchaser/provider split on their overall decision-making efficiency, and on the extent to which they were able to respond flexibly and effectively to consumer demands. Corresponding with Walsh's (1992, 1995) points about 'contract bureaucracy', they identified problems of 'over-bureaucratization' and 'over-proceduralization' arising from the complex contractual processes introduced by the authority to regulate purchaser/provider relations:

We [providers] agree to provide a service for the commissioners [Purchasers], and then the Service Development [contracts] manager will enable the thing to happen. They act as kind of go-betweens and negotiators between me and the commissioners. But . . . I question whether the Service Development bit gives any value added . . . I went to speak to a colleague the other day and he was clutching this great big document – a 50-page document, which was a service level agreement – written in this awful legal jargon, you know, whereby and whereat, the first named party etc., and he'd slung it in the bin and written a single sheet back to the commissioner saying: 'This is what we can do and it won't cost you any more and this is how we'll do it – if you're happy with it let me know', and he rang back and said 'fine', and that was it. Why are these people doing this – if they're saying let's cut the garbage, let's cut the fat in the structure, then why is this happening?

(Social Services provider manager)

Similarly, some Highways provider managers, although accustomed to a client/contractor split which had operated within the department for some time, were critical of the increased formalization and 'contract bureauc-racy' which had begun to characterize previously informal client/contractor relations:

> Whereas we [client/purchaser] used to go and have a chat with Joe Bloggs [contractor/provider] and say, 'Well, we ought to draw up a traffic signal scheme for this junction or whatever', and he'd say, 'Oh yes, I know what's to be done, yeah, I'll go and do it' – now, he's got to take one step back and say, 'Well, you [the Purchaser] write down exactly what you want me to do and I'll do it ... It's actually injected quite a wedge of form-filling and red tape into the organization. So whereas we were a nice close-knit organization and probably fairly efficient, I would suggest that perhaps we're less efficient.
> (Highways purchaser manager)

In addition to these contractual obstacles, which inhibited the achievement of productive and cooperative information exchanges between purchasers and providers, the latter were also concerned about the impact on their rela-tions with their end-user 'customers' – in a context where they were making strenuous attempts to move away from the traditional professional orienta-tion of providing services *to* people, towards providing services *with* people (Walsh 1989: 60). For example, the responsibility for obtaining and ana-lysing feedback from end-user customers now rested technically with the purchasers rather than with the providers who actually delivered the ser-vice: 'Theoretically, I have no contact with customers,' said one Highways provider manager. Similarly, Social Services provider managers complained that their capacity for responding quickly to changing/new customer require-ments were constrained by requirements to secure the agreement of the purchaser to any proposed changes in service provision: 'We have to come up with the good ideas, but then we have to sell them, literally now, to the purchasers.'

While the purchasers stressed the mutual involvement of both parties in such decision making, providers tended to emphasize their disadvantageous position – partly because of the purchasers' responsibility for formal service monitoring and evaluation, and partly because the purchasers represented the formal link between service specifications and departmental business plans, from which such specifications derived. The arrangements for pro-viders to contribute to these processes were less clearly defined, raising the dangers of increasing separation and distance between the direct service providers (with their first-hand knowledge of consumer needs) and the policy-makers who lack such direct day-to-day knowledge (Deakin and Walsh 1996). Similarly, purchasers tried to avoid using the term 'purchaser/pro-vider split' – 'it's not a split, it's a partnership', as one purchaser emphasized – and stressed the way in which managers from each function negotiated jointly over the initial contract and subsequent amendments. Providers, however – again, particularly in Social Services – stressed the unequal nature of the relationship, and the 'opportunistic' behaviour patterns which could arise during these negotiating exercises.

In general, provider managers' comments suggested that these heavily regulated quasi-market coordinating mechanisms represent, essentially, an extra *horizontal* overlay of bureaucracy between the purchaser/provider functions operating *in addition to* the still extant *vertical* hierarchical bureaucracy, which had always inhibited free information flows and speedy decision-making within the more traditional local authority bureaucracy.

Commercial Services provider managers' responses were slightly different from those of their Social Services and Highways counterparts, reflecting, in part, the different nature of their transactions. For example, managers in business stationery, furniture and other similar service areas experienced decision-making and informational problems arising from changes in the nature of the purchasers of these services. Former large and experienced corporate departmental purchasers had been replaced by large numbers of smaller, relatively experienced, end-user purchasers within, for example, schools and elderly people's residential centres. Because of central government legislation and BCC devolution policies, these purchasers had gained the freedom to buy such supplies on the open market. As a result of these developments, both the nature of the transactions and the managers' roles had changed:

> Under the old culture, there was more opportunity to talk to people – for instance, we involved the people in the Education Requisition Centre in decisions on products they were going to buy. There isn't a centre now. You can't go and talk to 800 schools . . . What's happened in reality, as I mentioned earlier, we're developing a bright glossy catalogue with a range of choice, and we're adopting a selling role rather than a coordinated purchasing role.
> (Commercial Services provider manager)

Commercial Services managers identified both inefficiencies and efficiencies within these new market transaction systems. There was certainly more responsiveness on their part to purchasers' demands:

> we have lost the captive market. Up until 1988, schools and departments *had* to come to us, they had to spend their money here, and the service we provided was appropriate to that status. It didn't matter if they waited three weeks for something, they had to come to us . . . But we now have customers to deal with who make their own decisions on their own budgets . . . we have to understand what they want more . . . We have to work harder to ensure that people still come to us.
> (Commercial Services provider manager)

Purchasers were also free to shop around in a highly competitive market for 'best buys'. Yet at the same time, the Commercial Services managers pointed out some of the inefficiencies arising from the purchasers' relative inexperience in the purchasing role and their lack of specialized information about certain products which could result in some costly 'bad buys' – especially in relation to more complex services or products, such as photocopiers. Moreover, the Commercial Services managers cited the increased transaction costs associated with the active marketing and promotional activities which were required to sell their products within the new competitive market environment, such as a new specialist marketing unit and the catalogue described above.

Opportunism

This refers to 'the guileful pursuit of self-interest' (Levačić 1993: 45), which can be exercised by one party taking advantage of differential access to information or to market power to exploit or mislead the other, or to misrepresent intentions. It is particularly likely to emerge when transactions are characterized by high levels of uncertainty and bounded rationality – when powerful and large purchasers can manipulate providers. This situation can occur even when individuals are aware of this danger and try to avoid it.

One of the benefits advocated for the use of market coordination systems is that it inhibits the pursuit of self-interest by managers. It removes the incentives existing under traditional hierarchical coordination systems for service managers to maximize their demands for resources, to 'empire-build' and to pursue, especially in the local government professional context, more narrowly defined sectional professional interests rather than to concentrate on the end-user and/or the overall local authority's policy objectives (Gray and Jenkins 1995). The argument is that competitive market mechanisms compel the providers to achieve cost efficiencies and to focus on meeting purchaser or consumer needs, rather than their own, as otherwise they will go out of business; the quotation above from the Commercial Services provider manager aptly illustrates this point. However, these benefits are less likely to materialize in regulated quasi-markets, where free market type price mechanisms and patterns of supply and demand do not exist, by and large, to regulate exchanges – as in the BCC Social Services department.

Social Services managers in particular commented on the swift appearance within their departments of undesirable forms of opportunistic behaviour arising from BCC's encouragement, under the new quasi-market system, to managers to become more 'entrepreneurial' in the sense of generating new business and additional income for their trading account provider units:

> it's an undesirable consequence of the split – *it actually forces people,*
> no matter how they try and resist, into some rather wary ... you

know, what are they after here? We often joke about it, you know: 'I'm not going to charge you for this discussion – if you come and ask me for some advice, this is free' . . . I think we have resisted the worst excesses of it in this area, but in other areas some of the commissioners [purchasers] are being really macho and draconian and saying 'We are going to put you out of business'.

> (Social Services provider manager, emphasis added)

Managers here emphasized the extent to which, almost inadvertently, they found themselves adopting these uncooperative forms of behaviour under the pressures exerted by the market system, reflecting the views that particular forms of organization regulation can encourage or discourage particular forms of employee behaviour (Pfeffer 1981; Langan and Clarke 1994; Hood 1995a). Within this largely internal quasi-market coordination system, the potentially conflicting demands made on purchaser and provider managers (to achieve simultaneously both competitive and cooperative forms of behaviour) were inhibiting adoption of the ideal 'collaborative' rather than 'selfish' forms of behaviour associated with more effective and informal *networking* forms of coordination based on trust and commitment rather than on control through contracts (Flynn 1994: 222–3; Hulme 1994).

> The purchaser/provider split has somewhat buggered up the [communication] chains . . . some stuff goes through Service Development who feeds the commissioner, and some stuff comes down the Service Provision chain, and again the value of good information networks is important. Quite often, John will copy stuff to me which says 'purchaser/commissioner'. But in other areas, given the almost conflictual relationship between the two, it's: 'I'm not going to give them that because that will *help* them', and certainly I'm concerned that John's stuff hasn't come by a direct route to me – it's only because of my informal . . . I think maybe it's become, the culture has become more closed because of the competitive spirit that has been generated and forced upon people, so people have become far more wary and suspicious. Without a doubt I've learned to become a bit more guarded and canny – there's sort of more sparring, and people bidding for power and trying to get bigger slices of the cake. There's a lot of that going on and it's very unclear and very unsavoury and very wasteful.
>
> (Social Services provider manager)

As in the discussion about bounded rationality in the previous section, managers emphasized that opportunistic forms of behaviour (such as inter-departmental and hierarchical power struggles) had existed in the pre-market hierarchical regulatory system. But, again, the market system was seen as providing an 'additional' forum for the expression of such conflicts, where purchaser/provider power struggles took place *in addition to* conflicts still evident within the coexisting hierarchical coordination systems.

In contrast, Highways and Commercial Services managers reported a lower degree of opportunistic behaviour within their departments' market systems, which, especially for Commercial Services, were more genuinely open and competitive than for Social Services. They were more concerned about the impact on provider roles of opportunistic behaviour by external private sector competitor providers, who were seen to enjoy unfair advantages in terms of opportunities for income generation in comparison with BCC providers, who suffered from both BCC and central government regulations limiting their competitive behaviour:

> I've got no choice about whether or not I take the [BCC] work on; we can't tender for outside work. It's window-dressing, the idea that we are free to compete or be equivalent to someone on the outside because we are competing with our hands tied behind our back.
>
> (Highways provider manager)

But these provider managers were concerned about their job security in the context of external competitive threats, and when the opportunity arose for more 'selfish' forms of behaviour in the context, for example, of sharing information within the department, a Commercial Services (provider) manager commented:

> Information is power, and power – people are very scared, I think, people are very scared about their jobs. Information is power, so you hang on to the information rather than – in times gone past, it was in everybody's interest to tell everybody everything. But now it's not, because it's my job that could be on the line. I mean, I've got to feel needed, wanted. We're all the same – I mean, being in a business environment, you don't necessarily pass on information which you think people may use against you.
>
> (Commercial Services provider manager)

Liaison roles

Many managers reported increases in collaborative project work with a wide range of individuals and groups both within and outside the authority. Differences between working with internal and external service providers appeared to be diminishing as a consequence of BCC's internal market, CCT and other legislation. One social service manager emphasized the importance of her own part in breaking down inter-agency barriers and encouraging collaborative working between them:

I liaise all the time. I think it's absolutely crucial. I spend a lot of time – I work incredibly hard and I see it as vital, as we're moving more into inter-agency work care. I think we're actually starting to look at the needs of the individual rather than the resource-led implications, which is sitting behind your carefully guarded agency walls and saying, 'We'll do it this way inside here, and we'll criticize you over there for doing it your way and doing it properly.' My definition of a middle manager is somebody who breaks the walls. You have to enable that, you have to get rid of this sort of defensive, protective mechanism, and that's what I do all the time. It's a prime objective . . . I chair what's called a Joint Care Planning Team for children's services, and that's the three main agencies plus voluntary agencies. I sit on inter-agency Child Protection Committee; I started up an inter-agency joint funding mechanism for learning disabled adults . . . I've made sure that we get together to make decisions on joint funding about children, with the health service and education, to get everybody together.

(Social Services purchaser manager)

Statutory requirements for more inter-agency cooperation – for example, required by the Children's Act for Social Services, by EU legislation for some Highways functions, together with the BCC's and the government's customer care requirements – also encouraged inter-group working. But, as noted above, contacts were tending to become more formalized. The following quotation was typical of many responses, illustrating the wide range and complexity of the networks of contacts and information exchanges within which they operated. Their involvement, while varying according to the precise nature of their functions and personal preferences, tended to be increasing:

I have probably four, five, six meetings a week sitting round a table. Telephone calls are legion – with Transportation, Traffic Systems, Planners [BCC sections], people from outside like Seeboard, Gas Board, BT, BR, Southern Water, National Rivers – landscape groups, conservation groups, Barset Trust for Nature Conservancy, pressure groups, planners, the districts [councils]. There's more and more legislation, more and more involvement – it's become more sensitive recently with the planning side of things and the landscape side of things. People are more environmentally aware than they used to be. You've got the green side of things now, people are more aware of their rights than they used to be – communication has increased public awareness and they know more about their rights – not everyone wants to know about what's going on, but there are more that do want to know, there's the Citizens' Charter . . . Materials suppliers and contractors; I've always dealt with those; you get more involved with contractors and things when you're on the construction side of things. We write the specification for these materials, and on site they deal with the guys who turn up with the stuff, so I'm less involved at the moment as I'm design. I used to do the odd lecture on aspects of geotechnics and things like that; recently, I talked to a girls' school on highways; it's probably about the same here – I've always enjoyed doing that sort of thing.

(Highways provider manager)

Many were involved in departmental working groups concerned with developing and integrating professional practice standards across their departments. These included a quality assurance group in Highways, a mental health professional development group in Social Services and a use of capital assets working group in Finance. Increases in their involvement tended to be attributed partly to meeting their own career and professional development needs and partly to the larger number of such groups. The growth in these groups derived from the council's policy of involving lower level managers more in decision-making and of integrating the operations of semi-autonomous business units.

Many of them reported increasing contacts with colleagues carrying out similar work – both inside and outside BCC. Social Services and Finance managers, who tended to be dispersed geographically, met regularly with their counterparts across the county. One Social Services manager commented on how contact with her peers was encouraged by senior management, 'whereas previously we weren't supposed to, because they felt it was a waste of time'. Some Finance managers mentioned attendance at meetings at County Hall under the 'dotted line' relationship between the devolved Finance managers and Centre Finance staff to facilitate professional updating and liaison between widely dispersed staff. In addition, reflecting the rapid and numerous changes taking place in professional practices nationally (partly in response to legislative changes), most reported receiving extensive and growing quantities of information about professional development which was circulated throughout their departments.

Increases in involvement in all these initiatives tended to be attributed to three main developments. First, more opportunities were being made available to managers to participate in such initiatives: 'You're encouraged to get involved.' Second, there was the need for new developments in work practices to be disseminated across the authority, thus avoiding duplication of effort: 'to avoid reinventing the wheel', as one manager put it. Third, they felt that they had to make more efforts 'to be seen', and to inform themselves about developments in both the organization and the outside world. This was for a mixture of reasons connected with personal career development and the need to raise the public profile of their work section or department:

The University of Barchester has just come to Prince Hill – I am on the local, the Barchester branch of the Institute of Marketing, and so they contacted me via that. And I said, 'Hey, hang on – you're a customer. Come and talk with me.' When I'm on *Working Together,* when I'm a SET adviser, when I'm on an ODAS course – I feel very much that, particularly the role I'm in now, but I think any role I've been in, that you are – when they see Barset County Supplies on your label, then you are Barset County Supplies to them, and the way you conduct yourself, and the way you input into it gives a flavour of what Barset County Supplies is about . . . I think it's the way forward for communicating. I think that within BCC and outside, it needs to be a symbiotic relationship – a two-fold thing that as times get tougher in the economic environment, then the best thing is to actually group together and make the best of it and learn from each other.

(Commercial Services provider manager)

I've a number of points of contact within other local authorities where we share problems, and try and help each other through difficult times . . . And then, just getting together with other people on an informal and formal basis, it keeps me in contact with things that are happening. But also I want to get beyond the point where I'm just managing my team, doing my job, earning money. I'm looking to future progression. Future progression is going to mean that I'm going to need to be involved in branch-wide activities rather than the team, and in learning. The first step on that ladder really, is to find out what happens elsewhere in the branch and get involved in it, which is why I asked to be involved.

(Highways provider manager)

Several of them explained how the proliferation of cross-departmental and county-wide project groups, together with the introduction of devolution, had broadened their network of informal contacts:

It's increased in the sense that because you have more contacts, you know more people. If I walk into the canteen at Greenwood now, I am just as likely to sit down and have lunch with someone from County Supplies or Finance, whereas before it would have been social worker type people. It's not necessarily on the grounds of doing it with some Machiavellian motive in the sense of getting something out of them – it's just that I've met them, and so I know them, and I'll sit and have lunch with them because they're friendly.

(Social Services twin-hatted manager)

The authority has introduced more sophisticated computerized management information systems to accompany the introduction of devolved resource management. When asked about the impact of new technology on their information processing roles, most focused on the value of the more extensive and detailed information provided on these computerized systems, which empowered them to make resource deployment decisions. They also commented on the ways in which these systems had enabled closer monitoring of these decisions by specialist staff (such as Finance) and senior management. The Highways managers were the only departmental group at the time of the research to have access to e-mail. This was seen in general as facilitating and enhancing communication and information exchanges across the department and, for some managers, with external agencies such as district councils. However, some found it unreliable, in that 'not everybody has got round to using it'. In addition, Highways managers reported the continuing development of more sophisticated computer-aided design and modelling software used to improve their service delivery.

A more 'open' information culture?

The managers' responses suggest they were becoming increasingly involved in developing and maintaining contacts with an increasingly wide range of individuals with whom they engaged in various forms of project work. They commented on the considerable increase in the amount of information disseminated from centre management teams about current and proposed future developments across the authority relating to policy and strategic issues; about changes planned in general organizational structure and systems; and central government initiatives impacting on local authority service delivery. All this was in addition to increased dissemination of information related specifically to their own work areas and professional spheres from their own departmental management teams. References were frequently made to feelings that the 'grapevine' had become slightly less important, in that 'people tell you things now', information access depended less on 'who you know' and there was less differentiation in terms of managers' access to information being dependent on hierarchical position. Many talked about a changing atmosphere where the 'information is power' assumption was no longer so tenable, largely due to the information requirements of those who held devolved decision-making responsibilities. BCC was also seen as having made a specific policy decision to improve communication flows, and to reduce hierarchical and departmental barriers:

> Yes. I think it's getting better ... There's our own management team – we meet on a fortnightly basis. But sometimes I feel there's always the possibility that things are filtered out before they get down to you. It's only as good as the person telling you, isn't it? Whereby, in *Working Together*, they send round leaflets every now and then, which is really good, and I pick up things which I haven't heard of before. They're doing the sort of Son of *Working Together* papers now, which is really useful; I think *Working Together* was something which really

brought all this to the forefront – people in my session were feeling that it could be better, and I think it has been – I think they've made a positive effort on trying to improve things. It's incredibly difficult with an organisation of the size we work with – really difficult. For me, *Working Together* has been a real breakthrough. I've been at meetings with the Chief Executive talking to us all, and we've got a chance to meet chief officers. Our two chief officers both offered that we could go and see them, which I took up and went to them individually which was really good – that's something I wouldn't have been able to do before. The Commercial Services Director is really good. He'll come down and come out to lunch occasionally and things like that. So it's nice to talk to him direct as well ... And I'm sure that if you were concerned about any particular section, I think now they would make the time to talk to you, or at least to answer you if you wrote about something. Yes, it's definitely getting better.

(Commercial Services provider manager)

Key improvements identified by managers were more structured systems of departmental management and briefing meetings, including circulation of minutes, which provided a useful vehicle for passing information down and for feeding information up the hierarchical chain. They also mentioned the dissemination of increased amounts of written information directly to managers (with contact names for further information), and attempts by more senior managers to become more accessible. Thirty seven of them considered that, overall, change management procedures had improved, largely as a consequence of increased information provision – 'you know what's going to happen, and you know why' – in terms of both more written information and more meetings with senior managers. However, many of them also mentioned constraints on the extent to which the organization's communication and information systems had become more open, and identified several barriers. These were: logistic or technical problems connected with the design of information/communication systems; the limitations of managers' own information processing skills; and 'political' barriers concerned with the reluctance of senior management to disseminate information concerned with sensitive departmental/organizational change and policy issues. These barriers overlapped in many cases. For example, the sheer quantity of information circulation was cited as a problem by many who had experienced difficulties in sorting out the relevant, in deciding what to pass on to their work teams, what to keep and how to file it. Some commented on the danger of missing important information because of the way in which they were 'swamped' and 'bombarded' with information, some of which was too detailed or of only marginal relevance to them. At the same time they emphasized that, in general, it was 'better to have too much than too little':

You get trivia about new arrangements for bicycle parking at Greenwood, cheek by jowl with stuff about reorganization of the central departments – you get absolutely swamped, and there's the danger of missing something important simply because you can't process it all. But, having said that, it's better to have too much than too little.

(Highways provider manager)

This 'swamping' problem raised issues concerned with communications systems design, the information processing skills of managers and organizational power struggles and 'politicking'. Thus, one manager speculated about the extent to which information 'swamping' was an inadvertent characteristic of a poorly designed system, and the extent to which 'You wonder sometimes if it's deliberate – they slip something vital in on the assumption that you might miss it!' In the same vein, several managers said that if they wanted to make sure a message would be read, 'You mark it as *strictly confidential* – and then you're sure everyone will read it!' Similarly, with regard to requests to comment on proposals for change, some criticized the inadequate length of time made available for them on some occasions to respond to such requests. They were unsure whether this represented a 'ploy' to discourage full responses or whether it was owing to poorly designed systems. Several acknowledged the logistic problems faced by an authority which was so large, with offices located all over the county, in designing communication systems that were quick and efficient.

While appreciative of increased information provision, many expressed concern about inadequate opportunities for consultation, and scepticism about the extent to which contributions passed up the hierarchy – whether verbally or in writing – were acted upon by senior management:

There's a fair degree of consultation on what is happening – my query would be that in theory there is consultation, but I don't believe people are actually influencing the decision-making process – it's cosmetic ... There's a lot of apparent consultation, but in fact the director and the department decide what they want to do, and that's what happens – everyone understands that.

(Highways provider manager)

Many felt that the county had made real efforts, with some success, to 'open up' the organization in the sense of adopting a formal well disseminated policy about free information flows and open decision making. Yet they felt that there remained behind the rhetoric of the 'open organization' sensitive policy areas at senior levels where only partial information was released, where 'hidden political agendas' were suspected and where consultation was largely a 'pretence' because decisions had, in reality, already been made. As noted earlier, the purchaser/provider split and threat to jobs from competition were seen as increasing the potential for power struggles in some instances.

In addition, some expressed doubt about the commitment to the new 'open' culture of a number of senior managers located at key positions in departmental hierarchies:

> Our boss – he went last month – but anyhow, he was on the departmental management team and he would have the minutes which he was supposed to show us. But we never saw them. Because he worked on the basis that that was what he was there for, to tell me what he wanted me to know. He was of the old school, you know, 'This is my job, and you just have your little bit', and he would tell me about finance, my bits, but he wouldn't tell me anything else. It put us in an embarrassing position when the director came down and said, 'Do you see the minutes of the DMT?' and we said 'Not always', and he turned to my boss and said, 'These are the key people in your branch and they should see them', and he said, 'Yes, of course I will.' But he didn't. The only time we saw them was when he wasn't there and someone else went and he would be given the file of them, and he and I used to read through them.
>
> (Finance manager, Highways Department)

Some resented the 'mixed messages' given out by the council, in the context of some of its culture change initiatives. For example, some Social Services managers commented on the contradictions between the customer care approach and the resource constraints which limited their scope for meeting consumer demand for services. Some considered that resource constraints and (party) political expediency limited to little more than consultation at best, and manipulation or 'tokenism' at worst, the involvement of users and other interest groups in service planning and policy-making. Social service managers, in particular, reported problems with the way in which user-group expectations could be unrealistically raised in terms of invitations to: ' "Come and tell us what you want", and then they do, and we have to say "Well, I'm terribly sorry but there's a cash limit", and they sort of look like a child that's had its sweets taken away.' (Social Services purchaser manager). Others were sceptical about the county's human resource management policies, designed to ensure increased levels of organizational commitment to the county – what one manager called 'the caring sharing employer crap'. They were critical about the coincidence of such communications with notes about cuts in their expenses entitlements, and with the insensitive handling of possible redundancies.

Finally, the managers were asked about the main reasons for the increases in their involvement in liaison and information roles. The single most often quoted factor identified as contributing towards the development of a more 'open' information culture was the introduction of devolution. This involved them in additional information-processing requirements as a consequence of their additional responsibilities for areas such as personnel and finance management:

> It's devolution – you as a manager have so many more options and so many more choices, that you *have* to have more information, you *need* more information. There's the feeding up of modifications and suggestions for change . . . There was this thing, you know, that information is power, which prevailed, which is not so much now. It can't survive; that type of regime can't survive because people need to have information to be able to function at all with devolution.
> (Finance manager, Social Services Department)

In addition, BCC's adoption of improved customer care, more risk-taking and entrepreneurial cultures, coupled with the internal market and the impact of CCT, required them to seek out increased volumes of information from a wider range of contacts, both inside and outside BCC. The pursuit of opportunities involved them in extensive discussion and negotiation with purchasers/providers, with superiors and with support staff. Increased levels of accountability for performance involved them in monitoring more rigorously both their own and their subordinates' performance. In addition, they were required to disseminate information upwards about their own work performance and feed back up suggestions for changes to the next year's business planning and policy-making processes. Underpinning all these developments were the requirements of central government legislation, CCT and statutory requirements for more involvement of external agencies and local groups in service planning, design and delivery. These combined with the Conservative ruling group's own similar policy orientations to push the council towards the 'enabling', 'fragmented' and 'competitive' model, which required the development of more open information systems, and closer collaboration between managers in different departments and agencies.

Overall, managers' responses suggested that some progress had been made towards realizing the authority's stated aims of improving managerial access to information and enhancing information flows, in the context of a move from a relatively closed and vertical hierarchy to a more open and networked horizontal form of organization. The respondents reported, in general, significant increases in their involvement in liaison and information-processing activities. Yet many of their comments suggested that some barriers to the achievement of a new 'open' culture remained. These included logistic or technical problems relating to information systems' design and to their own information-processing competences. Other obstacles identified by them reflected the existence of 'political' tensions within the authority. These operated both vertically between hierarchical positions and horizontally – particularly in relation to recently introduced internal markets. Thus, many felt there was only limited information dissemination on sensitive issues connected with resource allocation, policy decisions and organizational changes which could threaten some employees' job security or status. All of these, compounded by the resource constraints and public accountability requirements of local government, can inhibit the openness of decision making over sensitive policy and service delivery issues. Such tensions are analysed further in the next chapter.

6 New patterns of decision making

Changes in managers' interpersonal and informational roles both contribute to and derive from changes occurring in their decision-making behaviour (see Figure 6.1). Mintzberg (1989: 19) argues that, using the formal authority invested in his or her position, 'The manager plays the major role in his or her unit's decision-making system.' As entrepreneurs, managers act as voluntary initiators of change; as disturbance handlers, they respond involuntarily to pressures and events beyond their control, such as a supplier failing to deliver a product. As resource allocators, managers make decisions about the allocation of organizational resources – such as finance and personnel – to particular objectives. Each of these activities involves managers in extensive negotiations. Possible changes in these forms of behaviour are now discussed.

Resource allocator and entrepreneurial roles

An increase in managers' control over resource and deployment – through devolved management systems – forms a key component of the new 'managerialism'. Devolved management involves 'ensuring that within the Authority each individual manager has responsibility for delivering a service or for achieving a stated result.' This involves managers at the lowest practicable level within the organization having: 'more authority over resources; greater scope for decisions; accountability for achieving agreed targets' (Stoker 1989: 33). Under contract management approaches to service provision, involving the purchaser/provider split, the decentralization of resource management will take two forms. Purchaser managers have devolved powers to make decisions about using their budget allocations to specify and buy particular services. Provider managers are responsible for delivering services

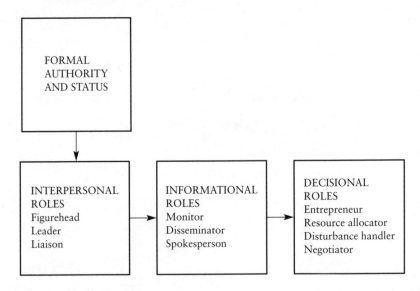

Figure 6.1 Managers' roles.
Source: H. Mintzberg (1989) *Mintzberg on Management.* New York: The Free Press, 16.

to the standards and costs set out in service level agreements. Devolution requires changes in the relatively centralized control systems which tended to characterize the traditional centralized bureaucracies associated with pre-1980s local government administration. However, many organizations may be reluctant to reduce their reliance on these. It can be difficult to design and implement financial control systems which can monitor effectively managers' spending decisions, or to identify performance criteria suitable for assessing and controlling managerial performance levels in some areas where specific, measurable targets may be difficult to set. The mechanisms required to regulate the new contractual relations between purchaser and provider managers can also result in the generation of new forms of 'contract bureaucracy'. These difficulties can be compounded by public accountability requirements, which hold elected members accountable for the actions taken by local authority staff (Stewart and Ranson 1988). This is likely to occur in politically sensitive service areas. Moreover, hostile organizational environments can result in moves towards (re)centralization – especially for public sector organizations such as local authorities, where spending levels are controlled by central government spending limits. Local authorities are therefore likely to be characterized by continuing tensions between relatively *centralized* and *decentralized* forms of decision making.

Failure to delegate decision-making *authority*, as well as *responsibility*, to managers is likely to reduce improvements in organizational effectiveness which devolution is intended to produce. The overall aim of devolved management is to enable managers to improve the efficiency of their resource utilization, and to achieve more flexible and creative service provision that is more responsive to local community needs and demands. It is then, important for senior managers to achieve the right balance between two extremes – complicated rules and procedures which are 'so rigid and minutely defined that the front line is purely an instrument for delivering what is still a highly centralised system' (Gaster 1993: 126), and a situation where the absence of suitable financial and performance control systems can leave managers uncertain and unclear about the extent of their authority (Lowndes, 1992). Either way, the benefits of greater control over resource deployment for both middle managers and the organization as a whole will be diluted with managers, frustrated by unfulfilled expectations, losing faith in the system and/or indulging in dysfunctional 'game-playing' activities to 'get round' the rules (Blake *et al.* 1991).

Linked with the requirement for appropriate control systems is the need for effective management information systems, designed to meet both corporate needs and the devolved managers' requirements for data tailored specifically to their own departments. This should be 'easily accessible, flexible in scope and content, up-to-date, and easy to interpret' (Rawlinson and Tanner 1990: 34). New technology can be used to reinforce both centralized corporate control as well as to 'empower' middle managers. Fincham and Rhodes (1992: 319) conclude that, rather than being used to maximize middle management autonomy, 'new technology tends to be treated as a "window of opportunity" to support the managerial instinct for centralised control'.

BCC managers' experiences of devolved management

In Barset, devolved management involved the allocation of authority over spending decisions to 'front-line' budget-holding managers (acting as purchasers or providers within the authority's still evolving internal market system). These were accountable, through the performance review system, for the management of resources, to purchase or provide services specified within departmental business plans and which ensured adherence to corporate standards (and ultimately elected member policies) and legislative requirements. In addition, managers had been urged to be 'entrepreneurial' under a programme of corporate culture change, which included a focus on customer care, 'leading' rather than 'managing'. The 48 managers were asked about the extent to which the objectives of BCC's devolved management system had been met, in terms of enabling them to exercise greater levels of control over service delivery and resource management. The majority of them – 45 of the 48 – responded that, overall, they had gained increased levels of control over the financial information and personnel resources which they deployed to deliver services to their customers. The importance which they attached to this is illustrated by the responses shown in Table 6.1.

Table 6.1   Impact of devolution on the managers' work

Response category	Number of mentions made by managers in selected departments				
	Social Services	Highways	Finance	Commercial Services	Total
More control over management activities	12	12	9	6	39
Specific mention of budgetary control	12	5	1	1	19
Increased responsiveness to customer requirements	1	–	8	10	19
Other responses	4	1	4	1	10
(Numbers of managers)	(12)	(12)	(12)	(12)	(48)

Note: Some managers made responses which fell within more than one of the response categories, so the total number of responses for each department amounts to more than 12 (the number of managers interviewed in each department).

The following are typical of many of their responses:

In a phrase, it's freedom to act. It gives a free rein to my responsibilities and ability to manage, it's about being able to make decisions and implement the decisions rather than necessarily – certain decisions anyway – having to go through a line of communication in order to get the final sanction. There's more financial control over budgets, so I can balance the books, so to speak, either by drawing in more resources if the money's available, or by how I use the budget, how I use the staff, over which I've got more flexibility and control now than I had in the past.

(Highways provider manager)

It has meant greater responsibility and accountability for what you are doing. You have greater freedom within the parameters of good practice guidance, regulations and financial controls – you're not continually having to ask the person above you for something so there is a general cultural shift.

(Social Services purchaser manager)

The difference in emphases on particular aspects of devolution appeared to derive, at least in part, from the various functional contexts within which they operated. Thus, the key impact on financial managers was related to their relocation within direct service provision departments – such as Education and Social Services – and the consequent requirements for them to be more focused upon the particular business needs of their line managers as 'customers'. The same emphasis on customer responsiveness was made by those in Commercial Services, although for different reasons. The devolution of resource management responsibilities to line managers in direct service provision departments meant that they could buy many support services on the open market. In order to compete effectively for custom from BCC and other public sector organizations, many Commercial Services managers had become far more aware of their customers' requirements and their competitors' products:

> they [departments, schools, residential/community centres] can go anywhere they like now – for everything, since 1988. They don't have to come to us. I mean, we didn't exactly have to pull the stops out before – it was like Henry Ford, you know, you can have any colour you like as long as it's black. Before, they more or less had to accept what we offered – and of course, we shop around in our purchasing role to get the best deal, and that's one of the problems now – they don't have our experience ... but now they've got their own budgets, they're making their own decisions, and they want dusters in different colours, and the kitchen units. We have a whole range now of different colours and finishes, whereas before it was just one or two basic designs ... We have to listen to what they want, we have to give them what they want when they want – none of the old, you know, 'Oh, I think we can let you have it next month.' Otherwise, they go somewhere else and we go out of business – it's as simple as that.
>
> (Commercial Services provider manager)

Forty-two of those interviewed were devolved budget holders and all of these indicated they had gained increased levels of control over resource management compared with the pre-devolutionary mid-1980s. They had become more accountable, through the authority's recently introduced staff development and performance review (SDPR) system, for achieving both resource management and service delivery targets. Within the authority's market system, which was still evolving, most operated as: (a) providers of services (to internal and, sometimes, external customers); (b) purchasers of services (from internal and/or external providers); or (c) 'twin-hatted' managers (finance managers allocated to service departments which had not yet adopted the purchaser/provider split).

Highways and Social Services purchasers held the budgets for the purchase of services from the provider units. They were responsible for producing business plans detailing – within the framework of objectives set out in departmental plans and budget allocations (representing elected member policies) – the costs, levels and quality of services required from providers. They were also responsible for monitoring spending and service delivery against these targets, and for amending service provision in the context of changing circumstances and requirements:

We are moving towards a more objective assessment of needs so that it may be possible, with a fair degree of objectivity in the not too distant future, to actually place the money where we really need to place it. The split of the cake will be determined by the needs primarily. At the moment, to be fair, it isn't totally needs, it's historical as well. But I think we are trying to move towards a total needs-based assessment ... Within that framework we set out an annual programme every year, but, inevitably, something happens which prevents us from doing the road resurfacing in one street when there's a bit of a disaster somewhere else. Now that means that at the present time, I have the power to make these changes myself. I obviously tell someone I'm doing it, but once upon a time I would have had to check with someone that I was able to do it from the financial point of view. So that's the biggest change, I think.

(Highways purchaser manager)

Social Services purchasers also highlighted the beneficial moves in their department away from resource-led to needs-based service provision mentioned in the last quotation. They commented on the way in which the business plan framework (reflecting elected member policies), and their own devolved responsibilities for resource allocation and service planning within it, had provided them with more structured opportunities to contribute towards setting overall service priorities on the basis of their knowledge about local demands for a particular service:

We can give messages very clearly about where there is a projected overspend. Last year I mounted a really strong campaign because we were under-funded for [a certain service – confidential information]. There was a projected overspend, and I was just letting the area director know each month where we were going. She was going upwards and now there is a county-wide review of how those fundings are decided. It's very different from feeling out of control a few years back. Knowing that there was a much greater need than you had a budget for, not knowing how to deal with it.

(Social Services purchaser manager)

Providers had acquired responsibility for planning, monitoring and controlling their budget expenditure to ensure provision of the service required by the purchasers (defined through contracts or service level agreements). They were also responsible for balancing costs against the income to be received from the purchaser to achieve financial targets of 'breaking even' or generating a 'surplus' (profit):

We have much more control. I think the creation of centre managers at lower levels is the starting point. That was never the case before – finance was controlled by senior management. I'm responsible for the budget of my team, which has a turnover of about half a million pounds. I have a trading account which means that each person costs so much money per hour which is a function of their salary – that's new – so I know that a person will provide income if he's provided to a client on a piecework or daywork or time basis; there's a surcharge on the cost rate which makes a profit ... I have to make a profit within my turnover, I make money doing work for the Purchaser. The fee is fixed, it is a function of the cost of the scheme. If I say my fees are going to be £10,000 for a particular project, and I spend £9000, then I've made a grand; if I spend £11,000, then I've lost a grand and I have no way of clawing that back from him. The profit gets rolled into my cost centre, and at the end of the year I have an outturn profit – or a loss, although I haven't had one yet.

(Highways provider manager)

Increased levels of control over financial resources were complemented by more control over personnel resources. Many emphasized the part played by the council's SDPR and performance-related pay systems in involving them more extensively in the monitoring of their staff's performance and in the identification of their training and development needs. Many also reported increased levels of control over other personnel matters, such as staff recruitment and selection, staff deployment and disciplinary matters. Social Services managers gained direct line management responsibility for clerical staff who had previously been under the control of area office administrative managers. Some experienced greater feelings of responsibility for their own staff management than previously:

Staff management has changed – like the performance review system – the whole sphere of staff management has changed. I think I feel much more responsible for the people here than I would have done 10 years ago because their targets are set by me, their money is coming out of my budget ... There's a much greater feeling of them belonging to a particular set-up.

(Highways purchaser manager)

Those operating within devolved management systems require various support facilities to enable them to carry out effectively their new functional responsibilities and to exercise their decision-making powers to the full. They require training to help them develop the necessary competences; they need easy access to support and advice from specialist staff, and to comprehensive management information systems. Most of the respondents reported that they had received some training on how to exercise their new devolved responsibilities. However, some were critical of the amount, the timing and the quality, and 22 felt they needed more training in financial management and IT skills.

Most of them expressed positive views about the level of support provided by specialist finance, personnel and information systems staff, who had been devolved to their own service departments. Here, their operational activities were expected to be directed towards the business needs of their line manager 'customers'. Finance managers were asked about the impact of devolution on their role *vis-à-vis* their line manager budget-holder 'customers'. Ten of the 12 reported changes in their roles which reflected Audit Commission (1989a) recommendations about the need for moves away from 'ivory tower accountant' or 'old-fashioned auditor-type' roles towards enabling budget-holder managers to compile, monitor and control their devolved budgets. Many finance managers stressed their freedom under devolution to design financial systems to meet the particular needs of their service managers' businesses. The following comment, from a finance manager situated in a Social Services Department area office, was typical of responses:

> As cost centre managers take on their devolved responsibilities, it means that me and my staff are crunching figures less, and imposing our figures less, and we are becoming more like trainers and facilitators – we are doing less of our own professional responsibilities ourselves, and more helping other people to do it ... We see the cost centre managers as customers, we try to emphasize that we are the support role, and we attempt to assist and guide managers in their financial responsibilities.
>
> (Finance manager, Social Services Department)

However, many finance managers acknowledged the limitations on their enabling role. They explained that there were occasions when the control element of their role inevitably took over, in the interests of ensuring adherence to sound financial practices and corporate standards: 'you still have to say *no*! although you try and do it more nicely – you try and persuade them and talk it through' (Finance manager, Highways Department).

In contrast to the negative opinions expressed about finance managers by line managers in a Chartered Institute of Public Finance and Accountancy survey (Holtham 1987), 24 out of the 36 service manager 'customers' agreed with finance managers' perceptions of themselves as being accessible and enabling. Terms such as *specialist advisor, partnership and consultancy service* tended to be used by line managers. Several emphasized the important role played by finance staff in providing training in budgetary management skills, while others stressed the value of access to finance staff located in the same office, where 'you can pop down and see them whenever you like.' One in Social Services explained that the appointment of a new accountant from another local authority had made her realize the extent to which the roles of finance officers had changed in recent years:

We had a local government – a district appointment to our finance manager last year. A really nice guy, but he was very used to financing and controlling everything in his district council – finance, the lot ... And he's had to learn that in our department he's (a) part of a team and (b) he's a support person – he actually supports the business, he doesn't run it. And that was difficult for him.

(Social Services purchaser manager)

Most made similarly positive comments about the changes in the roles of devolved personnel and information systems staff:

Information Systems – yes, they've moved towards providing us with what we ask for rather than telling us what we want. We've got a system called CMIS which is our Care Management Information System, and the care managers didn't use it because it wasn't relevant to them, and so they – they started to create user groups, and they've now modified and enhanced the system – it's still not perfect but ... We really are now in the position to say, 'That's not good enough, go away and come back. This is the business we are in and this is what we need out of that system.'

(Social Services purchaser manager)

When asked to evaluate the effectiveness of the computerized financial information systems recently introduced across the county, the majority of the respondents were extremely positive. Numerous references were made to the benefits of the new systems. These were compared favourably with previous systems in terms of being easier to use and to understand, and of providing 'live', well presented, accurate and trustworthy information that enabled the budget holders to have real control over resource management. Several emphasized that they no longer needed to keep 'ghost budgets', as they had in the past because of the unreliability of previous systems. Some had been involved in working parties, where information systems staff worked in partnership with line managers to ensure that the new systems met their needs. The following is typical of the responses made by many:

Before we had SATURN [the new system] there was a regular flow of large bundles of computer output which nobody read, because you didn't have time to sit down and wade through an inch of paper when you were only interested in two figures. The net effect of the new system is that the information is all there and all available and you can use it and you can access it ... it's real hands-on stuff. I can go to my little machine in my office and plug straight into it and tell you what my state of trading is – just like that.

(Highways provider manager)

Overall, it was clear that computerized information systems had enhanced the scope of their control over their resource deployment and service delivery. However, some managers, mainly within Social Services, reported continuing difficulties in terms of access, flexibility and clarity of presentation. Two managers were still using basically manual systems for their service delivery operations. Some of those in Social Services felt that the absence of adequate financial information severely impeded the effectiveness of their budget management:

> In terms of IT, we're still in the dark ages. Financial management information is out of date, it's unreliable, it's inaccurate, it's not always very easy to read, and the information is often highly aggregated as well, which isn't always very useful . . . The financial systems are supposed to allow people to act in an independent way but this really barely exists.
> (Social Services purchasing manager)

Finance managers highlighted the capacity of the improved information systems for enabling them to extract required information more quickly, and to carry out more detailed monitoring of their line managers' budgetary activities:

> IT has had a significant impact. I can get into all the line managers' accounts . . . I could before, but it wasn't so easy. We have been able to increase the visible part of our budget monitoring – to supply more information, and more types of information more quickly, and more often; it's more ongoing and there's more of it. We're able to supply managers with additional detail and also supply members with additional detail.
> (Finance manager, Social Services Department)

Many provided examples of the benefits which the Audit Commission (1989a) suggests should derive from devolution. These include enhanced motivation, more efficient and effective resource utilization and more accountability for results. Forty-six reported they had become more accountable and more 'visible' in terms of being required to meet more precisely defined performance criteria. This was attributed to a combination of factors, which included the new SDPR system, departmental business plans (reflecting elected member policies), clearer delineation of managerial responsibilities and a general 'cultural shift' towards a greater emphasis on results: 'If something is going to land on you, it will land squarely on you now, whereas before you could dodge out from underneath it because the tiered method was such that nobody actually took ultimate decisions . . . things are a lot tighter now' (Commercial Services provider manager).

Some emphasized the importance of devolved budgeting, of actually knowing what financial resources were available to them. This was contrasted with pre-devolution practices when their lack of budgetary responsibility made it impossible for them to manage financial resources or service delivery in any real sense. Many explained that their devolved powers had enabled them to be more efficient and effective in their resource utilization. They were able to be more flexible and creative in delivering services directly to precise customer needs. Overall, 39 managers reported increases in the extent to which they had become involved in 'continuous improvement' activities:

> There's been quite a shift in this respect. People are much more geared up to looking at what they're doing, and why they're doing it, and how it can be improved. We're encouraged all the time to find better ways of doing things, and cheaper ways of doing things. I don't think that was around so much before; people just went in and – that's probably unfair, but I think that under devolution there is much more visibility now in being a manager – of providing a better service. There is certainly more competition to go higher and get more senior management jobs – you have to look, you know, as if you're in the business.
>
> (Social Services provider manager)

All of them were able to provide examples of the way in which their devolved powers had enabled them to deploy resources more effectively and creatively. For example, one Social Services manager explained that her increased control over budgets had enabled her to make use of an empty local authority house to provide support care for some mentally handicapped clients rather than using the more costly and less effective alternative of a residential home:

> I've just been able to do it, whereas, say, four or five years ago, I'd have had to go up through the great paraphernalia of the hierarchy to get that agreed. But it's my money, it's my budget – I can do what I like with it within reason . . . Devolution means that I have the flexibility – within pretty strict criteria, there's not that much flexibility – but it does mean that we have some flexibility to use the money we've got more creatively. There's lots of small bits and pieces of projects – we're not so constrained now as we used to be when I first started by financial procedures and rules and regulations.
>
> (Social Services purchaser manager)

Entrepreneurial roles

All the managers were aware of BCC's requirement to adopt a more *entrepreneurial* style. Most of them (46) were able to provide definitions of what this meant. These focused primarily on the adoption of: (a) what managers termed a more 'private sector business style', involving the generation of income through actively seeking new business opportunities; (b) a more experimental and 'risk-taking' approach to service delivery, enabling them to be more innovative:

> It means freedom of action to come up with ideas of your own, to not have to be lead from the top. You can lead from the bottom and actually come up with good ideas and experiments, and try them out because you've actually got the money and the authority to do so.
>
> (Social Services provider manager)

In conjunction with their adoption of BCC policies about increased responsiveness to customer needs, and a greater focus on customer orientation, many examples were provided by them of their more entrepreneurial approach:

> I'm very much an entrepreneur. I develop new ideas for the authority – like the catalogue [of products for sale to internal and external customers], and, more importantly, how it's funded. £95,000 of the cost of it is funded by the suppliers, and that's by developing a new supplier approach. It's not just purchasing the product, it's also getting technical support, selling support, and developing those sorts of things, and a lot of that has been entrepreneurial.
>
> (Commercial Services provider manager)

> One of my colleagues has done a series of sitting in a High Street shop somewhere, and advertising it, and invited people to come in and ask questions about highways on his particular patch, and it's worked quite well. That's not entrepreneurial in terms of making money, but it's a fairly radical move compared with what we might have done in the past ... He would seek approval from his line manager, but we are encouraged to have this sort of idea, and go out and do it.
>
> (Highways purchaser manager)

Tensions of devolution and entrepreneurialism

Overall, then, most managers reported greater levels of control over their resource management, aided in many cases by more effective information provision, effective assistance from devolved finance, information and personnel support staff, and at least some training and preparation for their new responsibilities. However, most – 46 in all – reported that, in practice, they experienced a number of constraints which restricted the scope of their control over resource management and, hence, the benefits to be gained from devolution. Most of them identified areas where they wanted to be allocated more authority over resource management. These reflected the distinction noted earlier between devolution of decision-making *responsibility* and *authority:*

> There's a paradox – you've certainly got more responsibility, but you haven't got as much power – the appropriate level of power to go with that responsibility. They've always kept back more power than they've given you responsibility, so you have more things you are accountable for – that has increased under devolution – but for every 100 per cent they've increased the devolution, they've only increased the power to actually exercise that by – 70 per cent?
>
> (Social Services twin-hatted manager)

Despite the raising of the spending level at which changes required approval by the Service Committee (of elected members), managers' control over decisions to switch expenditure (or make virements) between various budget heads was inhibited by requirements to obtain authorizations from senior management. This was mainly to ensure adherence to elected member policy decisions. Indeed, the political environment was cited as a key reason for continued senior management monitoring of certain (politically) sensitive decisions. For example, in Highways:

> All letters to elected members have to be signed by one of the top men – not by me. And they have to be finished differently – you know, 'yours sincerely' instead of 'yours faithfully', something like that. It's the same with MPs. Because they like to keep control over sensitive issues.
>
> (Highways provider manager)

Although acknowledging that political constraints were an inevitable factor in local government – 'the price you pay for democracy' – some of those in Social Services nevertheless reported the adoption of various manoeuvres to 'get round' the regulations, such as recoding expenditure to avoid detection. They assumed that, in practice, senior management were concerned mainly with ensuring that budgetary spending simply remained within the set totals. However, they also felt that scrutiny was becoming increasingly tight, with reduced opportunities for middle managerial autonomy. This was considered to be owing partly to the introduction of more effective computerized budgetary control systems, and partly to clearer policy specifications (derived from elected member decisions) represented within departmental business plans.

Such comments about the importance of the role of elected members, and the need to ensure that managers were not able to use their devolved powers to alter the policy decisions made by elected members, illustrate the 'unique' characteristics of local government management discussed in Chapter 1. In response to specific questions about their relations with elected members, most managers had very little direct contact with them – apart from meeting them at the odd ceremonial or public relations occasion and, occasionally, responding to an elected member query about a particular service delivery matter. Yet these managers demonstrated their awareness of the way in which their own freedom to act, based on their own particular local knowledge or professional expertise, was limited by their requirements to meet policy objectives as set down by elected members. On the one hand, they accepted as an inescapable matter of fact of employment in local government that such constraints did and should exist, in the interests of maintaining public accountability through the elected members. But, on the other hand, they had their own professional (and political) beliefs and values, which were sometimes at odds with the political orientations of the ruling group of councillors about the most effective ways of meeting consumer demands for services, which made it difficult for them to identify with or support wholeheartedly elected member policy decisions. Such reservations were compounded by the consequent inevitable interference which they experienced with their freedom to deploy their resources as freely as they would wish under devolution, in the context of their own local knowledge about particular local service requirements. While, as illustrated above, purchasers had some scope for influencing such decisions through participation in the departmental planning system, the mechanisms for such contribution were less clear-cut for provider managers. As a consequence, the latter experienced a greater degree of difficulty in resolving these problems. In other words, managers experienced conflicting and plural accountability requirements (Glynn 1993): to the local community through the elected members; directly, via their service provision role, to their own particular local consumers; and through their own accountability to their professional community, for providing appropriate standards and levels of service.

Such difficulties were most severely experienced by social services managers, where, in any case, the dividing line between policy (set by elected members) and operational matters (the actual delivery of services based more on professional expertise) was, as stressed in the local government literature, very difficult to determine. For example, decisions, say, to switch service provision from residential to home-based care for a particular client group can be seen as representing both policy issues (the preserve of elected members) and operational matters (concerning professional expertise). Such difficulties were much less evident among, for example, the Highways managers, who operated in a service area where policy/operational distinctions were more easily made, and where service objectives were more easily established, with clearer indicators for assessing success or failure of particular service initiatives, such as traffic calming measures. Several Highways managers noted the greater areas of certainty in their service areas, in comparison with their social service counterparts whom they encountered at interdepartmental seminars:

Our reason for being is to look after the structure and fabric of these roads – whether that's cleaning the gutters or resurfacing the road, that is our function in life. We have no freedom to say 'we don't think that's the best way of doing it, we'll make the railways better instead', whereas Social Services to some extent have – they may think 'that's not a suitable task, we'll try another task', and solve the problem in another way. We don't – we have a *defined* task.

(Highways provider manager, his emphasis)

Flexibility within the managers' resource deployment activities was also inhibited by the lack of funds made available to purchasers to develop services and by the commitment of resources to fulfilling statutory obligations. Purchasers did not yet have the freedom to choose between internal and external service providers. This was because of the authority's own policy about maintaining a degree of service provision in-house. *Ad hoc* 'clawbacks' by senior management to offset overspends elsewhere made it difficult for managers to draw up their business plans with any degree of certainty. They were not allowed to 'roll forward' underspends in one year to spend in future years.

Provider managers also identified constraints on their autonomy to make resource deployment decisions, and to adopt more entrepreneurial forms of behaviour. First, their opportunities to generate business from internal customers were limited by tight constraints deriving largely from central government funding restrictions. At the same time, they experienced tight government regulations about cross-boundary tendering, and the authority's own restrictions on the amount of external work which they could pursue. These placed what were perceived to be unfair and frustrating checks on provider managers' attempts to generate new markets for their services and to become, as urged by both the government and BCC, more entrepreneurial and competitive:

There's no change [in relation to becoming more entrepreneurial]. We can't tender for outside work and we're not allowed to compete with our own internal business units to get work – and we wouldn't want to do this anyway, to put our colleagues out of business. It's a joke to see us as having the same freedom as a private sector partnership to get new work – the level playing field idea simply doesn't operate for us.

(Highways provider manager)

In addition, many providers - particularly in Highways and Social Services – felt that in practice their control over resource deployment on a day-to-day basis was limited by a number of factors. They expressed concern about budgetary items over which they exercised little or no control, to the point where 'your budget's not yours'. Mention was made of staff costs (salaries and conditions of service were centrally determined for the whole workforce,

and these costs formed the major element in many of their budgets), building costs, such as maintenance, and set charges levied for support services,
such as personnel, finance and computing. One commented, 'I'm responsible
for spending tens of millions of pounds, but if I want a new pair of bloody
boots, we almost have a public enquiry.' The lack of control over these
and other items led some managers to comment adversely on the frustrating
paradox of being held responsible for resources over which they had no
real control:

> I don't want to sound power mad, but I actually think that if you are
> going to take responsibility for things, you've got to be accountable
> for them . . . Like they've given us our budgets. Now, if you give me
> my budget, then I'm accountable for that budget, but I've got to have
> sole control over it. It's no good you saying to me: 'Well, it's your
> budget but I'm going to take this bit off.' Or 'You don't have any-
> thing to do with the maintenance of the building; we'll do that but
> you'd better put £2000 aside on your budget.' This sort of thing. To
> me, that's a nonsense.
>
> (Social Services provider manager)

Some felt the authorization required from their line managers and specialist staff to make various resource decisions amounted basically to 'rubber-
stamping', which did not greatly constrain their autonomy. Others resented
what they saw as unwarranted and increasing interference with their managerial autonomy, arguing that they should be free to make decisions as
long as they met their service delivery and financial targets. For example,
some of them commented adversely on the requirement, recently imposed,
to obtain line manager authorization to employ temporary agency staff:

> There is a recent constraint on that, on employing agency staff. My
> view again is, as a cost centre manager, if my cost centre can stand the
> cost of bringing in that extra person to cover the peak in the work-
> load, why shouldn't I do it? Why have to get approval from all and
> sundry? . . . Because of concerns about the increasing number of agency
> staff employed there has been a controlling imposed on that in that I
> now have to get approval from my line manager.
>
> (Highways provider manager)

Similarly, on making changes in staff deployment:

> If we say, well, we'll take out these managers and turn them into
> practitioners, or take three people from there and put them there, it's
> not my decision. It's in negotiation with the general manager [his line
> manager], and usually the final clearance would come from the area dir-
> ector. Then, as providers, we also have to consult with our purchasers.
> It's a bit anomalous really – you're told that you're autonomous, that

you've got a responsibility as an accountable manager, but the reality
is very different.

(Social Services provider manager)

Some managers, as a consequence of experiencing these constraints, expressed doubts about the validity of applying the term 'devolution' to their
newly acquired resource deployment responsibilities. They argued that these
amounted to responsibility for budget administration and monitoring, but
little else:

> In theory, there is devolution down, but the reality is that devolution
> doesn't really exist at this level. It is really very cosmetic. There is very
> little equipment on my budget, my cost centre is effectively staff, and
> that is dictated . . . If I was, say, underspending on that budget, then
> in theory I have the ability to spend that money on additional staff or
> some bits and pieces. But the reality is that the group manager would
> want my underspend to balance someone else's overspend. Profits too
> – if my team was doing well and making an income, then that income
> wasn't mine to spend because that was wanted for the department
> generally. So it is very cosmetic. We are the muggins playing on the
> screens and plugging things in, but the reality is, because staff form
> such a high percentage of it, there is no real control, not real control.
>
> (Highways provider manager)

Finance managers reported that their own operational budgets, as opposed
to those of their line manager customers, were concerned largely with staff
salaries. Their comments reflected those of the managers outlined above –
'the degree of freedom or flexibility is not great'. Their concerns over controls on their devolved powers related more to their roles *vis-à-vis* their line
manager 'customers'. Finance managers allocated to area offices – in Education
or Social Services – cited resource shortages of time and personnel as limiting
the achievement of desired service levels to line managers. These respondents
expressed concerns that the reintroduction of a degree of recentralization
of financial functions and control systems was reducing the scope of their
autonomy over their own area budgetary management:

> Greenwood [where departmental directorates are located] is like the
> phoenix out of the ashes – it has re-emphasized itself. What we are
> finding of late, probably the last 18 months to two years, is that there
> has been a bit of back-tracking, the areas have begun to be more
> dictated to, to some degree, and of lesser importance. The budget
> preparation that we do, we get quite a detailed pack of guidance and
> rules and how to do it – literally, we must do this, we must provide
> that, we must do that, must do it then, and so forth . . . The budget
> for this year, for example. We have got certain budgets which are
> demand-led, or quite likely to overspend – statutory rights like school

transport and free school meals. You are duty bound to keep going, so you go into overspend. The Education Department are fully aware of this, so they asked us all in the six areas to save between us about £2 million, and that was going to go into a back-pocket, so to speak, and sit at Greenwood as an underspend, so we are all overspent in the areas, we have got all the pressure of the overspends ... Greenfield [the centre], who has taken this money away from us, is sitting there with a pot which is £2–3 million just available with no expenditure against it, so it is an underspend ... We are told it doesn't matter when we are looking at education as a whole, but then why have we got *area* budgets and *area* finance managers, *area* directors?

(Finance manager, Education Department)

Similarly, a finance manager located at Central Finance commented on the difficulties he was experiencing in reconciling corporate strategic requirements with pressures from departments to go their own way, and explained why devolved budgetary management required a growth in written, formalized procedures:

There were financial regulations but they were very limited in their scope – there wasn't a great deal of documentation because it wasn't necessary. Before, at the centre, you [finance staff] just knew what to do, there was no need to have it written down; everyone either knew or could consult with somebody down the corridor – how do I do this? But that no longer applies – hence the need to have much better documentation on what those processes are.

(Finance manager, Corporate Services, County Hall)

Several finance managers also commented on the way in which the new, more sophisticated financial management systems had enabled them to scrutinize in more detail the resource deployment of their line manager 'customers', and to ensure that rules about, for example, moving money between budget heads were followed:

We make the [computerized financial] system so they [the managers] won't do it ... one of the managers said to me, 'you keep closing the loopholes', but it's only because I know about the loopholes that I can close them, and the door's never slammed and locked. They can do it the official way – like they can apply to move money and it will go up the line of responsibility and back down again, and if it's agreed right at the very top, it's fine. What I'm stopping them doing is this quick shift across without telling anyone. They accept it as a challenge to see if they can beat me.

(Finance manager, Highways Department)

The same manager went on to give several examples of how the more effective computerized information system had enabled him to monitor, in more detail, expenditure on items such as overtime, pay and lease car charges: 'It would have taken too long before, with 700 people in the department.'

Social Services managers tended to express the view that their service delivery had become subject to closer regulation, resulting in a reduction in their professional autonomy. They considered that the introduction of formal procedural manuals and handbooks, including detailed specifications about service delivery methods (deriving partly from new legislation, as well as BCC policies), had limited the extent to which they were able to use their own professional judgement:

> What devolution has done is generated a bookshelf of rules which didn't exist before.Those manuals [pointing to a shelf] – for years, we had nothing. I remember when I joined Barset, the divisional manual was that big [pointing to half-inch thick book]. Then, back in the eighties, they produced a half-baked children's manual, which was that big [1 inch], and now we've got, we've got this [3 inches thick]. That's an interesting – it links in directly with what I said about the counter-thrust. You've got nominal devolution, and yet you've got – a tighter at the centre, from the policy makers; nearly all this stuff has come from the centre . . . My overall view on this is that the organizational changes have been under the *guise* of devolution, but it's actually been around, yes, tighter organizational control.
>
> (Social Services provider manager)

The introduction of control systems based on financial and service delivery outcomes was seen as constituting an *addition* rather than a *substitute for* detailed procedural regulation of resource utilization and service delivery management:

> We've always had a hierarchical structure within the department, but overlayed on to that, or within that, has been the performance-related pay and the target-setting process . . . I don't think much has changed in my judgement. We just got something overlayed on top of what already existed.
>
> (Highways purchaser manager)

Overall, 34 of them considered that there had been an increase in the scope and amount of rules and procedures governing their operational management autonomy since devolution was first introduced. These continuing tensions between centralization and decentralization were illustrated graphically by a Highways manager who expressed the changes he had experienced in the authority devolved to him since the introduction of devolved management (see Figure 6.2).

Managers attributed the move towards centralization to a number of reasons. These included the need for the authority to control costs more

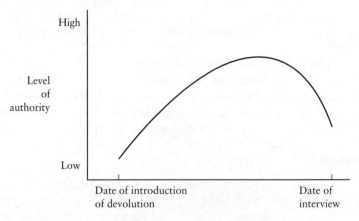

Figure 6.2 Changes experienced by a Highways manager.

tightly because of increasingly rigorous central government (and local member) determined spending limits, and a feeling that devolution was expensive in terms of duplication of facilities such as financial service provision. Managers also raised the continuing impact of constraints relating specifically to public sector organizations, including restrictions on income generation and investment opportunities, the political sensitivity of certain service areas and the need for public accountability. In relation to the last, the following quotation illustrates the managers' recognition of the unique constraints placed on local government managers and staff by the public accountability requirement, of the way in which elected members are held accountable for their officers' activities, and hence seek to avoid adverse publicity which might cast doubts on their competence to run their authority:

> It feels peculiar that they've given you all this authority, and then suddenly they will issue instructions about what you shall do in the event of child abuse with every 't' crossed and every 'i' dotted twice, and yet I know why – it's because they're concerned about headlines in the *Sun* or whatever.
>
> (Social Services provider manager)

They also mentioned a reluctance by senior managers to relinquish control:

> I've got the feeling that it's started to reverse again – not because devolution hasn't worked, but because the centre are now feeling threatened by the power of the areas, and are trying to pull it back because they see themselves dissolving. In true devolution this would be the ultimate end, and they see this and they don't like it, and they are trying to reverse it – not for the benefit of the service but for their benefit. If I was sitting in the centre, I might have a different view of course.
>
> (Finance manager, Social Services Department)

Several managers suggested that, when devolution was introduced, senior management had paid insufficient attention to the need for clear delineation of authority. One working in Social Services emphasized the extent to which, initially, she had operated on a 'trial and error' basis in terms of finding out what she was and was not permitted to do in terms of decision making. She felt that this had since been addressed, with the consequence of increasingly tight controls over devolved managerial activities. A recent external auditor report had also raised the authority's awareness about the nature of its financial control systems:

> They [Central Finance] opened the stable door, and everyone rushed out, and now they are saying, 'Christ, I've got no control', and they are trying to haul everything back in again, you know . . . They said, 'Away you go', and we started heading off in our own direction – so did Social Services and so did Education – and then last year, the auditors came along and brought them up short, hence the review in this department. It was felt that control had been loosened to such an extent that the Treasurer could no longer exercise the control over his fiduciary duty . . . They didn't plan the devolution, they let it happen.
> (Finance manager, location withheld to protect identity)

As noted in Chapter 5, the recently introduced purchaser/provider split had caused some provider managers to express concern about the potential of the new internal market system for replacing the pre-devolution vertical bureaucracy with a new horizontal 'contract bureaucracy'. The latter was reflected in the complex rules and regulations governing the relations between the purchaser and provider managers through service-level agreements and contracts. New procedures had been required for arranging initial contracts to be drawn up between purchasers and providers, and for enabling subsequent changes to be made to these agreements by both parties. Previously, 'twin-hatted' managers (responsible for both functions) had been able to make all the decisions about service delivery methods and resource deployment on their own (in consultation with line management). For example, one Social Services manager explained that, in the context of attempting to develop new services at her elderly person's residential and community centre, she had to secure the agreement of her purchasers, as well as the agreement of business manager support staff and her line manager. Unproductive conflicts had developed between some purchasers and providers, arising from the aim of the former to minimize the cost of service provision and the aim of the latter to maximize the generation of 'surplus' or profits. This had resulted in problems for some of them in attempting to reconcile sectional interests with the shared aim of achieving organizational goals. This could result in 'selfish' and 'opportunistic' rather than 'collaborative' behaviour between them:

Some of my managers became like landladies, you know, arms folded – 'You've used an extra piece of toilet paper, that'll be another 25p' ... We created these diverse cultures which have been very unhelpful and very unhealthy, and I've had to find a lot of time to bring all this back and say: 'We all still work for BCC'.

(Social Services provider manager)

As noted earlier, the Commercial Services managers had operated longer than the other managers within a market system, and thus had time to be accustomed to the procedures involved. The nature of their products/services, such as printing services or the supply of business goods like paper and furniture, also appeared more suited to a purchaser/provider split. Thus the key potentially problematic issues identified by Walsh (1992, 1995) – such as service specifications, forms of contract and packaging work for competition – could be more easily resolved. Complex services such as social work – where outcomes are less easily specified in advance, and where the division between service policies/objectives and service delivery operational activities is less clear-cut – tend to be less susceptible to contractual forms of service delivery.

Negotiator and disturbance handler roles

The acquisition of devolved responsibilities, together with the introduction of the purchaser/provider split, tended to involve managers more extensively in *negotiation* and *disturbance-handling* activities. The competences required include: 'those of the honest broker and negotiator, requiring qualities of peacemaking and peacekeeping between conflicting interests, and a temperament which maximised agreement and mutual benefit ... a capacity to cope with ambiguity, uncertainty and change, and view problems as opportunities or challenges' (LGMB 1993a: 15, 24). Such skills were identified by the LGMB as necessary for managers operating within the new 'enabling', 'fragmented' and 'competitive' local authority. The BCC managers reported increased levels of negotiation as a result of the purchaser/provider split. This was in connection with drawing up initial contracts or service level agreements, and in interpreting and amending these contracts when problems arose or circumstances changed:

We have joint meetings – I am going to be meeting with the Service Development Manager tomorrow because we're looking at another contract I want to establish with some voluntary counselling agencies. I would meet with him first and tell him what I want and then we'd have a three-way meeting with the contracts manager, the provider, and me. I would say what I want, the provider would say whether they could do it or not and what price they wanted, and then you'd negotiate around that. So it's sort of joint negotiating.

(Social Services purchaser manager)

We bid for finances through various systems to the Department of Transport (DOT), and they allocate us some money. We write contracts which have to be in accordance with their requirements . . . What's changed is that I'm it with the DOT, if you like, with the county. I am the chief person responsible for running that agency agreement and everything that goes with it. In days gone by, that wouldn't have been the case – someone higher up would have been *the* person. So most of the negotiations which go on with the DOT, between BCC and the DOT by and large come through me, and before, they would have been done at higher levels and I would just have carried out.

(Highways purchaser manager)

It is, however, important to note, as discussed in Chapter 5, the ways in which the opportunistic forms of behaviour associated with the internal quasi-market system impacted on such negotiations – especially within Social Services. Thus, despite the ideal of collaborative negotiations between equal parties, the reality sometimes involved manipulative behaviour between the two sides in the absence (largely) of free market type pricing or supply and demand mechanisms, and in the context of the contract bureaucracy required for governing purchaser/provider transactions within such a complex service area. Provider managers tended to see purchasers as taking unfair advantage of their relatively more secure and essentially monopsonist position within the authority to impose rather than negotiate changes in service level agreements. Purchasers considered that providers were becoming overly concerned with the impact of any proposed service changes on their account 'surpluses', which inhibited the flexibility and speed of their responses to changing purchaser demands.

Finance and other managers who were responsible for providing support services across areas and departmental boundaries reported that devolution, in conjunction with the new 'customer' status of service line managers, had required them to become more involved in negotiating activities, rather than in 'issuing orders'. They were required to negotiate rather than simply impose new systems or amendments on service managers, although it is important to bear in mind that many line managers considered that a degree of recentralization of authority was emerging:

It [devolution] had an impact in terms of the difficulty of being able to implement corporate standards or corporate systems or facilities across the organization . . . it was partly a question of authority. Control was something that was taken out of the vocabulary. The pre-devolution

days were such where the old County Treasurer wielded very significant control over the organization. He could quite easily determine how
a service developed on the basis of what resources were available to it.
So we're talking about a central power base which has shifted . . . So
the emphasis moved away from control to democracy if you like. So,
as a result of that, it becomes increasingly difficult if there is a corporate
policy, or if you want to try and install something, you talking about
a consultation process, a negotiation process rather than a directed process. An example of that was in developing systems . . . we had a team
of people working with 20 different departments, all with their different
ideas, trying to give them as much flexibility and freedom within the
corporate framework. There were certain facilities in this system which
you could tailor to your own requirements, so to all intents and purposes it was theirs – they owned it – to try and make it look as though
it was something they had absolute control over, whereas, in fact, it
was something that did still need some central direction.

(Finance manager, Corporate Services, County Hall)

In addition to mentioning their customer and supplier negotiations, Commercial Services providers mentioned the significance of their interactions
with the various support service personnel, with whom they negotiated
service agreements and prices:

The budget is now more or less down to each individual unit, and you
negotiate with personnel, marketing and all the other subsidiary services, whereas before, they would say, 'well, it's going to cost so much
to keep the computer running', and that sort of thing. Now they come
over to you, and you haggle about it more, and see whether you can
afford it.

(Commercial Services provider manager)

Overall, these various developments had resulted in an increase in situations where managers were required to adopt negotiating styles of behaviour. These developments included: devolution; the purchaser/provider split;
the council's customer care policy (requiring more extensive liaison, consultation and negotiation with a range of internal and external customers,
including community groups); managers' increased involvement with inter-
disciplinary work groups which operated across sectional, departmental
and organizational boundaries. In addition, their personnel responsibilities,
increased under devolution, had involved them more directly than before
in a variety of human resource management issues, such as staff performance monitoring and review, training and development, disciplinary and
grievance incidences. Here, as one put it, 'You need an understanding and
a negotiation – a dialogue.' Thus, as a consequence of the new SDPR system,

they were required to negotiate with their line managers about their own performance targets, and with their staff about their targets and development plans. Most managers' performance targets included some that were derived from the departmental business plans, and some that they had suggested themselves and put forward for negotiation with line managers:

It [setting performance targets] started out with my line manager really saying what the targets should be, but in discussion. There's been a shift in emphasis in recent years to the point where I've just received a memo from my line manager saying that my interview is on May 24, and will I prepare four targets for that date. So I'm setting my own targets in a way – there's more of a dialogue.

(Highways provider manager)

In connection with target-setting for his own staff, this respondent went on to say: 'increasingly the interviews, because staff are more aware of what the system is doing, it's not a point of conflict – the idea is to come to a joint consensus opinion, and that requires negotiation, I think.' Many mentioned negotiation, diplomatic and influencing skills as a competence where further training was required.

Within the context of new devolved responsibilities for negotiating service delivery contracts and the more rigorous exercise of leadership, their responses also indicated that crisis management and problem-solving had become a more important part of their work. Increasingly, they saw *themselves* as having responsibilities for sorting out problems which arose in relation to budgetary management, personnel and service delivery activities:

In the old days, if something unexpected came up, you'd have said, 'Oh!', and phoned your senior up. You can't do that now – it's your problem. If a kid walked into the office from one of our children's homes and said he had been beaten up, I would have handled it by phoning central office – you know, 'What should I do?' kind of thing. If it happened *now*, I would be expected to get on and deal with it and *then* phone central office – keep them informed, but deal with it then and there, immediately ... like with the flood disaster thing. In my particular role, I'd got lined up all these BT engineers, word processing companies and Christ knows what else willing to donate furniture and equipment – we had so many offers that we actually couldn't handle it all. Now that was rather a special situation, OK, but you put it into context – with any normal kind of situation, dealing with any emergency, I think that the onus is on you, the expectation is that you get hold of it yourself – but God help you if you get it wrong!

(Social Services twin-hatted manager)

Such responses were encouraged by the authority's service charters and customer care policies. Similarly, with personnel and finance problems, managers saw it as their responsibility – in conjunction with the help provided by specialist staff – to resolve difficulties. Speedy responses to problems were also required in the context of the increasing pace and volume of change, both of that introduced by senior management and of that arising from managers' own 'continuous improvement' activities:

> It's constant change – it's one reorganization after another – you know, we joke about it – when's the next reorganization? You've no sooner got to grips with one, than the next one's on the way. You're constantly having to deal with the bits that go wrong – inevitably, things go wrong – and you have to deal with them, and try and keep your staff happy, and keep a reasonable standard of service going at the same time.
>
> (Finance manager, Social Services Department)

Overall, the responses suggest that extensive changes had taken place since the mid-1980s in the managers' role behaviour across all four of Mintzberg's decisional roles: entrepreneurial, resource allocation, negotiation and disturbance handling. The key factor was the introduction of devolved management. For the first time for many of them, they were given responsibility for managing resources along with clear accountability for achieving targets within the context of a new 'performance culture'. They also identified benefits arising from these changes which had accrued to the organization and to the customer/community in terms of more efficient and effective resource utilization and service delivery. However, they also identified limits on the extent to which changes in their role behaviour had occurred. It appeared that, for many, decision-making *responsibility* and *accountability* had been clearly devolved to them to a considerable extent. Yet the scope of their decision-making *authority* was becoming inhibited by detailed regulations and procedures. The introduction of the purchaser/provider split was seen by many as generating procedural rules and limits on their autonomy, particularly by provider managers. They tended to feel less empowered to contribute to strategic planning decisions than their purchaser counterparts, who perceived themselves to play a more direct part in the policy-making process – both in terms of customer/public contact and in terms of drawing up service delivery specifications.

In general, their responses suggest the authority's practices corresponded with the tendencies of large organizations subject to strong visible external political control to adopt only limited forms of decentralization. Control systems had moved towards an emphasis on performance measurement against financial and service delivery criteria reinforced by a corporate culture introduced by the Chief Executive. Yet such systems were also being supplemented by additional operational rules and procedures, with more detailed control systems and more regulation of professional service delivery activities. The introduction of the internal market was also seen by many managers as generating additional procedural rules and limits on individual managerial autonomy, although the nature of these tensions or 'pulls' across the organization appeared to vary between departments.

Finally, changes in their work roles seem to have had significant implications for their levels of job satisfaction as well as for their skill requirements. The impact of these is analysed in the next chapter.

7 Managers' motivation and morale

Recent studies have identified various changes in the levels of job satisfaction experienced by managers as a consequence of organization restructuring and changing managerial roles. Not all of these delineate middle managers, nor do they all distinguish between private and public sector organizations. None of them deals exclusively with the job satisfaction levels of local authority middle managers. However, they do provide a useful framework from which to approach the identification of changing patterns of job satisfaction among managers working for Barset County Council.

The introduction of flatter organization structures, with reduced hierarchical levels which usually accompany devolution, can also involve reductions in the numbers of middle management posts (Dopson and Stewart 1988, 1990a; Scase and Goffee 1989; Smith 1990; Stewart 1991). It is likely that the overall impact of such organizational changes, including the adoption of more flexible (numerical and functional) human resource management strategies, is 'to challenge the relative "stability" and "safety" of local authority employment' (Fowler 1988; Stoker 1989). A number of studies provide evidence for increased levels of dissatisfaction with the decreasing security, promotion and career opportunities arising out of flatter organizational structures and reduced middle manager numbers (Goffee and Scase 1986, 1992; Scase and Goffee 1989; Lockwood *et al.* 1992), to the point in one study where some unfortunates 'feel that they are "fighting daily" for their lives' (Coulson-Thomas and Coe 1991: 12). Scase and Goffee (1989: 79) emphasize the threat posed by such changes to managers' conception of a career as 'a meaningful progression through a series of related jobs'. Thus, managers, who gain their sense of personal identity and related ideas of success or failure through such an orderly career progression, can feel threatened by actual or possible reductions in promotion and job security; especially those managers 'anchored' (Schein 1978) to their careers through desires for career stability and security or through 'vertical' career growth by climbing the corporate ladder to more senior positions. In addition, increased dissatisfaction with pay levels was found by Scase and Goffee, and, among public sector managers, by Mansfield and Poole (1991).

By contrast, Wheatley (1992), in the most recent of these studies, found considerable optimism among middle managers about both their job security and future career prospects, despite the prevalence of 'delayering' within their organizations. Many of the managers in one study (Dopson and Stewart 1990a) reported increased levels of intrinsic job satisfaction arising from the role changes, involving new freedoms to take on challenges, to reallocate resources according to job priorities, to innovate and risk-take and to develop and extend their management expertise. Moreover, those managers who had 'survived' the reorganizations had, as a consequence, gained confidence in their own abilities. Some also felt that they were 'more in control of their own destiny' (Dopson and Stewart 1990a: 14). Comparing the views of private and public (although not local government) sector managers, Dopson and Stewart (1990b: 37–8) found that 'most of the public sector managers . . . enjoyed their work more because they were more accountable; jobs were also viewed as more interesting, both because of the increased responsibility and because of the new management systems that had clarified objectives'. They did, however, find evidence to suggest, for a number of reasons, a less positive attitude to organizational and management changes among the public sector managers, arising largely from the political constraints and the associated requirements for public accountability. These inhibited the degree of middle managerial freedom to innovate. Moreover, the advantages gained from organizational changes were diluted to an extent by increased levels of work stress arising from increased workload, decreased resource levels and demoralized workforces. Such pressures can result in decreased levels of job satisfaction. Scase and Goffee found evidence to suggest the adoption by many of their managers of more calculative work orientations (involving little identification or attachment to the organization itself: Williams *et al.* 1989), with declining levels of commitment, decreased levels of intrinsic job satisfaction and fewer opportunities for exercising independent judgement and thought, and for personal growth and development. These factors, combined with the reduction in promotion opportunities and planned career progression mentioned above, had resulted, for many male managers, in a reduction in the centrality of their work and career as a major source of life satisfaction: 'unfulfilled career expectations, together with the increasing dissatisfaction and uncertainty associated with programmes of organisational restructuring, have encouraged them to withdraw psychologically from work, and to seek greater personal rewards in their private lives . . . managers are no longer prepared to "sell" themselves to their employing corporations at the expense of their family relationships and personal lifestyles' (Goffee and Scase 1992: 378–9).

Evidence for increased work pressures on middle managers also emerged from most of these studies. Those managers remaining in an organization after job restructuring and/or redundancies were frequently required to absorb additional work responsibilities, resulting in many organizations in 'fewer managers doing more work' (Coulson-Thomas and Coe 1991: 23), with inadequate resources, reduced staff numbers and significant increases in the hours worked (Scase and Goffee 1989). Dopson and Stewart (1988: 45) found that even those managers who welcomed the challenge of larger and more responsible jobs, in the context of the introduction of 'empowering' devolved management systems, felt pressurized by increased workloads, to the point where one manager said 'it's fine if your hobby is the job'.

Despite such findings, there is little data on changing patterns of work satisfaction among middle managers in local government. A recent Local Government Management Board and MORI (1994a) survey provides some information about current levels of work satisfaction among local government senior/principal officers (these grades include some middle management positions). This survey reported that, overall, 63 per cent of these officers were 'very/fairly' satisfied with their jobs, in relation to factors which equate broadly with the *intrinsic* rewards mentioned above. In relation to *extrinsic* rewards, scores were lower, especially in relation to job security and promotion opportunities. A recent survey of change practices in 16 local authorities reported that in most cases job motivation remained high, but that: 'In all cases, middle managers felt that they faced higher expectations, increasing pressure, longer hours and the need to develop a range of skills relatively quickly' (Leach *et al.* 1993: 16).

During the interviews with Barset managers, they were invited to complete a short questionnaire about their levels of work satisfaction, using the scaling techniques and measures adopted in the studies by Scase and Goffee (1989), and Mansfield and Poole (1991). They were asked to grade from 1 (low) to 7 (high): (a) the extent to which they considered that their jobs offered opportunities for obtaining the various rewards; and (b) the level of importance which they attached to these rewards. The mean scores are reproduced in Table 7.1. The third column – obtained by subtracting the mean scores in the second column from those of the first – provides an indication of their levels of work satisfaction in terms of how far they perceive the opportunities for rewards to match their wish for them. The closer these scores are to 0.0, the closer is the match between the desired and perceived opportunities for obtaining that particular aspect of work satisfaction.

These results show that the most significant source of job dissatisfaction was lack of desired levels of job security, with opportunities for promotion

Table 7.1   Sources and desirability of job rewards and levels of job satisfaction as perceived by all managers

	How much (mean scores: low = 1, high = 7)	How desirable	Indication of work satisfaction levels (difference between columns 1 and 2)
Independent thought, action	5.5	6.2	−0.7
Personal growth, development	4.9	5.3	−0.4
Self-respect, esteem	5.4	6.0	−0.6
Job security	3.4	5.3	−1.9
Pay	4.8	4.9	−0.1
Promotion	3.1	4.3	−1.2
Close work friendships	4.2	3.7	+0.5

Table 7.2   Changes in managers' levels of job satisfaction

	Number	Percentage
Overall *increase* in job satisfaction	38	79.2
Overall *decrease* in job satisfaction	8	16.7
Remained the same	2	4.1
Totals	48	100

ranked second. The managers' wishes for intrinsic rewards, such as independent thought and action, self-respect and esteem, and personal growth and development, were not met fully by the opportunities in their jobs. Pay almost exactly matched expectations, while the opportunities for developing close work friendships exceeded significantly the importance which the managers attached to them.

Managers were asked to indicate whether their overall levels of job satisfaction had increased or declined as a result of the changes introduced since the mid-1980s in their management roles and the authority's management systems. They were then asked to identify the main reasons for these changes, if any, in their work satisfaction levels. The results are given in Table 7.2.

Increasing levels of job satisfaction

Reflecting the generally positive responses of Dopson and Stewart's middle managers, these results suggest a general increase in levels of work satisfaction experienced by the majority of the BCC managers – over three-quarters

– since the mid-1980s. The reasons for this were explored in interviews. Many of them attributed their increased work satisfaction to perceived increases in personal growth and development, as well as independent thought and action. This appeared to derive from their experiences of greater personal autonomy, arising from the introduction of devolved management. The following quotation is typical of many such responses:

> It's more satisfying – with the devolution, I've definitely taken on more responsibility in dealing with day-to-day matters. I don't have to refer things upwards as in the past, and I have the confidence that the management above me have confidence in me, and I do things automatically now that perhaps years ago I would have thought, well, I'd better check this with someone. I'm making decisions, and I feel I'm actually contributing to things. When you've got a brain as we have, you want to use it. You don't want to be told forever, well, you've got to do things this way. I think everyone feels that if they can use their potential, or get somewhere near their potential, they're working better, they're in a better frame of mind, and that means you're giving more to the organization, and the organization's benefiting.
>
> (Highways provider manager)

Numerous examples were given by managers of increased work satisfaction arising from their greater decision-making autonomy. These ranged from their recently acquired authority to sign their own letters to increased control over service development and resource deployment. This was the single largest source of increased work satisfaction reported by BCC managers. Another important source was the increased feelings of recognition deriving from a greater emphasis on results – on what one manager described as the new 'performance culture':

> In some ways, because it's longer working hours, the job is less satisfying, but there's more satisfaction at the end of it in the performance attitude. Achieving. You actually feel you can achieve something, rather than just doing something.
>
> (Commercial Services provider manager)

> Power has devolved downwards. You stand or fall by your own results, and therefore, if your results are good, then the corollary to that is, then, that you stand up there as being the person that's done it, you get the recognition, you have a higher profile because of it.
>
> (Highways purchaser manager)

In addition, some of them commented on the satisfaction they derived from overcoming problems which had arisen from Barset's moves towards the 'new' management systems. These problems included increased competition from deregulated markets and the needs within the new culture to focus constantly on opportunities for achieving improvements in service delivery efficiency and effectiveness:

> There are more opportunities for job satisfaction, simply because if you win through a difficult – I mean, there are more difficult situations now, so when you win through a difficult situation then you feel quite good about it. You feel as if you are getting a positive result.
>
> (Commercial Services provider manager)

> I complain about the fact that there's more to do and there's only the same time to do it in, but that's another challenge. And I prefer a job where I'm being challenged rather than a job where I'm coping.
>
> (Highways provider manager)

Some clearly derived considerable satisfaction from introducing more private sector style, 'business-like' improvements to service delivery, and from running a 'tighter ship' (Finance manager). They appreciated the opportunity to overturn the traditional adverse image of local government as 'having, if you like, dead-legs who will hide under all the bureaucracy and administration and not make any decisions' (Highways manager). There was a feeling among them that organizational restructuring had weeded out some of the 'dead wood' managers who were unable or unwilling to become more innovative and entrepreneurial. This meant that, almost by definition, those managers (i.e. the respondents) who had survived the changes constituted a 'new breed' of local government managers who were, in many cases, more concerned about, and more able to manage more efficiently and effectively, services which were responsive to consumer demand. Many of them expressed considerable satisfaction with the improvements they felt they had made to service provision. A Social Services Department manager explained:

> There's been a huge change to actually looking at needs-led services rather than resource-led services – using family aids to actually do the things you feel the family needs, rather than what the family aid resource said they could offer to start off with. Before, your resource would be – you would know that your resource was there to provide a support and cleaning service. Now, we're saying what we need is somebody who will help that mother play with her kids . . . Resources used to be cast in stone. It was this feeling of security, you know, that people were appointed to do a job. That they stayed. Now, they're appointed to provide a service and there's a great deal more emphasis on training and negotiation and clarity of purpose . . . you're actually talking to the person who needs the service, and you're talking to the service provider – you know, it's actual person-to-person negotiation. And it's great. My God, the changes we've brought about in some of those families' lives was just astonishing. So I'm a great fan of that way of working. The value is so clear.
>
> (Social Services purchaser manager)

Declining levels of job satisfaction

It is important to note that most of these respondents, although experiencing overall increases in work satisfaction, also mentioned areas where work satisfaction had been reduced by some of the changes introduced since the mid-1980s. The factor most stated was the sheer pace and volume of change. Many, while taking care to emphasize they were not 'dinosaurs' and not anti-change as such, expressed concern about the amount of change they were expected to cope with:

> The problem has been not the changes – I agree with every one of them individually – the major problem we have is the quantity of change which has taken place, one on top of the other. Very often without being able to digest them – your feet don't touch the ground. I mean, we had an occasion 18 months ago where we had five reviews taking place at the same time in this department and we were spending more time being interviewed by people than we were doing our work. I mean, that is all very well, but when it comes to all of those reviews being put into effect at the same time, it is a nightmare trying to make sense of it.
>
> (Finance manager, location withheld to protect identity)

In addition, some expressed concern about the introduction of 'change for change's sake', with insufficient attention paid to the analysis of the real need for change in some instances. They commented adversely on BCC elected members' policy of being seen as a 'flagship' authority by a central government of the same political persuasion, which they saw as intensifying unnecessarily the pace and timing of some changes. Others were critical of inadequate levels of consultation and planning, resulting in difficulties at the implementation stage – although they acknowledged that the authority had made strenuous attempts to adopt effective change planning and management strategies through a number of carefully designed consultation, communication and involvement exercises. Some said that they actively enjoyed the continual change and found it stimulating, and that they preferred a dynamic work environment. Many, however, appeared to adopt a strategy that could be described as one of resigned acceptance in the face of what they perceived to be unstoppable and inevitable trends arising from central government policies towards local government, and BCC elected member decisions to support – and to pioneer in some cases – these central government initiatives.

Essentially, their views about change reflected a number of points made in the public sector literature concerned with effective change management (Dopson and Stewart 1990a; Leach *et al.* 1993). Thus, in general, they supported those changes – such as the emphasis on devolution, entrepreneurialism and customer care – which were perceived to improve service delivery effectiveness and responsiveness to consumer needs, enhance their own levels of motivation and morale, and generally improve overall organizational performance. They were significantly less positive about other aspects of the changes – such as the purchaser/provider split and the sheer quantity of change – which were not perceived, in general, to improve organizational performance or their own effectiveness. These were seen (and resented) as arising largely from 'doctrinaire' or (party) 'political' motives on the part of elected members and some senior managers seeking to establish BCC as a nationally recognized exemplar of the 'new managerialism'. They were appreciative of the authority's attempts to adopt good change management practices, but sceptical that some of it, particularly in view of the 'political' motivations behind some of the changes, amounted to little more than 'tokenism', with little real attention paid to their views or to the problems they were experiencing.

The second most significant source of dissatisfaction for the overall more *satisfied* managers related to limits on the scope of their devolved decision-making autonomy. Reflecting the contradictions of increased levels of bureaucratization which, paradoxically, frequently accompany the introduction of devolved management systems (Mintzberg 1989; Hales 1993), some managers resented the restrictions placed on their devolved authority. In relation to their control over the deployment of financial and personnel resources, they commented adversely on the development of increasingly rigorous management control systems, to the point where they felt that devolution had not 'matched up to the expectations' raised by the authority's stated policy intentions, and where they felt frustrated by these constraints:

> A manager has the 'buck stops here' sort of thing, and that's not the case at all for me, almost to the point where I feel I'm deskilled on some levels as a manager. Almost as if I'm not trusted to make management decisions on my own and take the rap for it if it goes wrong . . . I always feel like Gulliver, you know, sort of pinned down. I don't feel they've delivered what they promised in terms of managerial responsibility and accountability. They don't actually trust us – it's an insult to our intelligence.
>
> (Social Services provider manager)

There were other constraints identified by many managers as continuing to distinguish public sector management from its private sector counterpart. These included: the requirement for public accountability (of both ends and means); the public visibility of both the process and the outcome of decision making, especially in sensitive areas like childcare; the constraints of the central government legislative framework within which local authorities are required to operate; and the nature of public sector funding, where, unlike in the private sector, opportunities for investment and income generation are severely limited. A number of them generally accepted the inevitability of such constraints in public sector organizations. They nevertheless felt frustrated by the restrictions thereby placed on their managerial and professional autonomy, and this affected their levels of work satisfaction. These were exacerbated when the legislation was seen as placing essentially 'unfair' restrictions on managers: for example, where the cross-boundary tendering regulations prevent local authorities from competing on equal terms with their private sector competitors. Similarly, the impact of potentially beneficial new initiatives, such as the new 'customer care' culture, was seen as limited in practice by resourcing constraints, and by both national government and BCC's restrictions on the extent to which income could be generated from customers or purchasers outside the authority. Some expressed dissatisfaction with increased levels of routine administration arising from their new responsibilities for budgets and personnel. They suffered from the contradictory pressures of being required to operate in a more entrepreneurial manner within a culture that was only gradually shifting towards acceptance of the mistakes which would inevitably arise from such risk-taking. At the same time, performance was becoming more 'visible' through the new appraisal system, combined with the pressures of increasing workloads and working hours, reductions in career opportunities as a result of restructuring and the need to develop and use new managerial competences.

Only eight of the 48 managers had experienced an overall *decrease* in work satisfaction. Three of these had lost their jobs at the time of the recent restructuring and had been given posts at a lower grade. All three reported feelings of stress and reduced self-respect as a consequence:

> I got my redundancy notice in a fax. I got a fax that was signed by a clerk – by a secretary in there [the office]. My name was on it, you know – it was a 'Dear Nigel', a faxed letter saying that as a result of impending changes I was likely to be made redundant. All my colleagues in the area got the same thing. Then, the next time, we got a nice letter from the same person when we actually got it confirmed. It was a much more pleasant letter which said thank you for your continuing support and all that crap . . . I think I suffered psychologically because of what happened to me. I became very burdened by it all and I actually went off sick in the November for two weeks, and that gave me the space to pull things together. I've always been quite a go-ahead, quite dynamic sort of person – not in a big way, but a positive person. But this year, I've found it very difficult to motivate myself.
>
> (Social Services provider manager)

One attributed his feelings of dissatisfaction to decreased job security and uncertainty about future developments. Three managers attributed their declining work satisfaction to changes in their job content. The situation of one manager clearly reflected the tension which can be experienced by professionals who derive their work satisfaction from their specialist roles.

He regretted the reduction in his professional service activities and derived little satisfaction from increased management responsibilities: 'I came into local government because I wanted to do civil engineering and serve the public – not run a business.'

Thirty-eight of the 48 BCC managers felt that their working hours and general work pressures had increased. About one-half emphasized the substantial nature of these increases. When taken together with the associated pressures of the new 'performance culture', reduced job security and increases in the volume of work with restricted resources, these factors clearly posed considerable strain for many of them. Such strain is illustrated by the comments made by a finance manager who had moved, as part of the devolutionary process, from County Hall to a devolved post in the Education Department:

> When I was at County Hall, you would be busy in the budget period and you would be staying late, or taking work home or whatever, but by and large you could see where your big pressure points were going to come, there was more stability . . . Now, the authority has streamlined and most of the changes end up with slightly fewer people and more work. You feel you are never quite doing enough; however long you stay, there are 10 other jobs . . . The job's changed – you get the parents, the public, the headteachers – you just didn't come across this at County Hall, you're more in the front line now. Then you have also got to do the accounting type of job, spreadsheets to write, and you think what should you delegate, and what you should sort out, and it all tends to load up, so there is a tendency – you think, well I got in at 8 and I'll do about nine hours so I will go home at 5, and then you stay till 5.30, then 6; then it is nearly 7 and it creeps round, and you think there is something wrong with you, you're not actually coping, you're not getting on, and then you can see that the other manager is still here as well, and there are two more downstairs.

Some of them felt that the extra hours were an inevitable consequence of increased work pressures; others emphasized that they were, to an extent, a matter of personal choice. Some claimed that they chose to work longer hours because of the personal pride and satisfaction they derived from doing a really good, as opposed to an adequate, job. Others had adopted a policy of deliberately restricting the potentially endless hours they could work as a kind of self-protection measure. Some managers, both men and women, strongly resented the 'macho work culture' which they felt pervaded the organization (stemming from the Chief Executive's own well known 'workaholic' attitude). It was considered that this was used to assess the extent of managers' organization commitment: 'There's something wrong with you if you're not seen putting in the overtime.'

All the managers felt their job security had declined as a consequence of the changes in the local government environment; 'What job security?' was a common response. Only eight reported feeling 'reasonably secure' in their jobs. This decline was particularly regretted by many managers who specifically mentioned the high levels of job security traditionally associated with local government at the time of their seeking employment in the service: 'I was made redundant twice in three years before I came here – I didn't ever want to experience that sort of thing again, and I thought I'd be safe in local government – but that's not the case any more, it's a thing of the past – you're not safe anywhere' (Commercial Services provider manager).

Others regarded high levels of job security, which they had expected to experience within the public sector, as compensation for the generally lower levels of pay which they considered existed within local government by comparison with private sector pay levels. Plans for further organizational change, in part related to the forthcoming extension of CCT to white-collar services, were also raising anxieties. The purchaser/provider split appeared to threaten the job security of provider rather than purchasing managers. This reflected a concern that, increasingly, public sector organization employees are becoming divided into a core organizational 'elite' of purchasers whose job security is relatively secure, and more peripheral providers whose employment is at risk from private/voluntary sector competition and/or externalization.

Responses about the impact of changes on career prospects were very mixed. Positive comments mentioned how changes had 'opened up' opportunities for obtaining new posts and for career development – partly because of early retirement schemes accepted by older managers, and partly because of opportunities to develop new management skills useful for career progression:

> With devolution, you've got a wider range of responsibilities, you gain more experience and more breadth of knowledge which makes you a better candidate when you apply for jobs. As services devolved, we've taken on new responsibilities such as the audit role, which we received quite recently, the welfare benefits role, which was previously at the centre – we didn't do that at all. We're soon to get fostering and boarding out payments.
>
> (Finance manager, Social Services Department)

Some expressed the feeling that appointment processes had become more 'meritocratic', with more reliance on 'objective' criteria of competence and performance capability. This derived partly from the new 'performance culture', which meant that opportunities increased for competent and committed staff: 'It's an improved situation for me. I think they are actually looking at the people who are put in post a little more rigorously, and, to be honest, if you are performing, it's acknowledged more – it's calibre that counts more' (Highways purchaser manager).

Negative comments referred mainly to the reduced number of posts available at more senior levels and the greater numbers of 'competing' colleagues owing to the delayering and flattening of structures. Some women felt that they suffered in terms of career opportunities from the authority's advocacy of a 'macho' managerial style. This was seen as represented by BCC's strong 'Maggie Thatcher' leadership culture, by the few women managers present at senior levels, by the 'workaholic' pressures (particularly onerous for women with families) and by the quasi-military terminology used for some of the cultural change motifs, such as: ' "Ready, Fire, Aim" – it sounds like a very masculine thing, you know, like summing up at the end of a meeting: "can we have some *bullet* points" – these awful male expressions' (Social Services provider manager).

Overall, the majority of the managers reported increased levels of intrinsic work satisfaction, relating primarily to increased opportunities for independent thought and action, and for personal growth and development. These arose primarily from the introduction of devolved management systems, the new 'performance culture' and the new emphasis on improving service design and delivery. Those reporting declining work satisfaction referred to reduced career opportunities and job security. Apart from the two key exceptions of promotion prospects and job security, satisfaction levels appeared fairly high. However, for many managers, job satisfaction was offset by increases in both volume and pace of change, together with increased working hours and work pressures. These results correspond closely with those of Dopson and Stewart, which demonstrated a generally positive view of the impact of change on middle managers' job satisfaction. Individual managers' levels of work satisfaction will tend to vary according to perceived changes in their general organizational environment, in their specific departments and jobs, and in their personal circumstances (Tyson and Jackson 1992). This appeared to be the case with BCC managers. Thus, for example, managers' age, sex and position in the career cycle will influence their job satisfaction levels. The importance attached to promotion opportunities was lower among the older managers, and the 11 women managers were twice as dissatisfied with their promotion prospects as their male counterparts. All except one of these women had strong career aspirations and wanted to progress further up the organizational hierarchy, and some felt that this was harder for women to achieve than men.

BCC's careful attention to its change management processes certainly appeared to contribute to increased job satisfaction levels among managers. A more crucial contributory factor, however, appears to be increases in managerial autonomy, arising largely from the introduction of devolution. This was identified by many as the primary source of their increased satisfaction levels. Yet these increased decision-making powers are beginning to be eroded by 'counter-tendencies' towards organizational recentralization. These, together with doubts expressed by many about the efficacy of the purchaser/provider split, and their concerns about the accelerating pace of change – including fears for their own job security and career prospects – pose potential threats to the continuation of their current high levels of job satisfaction. Such issues raise a number of important points about the management of change in public sector organizations. These are discussed in the next chapter.

8   The 'new managerialism' and the future of local government

A number of significant issues emerge from the foregoing analysis. Most importantly, to what extent did managers change their behaviour according to the role prescriptions stipulated by the 'new managerialism'? In general, the interviews suggest that real and substantive changes have taken place across all three of Mintzberg's managerial behaviour role sets: interpersonal, informational and decisional. The interviews also suggest that this was as a consequence of the roles prescribed for them by the authority's adoption of the 'new managerialist' model. Thus, they were attempting to adopt more charismatic and inspirational leadership styles. They were 'enthusing' staff by setting clear policy directions, and encouraging them to develop positive attitudes towards BCC's 'new managerialist' culture. Within the recently introduced staff development and performance appraisal system, the managers were focusing more on identifying and meeting their staff training and development needs. Staff were encouraged to 'stretch' themselves by taking on more challenging work, and were being 'empowered' by being given more responsibility for planning and carrying out their tasks within a structured framework of clear performance targets. Managers were also placing more emphasis on participative and/or consultative leadership styles. They were involving staff in decision-making processes, and were developing more structured systems for ensuring that staff were kept informed about wider departmental and organizational issues.

In terms of liaison and informational roles, most managers reported increased levels of involvement in information processing and exchange. This arose largely from their new functional responsibilities under the devolved management system and the recently introduced purchaser/provider split. BCC's moves towards a more 'open' and flexible organization also involved them extensively in various communications processes which had been set up to operate both vertically and horizontally within the authority. The market system of service delivery required considerable liaison between purchasers and providers. Within the framework of a 'customer care' philosophy, managers reported working more closely with consumers to plan, provide and monitor services which were more responsive to local needs. As a consequence, most reported an increase in their level of involvement in inter-disciplinary project working-groups, which operated across departmental and organizational boundaries.

Under BCC's devolved management system, managers reported significant changes in their decision-making roles. They had gained responsibility for new functional areas such as finance and personnel within a firm framework of accountability in relation to resource utilization and service delivery targets. These were derived from departmental business plans within a new 'performance culture'. Many had attempted to adopt a more entrepreneurial approach in the sense of actively seeking opportunities to innovate and to improve the efficiency and effectiveness of their service delivery operations.

The broad scope and nature of the behavioural changes reported by these middle-level managers suggest that this authority was moving towards the achievement of 'transformational change', which involves significant shifts in organizational processes as well as in structures, and where 'a majority of individuals in an organization must change their behaviour' (Blumenthal and Haspeslagh 1994). Ferlie *et al.* (1996: 94) identify several indicators of 'transformatory change', which involve: 'multiple and interrelated changes' across the organization that impact on lower level units and individuals; 'novel organizational forms'; changes in products/services and delivery modes'; new leadership and power configurations, including redefinitions of professional and managerial roles; and the development of a new organizational culture and values. Clearly, from the perspective of the middle managers who were the focus of this study, each of these indicators of transformational change was manifest to a significant extent within the case study authority.

How, then, does the nature of change in the behaviour of these managers compare with the views put forward by both the advocates and critics of the 'new managerialism'? As noted in Chapter 1, advocates of this new approach claim that 'decentralization via markets liberates both organizations and customers' by increasing accountability (through a focus on goals and results), improving organizational efficiency and effectiveness (including the performance levels and motivation of staff) and ensuring that public sector organizations become 'more consumer (or citizen) responsive' (Gray and Jenkins 1995: 86). Alternatively, critics claim that, apart from the terminology, little will really change. Advocates are seen as ' "cherry-picking" success stories' (Jordan 1994: 279), and as discounting the 'unintended side-effects and reverse effects' of the 'new managerialism'. These include (among others) increasing bureaucratization, over-regulation of professional work activities, increased scope for opportunistic forms of behaviour, demotivated employees and a focus on 'endless reorganization' at the expense of concentration on 'large-scale substantive problems' (Hood 1995b: 114–16).

It is extremely difficult, if not impossible, to make any 'objective' assessment of the relative efficiency and effectiveness of the 'new management' systems in relation to the 'old' (Walsh 1995; Ferlie *et al.* 1996), and no attempt to do so has been made in this study. However, the managers in this study offer numerous examples of the benefits which, in their opinion, had resulted from their adoption of the new managerialism and which correspond closely to those identified elsewhere (see, for example, Gray and Jenkins 1993, 1995; Farnham and Horton 1996). They pointed to wide-ranging improvements in overall organizational efficiency and effectiveness, including better management of resources (especially finance, personnel and information), which were deployed to provide services targeted specifically to fulfilling more carefully defined consumer requirements. Overall, it appeared that many managers were moving in the direction of becoming 'entrepreneurs' who were using resources in new ways to maximize their productivity and effectiveness (Jordan 1994: 271). More time and effort was devoted to involving local consumers and community groups in decision making about both service policies and service delivery methods, as well as to monitoring satisfaction levels with the services provided. Purchaser managers, in particular, stressed the benefits, under the new market system, of the ways in which they were able, on the basis of consumer-based information, to make better argued cases for particular service and resource requirements. In addition, most managers' levels of work satisfaction and morale had increased, arising largely from their additional opportunities for exercising personal judgement and discretion as well as for enhanced personal growth and development.

However, the managers' views also indicated a number of constraints on the extent to which they were willing or able to translate into practice the dictates of the authority's new managerialism. Thus, the prescribed charismatic, inspirational and participative leadership styles were seen by some as simply alien to their own abilities and preferred ways of working. Others appeared to experience tensions between requirements to adopt more participative and enabling management styles and, because of pressures to drive change forward quickly, the need to adopt more directive – and even autocratic – methods to ensure speedy implementation of change. Some experienced tensions between the way in which they were held more tightly accountable for achieving results and the expectations that they should adopt more 'empowering and enabling' management styles. They felt there was an unacceptable degree of risk in delegating operational control to their staff over achieving results for which they (the managers) were held accountable. Similarly, the tighter performance monitoring experienced by their staff, through the formal performance appraisal system, resulted in a reluctance on the part of some staff to take on more challenging or 'stretching' work targets. Perceived links between 'success' or 'failure' in meeting performance targets and the performance-related pay system exacerbated such reluctance. Moreover, the idea of 'payment by results' also encouraged more calculative attitudes to work among staff, especially as the opportunities for gaining the higher performance pay grades were perceived as very limited.

Managers also identified various factors which inhibited the achievement of collaborative forms of behaviour, and 'open' information flows. They experienced tensions within the purchaser/provider split between the demands placed on them for 'collaboration' (required to ensure effective partnerships between the two sides), and for 'selfish' forms of behaviour (Hulme 1994). The latter arose from purchaser managers' objectives to minimize the cost of service packages and provider managers' objectives to maximize income from service provision. These tensions were particularly evident in the absence, for the most part, of true market mechanisms for resolving such conflicts. Other barriers inhibiting free and open cooperation, communication and information flows included: the limitations of managers' own negotiating and information-processing skills; the design of new information/communication systems; and various logistical or technical problems concerned with, for example, the new 'contract bureaucracy' involved in the purchaser/provider split.

A key problem identified by the managers in their devolved decision-making roles reflected the crucial distinction highlighted in the literature, of the devolution of operational *responsibility* as opposed to *authority* to lower level managers (Audit Commission 1989a; Hales 1993). Many of them identified limits on their decision-making autonomy over their newly acquired resource management and service delivery responsibilities. Moves towards more decentralized forms of control exercised through the performance measurement system – focusing on outputs and outcomes – were accompanied by the introduction of increasingly rigorous operational controls over their work processes. Many managers considered that these constraints on their own operational autonomy restricted the realization of the benefits associated with devolution. They felt limited in their capacity to act in more entrepreneurial ways of working, to achieve more efficient and effective resource utilization and to become more responsive to consumer needs and demands.

These views reflect a key area of debate within the 'new management' literature addressed in Chapter 1: the extent to which problems experienced within public sector organizations with the new managerialism can be seen as reflecting 'technical' or 'neutral' problems (of a sort to be found within any organization, public or private, embarking on a radical change programme), or as reflecting the 'the public sector is unique' approach (Gray and Jenkins 1995). Certainly, many of the barriers to the realization of the full potential benefits of the 'new managerialism' are clearly 'technical'.

Such problems – all raised by the managers in this study – can be categorized into four main areas: (a) system design; (b) political/personal factors; (c) time-scale; and (d) strategies for managing change. *Systemic* problems arise with the design and implementation of any new operating system. These are particularly associated with the difficulties of maintaining control over more decentralized organizational forms, as well as with setting performance targets for certain difficult-to-quantify areas. Many organizations, when threatened by the need to cut expenditure, will tend to adopt more centralized decision-making systems, and try to reduce the operational autonomy of lower level business unit managers (Mintzberg 1989; Flynn 1993). Such tensions between different, and often conflicting, elements of new forms of organizational structure are likely to become pronounced. In relation to *political/personal* factors, the impact of any change on the interests of specific individuals can distort both the design and the implementation of new systems. As the managers in this study observed, senior management can be fearful of losing power and status within more decentralized organizations. Lower level staff will be resistant to attempts to diminish their own areas of autonomy, and all staff will differ in the extent to which they feel 'comfortable' with, and are able or willing (even with effective change management, training and other assistance) to adopt, new forms of behaviour. New arenas will emerge, at least initially, for the manifestation of new forms of 'opportunistic' behaviour as individuals seek to protect and advance their own/sectional interests. *Time* is also a significant factor. All new systems need time in order to become effective, and individuals need time to learn, and become competent within, the required new forms of behaviour (Walsh 1995). The more far-reaching the nature of the changes, the longer will be the time period required for adjustment of systems and behaviour. Finally, *management strategies* for designing and implementing transformational changes influence strongly the extent to which change will be accepted and will achieve its desired ends.

However, some of these problems are exacerbated by, and derive in part from, the 'unique' characteristics of local government. Indeed, it is argued that the 'new managerialism' cannot be seen solely in terms of a purely 'technical' or 'neutral' system or mechanism which can be imposed upon local authorities, if only because of the role of publicly accountable elected members. Thus, for example, Hood (1991) identifies three sets of core values (and standards of success) which underpin all public administration systems: lean and purposeful (frugality); honest and fair (rectitude); robust and resilient (resilience). He suggests that the 'new managerialism', with its emphasis on cost-cutting and 'doing more for less', tends to represent mainly the first value set at the expense of the others. In similar vein, Gray and Jenkins (1995: 94) suggest that the 'new managerialism' may result in a downgrading of significant public administration values: 'Examples of such difficulties include the championing of results over administrative processes, the imposition or substitution of economic values for legal values and a conception of accountability that replaces or redefines traditional mechanisms by quasi-markets and producer/consumer relationships.'

Such debates about the 'new managerialism' and its representation by critics as a largely 'inappropriate and imported model of private sector management' (Ferlie *et al.* 1996: 11) have developed further during the 1990s as various aspects of the 'new management' policies and practices have been widely adopted by many local authorities. These illustrate variations on the initial 'new management' theme, in the context of a greater emphasis by central government on service quality and consumer choice, as well as value for money and competition. More than one 'new management' approach has been identified. For example, Stoker (1996: 21) has drawn up three different types, each representing a different set of predominant underpinning values: the *commercial approach*, with an emphasis on business values, choice (exit capacity) and competition; *community governance*, stressing citizenship (city-wide), networking and representative democracy; and the *neighbourhood approach*, focusing on citizenship (local), participative democracy and community.

Yet, despite these different models with their varying emphases on the transferability of various private sector style management practices to the public sector, the debate continues about the extent to which different elements of the 'new managerialism' enhance or inhibit the achievement of complex objectives. It continues to be argued by many that, although private/public sector differences may have been overstated in the past, and although some elements of private sector management can be adopted by local authorities, there remain several distinct differences between them (Ackroyd *et al.* 1989; Ranson and Stewart 1994; Farnham and Horton 1996; Stoker 1996).

Certainly this contention is supported by the views of the middle managers in this study. They commented on the nature of the constraints placed on their autonomy by the authority's political control system, although very few of the managers had any direct contact with elected members. This was attributed to the sensitive nature of officer–member interactions, which were therefore seen to be the prerogative of senior managers. However, the concept of public accountability – through elected members to the local community – permeated the managers' working lives. Constraints ranged from the relatively minor, but symbolic, requirement in some departments for managers' communications with elected members to be scrutinized by senior management (and to be written in a particular style) to the limits set on viring between budgets in order to meet particular local needs which might, if not properly authorized, alter the spending policies set by elected members.

Similarly, the close regulation of professional service delivery activities – of operational as well as policy issues – reflected the fact that, if mistakes were made, especially within sensitive work areas such as child care, it was not just the managers who were held accountable in the eyes of the public, but also the elected members. As Hood (1991) and Gray and Jenkins (1995) point out, service delivery in local government is not just about efficiency but about a criterion of effectiveness which rests on 'good administration' and values concerned with fairness, legitimacy, equity and due process. All of these require a degree of regulation over 'means' as well as 'ends' (Stewart 1992). Moreover, as Stewart (1996) suggests, there are difficulties, in practice, with separating policy from operational decision-making within service areas with ambiguous, ultimately political, value-based outcomes such as social work. Although elected members are expected to focus on policy, the dividing line is blurred; policy changes can emerge from operational professional decision-making, which can limit the degree of autonomy that can be exercised by public sector professionals (Mintzberg 1989). Such requirements contribute to problems of 'contract bureaucracy' problems when, because of the interpenetration of policy and operations, complex mechanisms are required to ensure that provider activities are accountable, through purchasers, to elected members. Such tensions – between elected members and professional operational judgements – will be evident under any publicly accountable management system. The irony is that the 'new' public management approach espoused by the authority caused greater problems for managers' own operating activities precisely because of one of its explicit aims: to reassert elected member control over the authority's service design and provision. It was more difficult than hitherto for them to evade senior manager/elected member policy decisions in their day-to-day professional activities. The 'new managerialism' had given them a degree of freedom over resource deployment and service provision that they had not formerly possessed, but, because of more transparent and extensive control systems, they had become simultaneously more empowered *and* disempowered.

Such tensions were exacerbated by other 'unique' characteristics of local government management. Thus, an emphasis on 'customer care', user participation, and service quality and standards was diluted by expenditure cuts. These can weaken the beneficial impact of consultation with consumer groups about the services which they wish to see provided, and clearly limits managers' abilities to meet local service demands. Indeed, as Sieber (1981) suggests, over-ambitious attempts to achieve the unachievable can actually result in greater levels of disillusionment on the part of consumers than would otherwise have been the case. In addition, the peculiar nature of the local authority 'customer' – in relation, for example, to the 'compulsory' utilization of certain services and statutory requirements – limits the scope of choices made available to consumers as well as the range of services which the authority is permitted to provide. The rhetoric of 'entrepreneurialism' can only partially be turned into reality under such circumstances.

In general, from the perspective of the managers participating in this study, the 'new managerialism' amounted to both rhetoric *and* reality. Substantial and real changes had undoubtedly occurred in every aspect of their work. Significant benefits had also accrued to their consumers, through more responsive service provision, to the organization, through increased performance levels, and to the managers, in terms of increased levels of motivation and morale. Yet the picture is also one of ambiguity and paradox: the rhetoric of empowerment as opposed to the reality of 'coercive autonomy'; requirements for better standards of service quality and responsiveness accompanied by diminishing levels of funding; the adoption, simultaneously, of conflicting charismatic, top-down, and participative, bottom-up, leadership styles; pressures to adopt entrepreneurial (and possibly 'risky') forms of behaviour alongside the still essentially 'risk-averse' local government culture; and the focus on a 'performance culture', but with performance criteria based upon quantitative input/output criteria rather than qualitative outcomes.

Particularly significant are the contradictions between a rhetoric of partnership and collaboration and the reality of a functional purchaser/provider split. This encourages opportunistic forms of behaviour, which involve multiple, pluralistic and conflicting accountabilities, which largely remove providers from first-hand involvement in the policy-making process (and purchasers from direct service provision) and which are establishing two tiers of employees with differential degrees of job status and security.

Clearly, there are likely to be functional and departmental differences in managers' experiences of the new systems. Provider managers appear generally more critical of the market service delivery systems than purchaser managers – for reasons connected with their disadvantageous position in relation to their power, influence and job security, as well as their perceptions about the negative impact of the market system on policy-making and service delivery processes. The application of devolution and market systems appears to be more problematic within Social Services than in other departments because of the nature of their public accountabilities. Social Services provide personal, high-risk, highly politically sensitive services – such as child abuse work – to vulnerable end-users, based on their needs and/or their statutorily or locally politically determined entitlements. Policy and operational distinctions are not clear-cut, the relationship between particular work activities and particular performance outcomes is not clearly demonstrable and it is more difficult to specify precisely in advance the desired outcomes of complex work processes characterized by a high degree of uncertainty. As a consequence, service level agreements between purchasers and providers (operating within a highly regulated quasi-market system) are more difficult to specify. They are more likely to require ongoing amendments, and are more likely to suffer from the problems of 'contract bureaucracy' and a high degree of opportunistic behaviour (Levačić 1993; Walsh 1995).

In contrast, Commercial Services provide low-risk, non-politically sensitive goods and services to a much wider range of non-vulnerable customers located within a private sector style open market. Providers compete within an essentially free market, governed largely by price mechanisms and normal patterns of supply and demand, to supply a large number of genuine 'customers' both inside and outside authorities. Performance outputs are unambiguous and fairly easily predetermined – turnover, sales targets etc. – in the context of the provision of more impersonal, relatively standardized goods and/or services. Essentially, local authority departments differ across a range of dimensions, such as: the nature of the services provided and the work processes associated with these; the different expectations, orientations and skills of managers and their staff; the nature of their customers and markets; the degree of political sensitivity; and the extent to which service object-ives are ambiguous, measurable and susceptible to predetermined outcomes (Stewart 1992, 1996). These differences are important because they raise questions about the optimum degree of centralized/decentralized manage-ment systems and the use of market systems which can most profitably be adopted for ensuring maximum efficiency and effectiveness of service delivery. As Gray and Jenkins (1995: 94) suggest, 'contingency theory is alive and well', and recognizes, by definition, the need for a variety of alternative organiza-tional forms to be considered. With regard to devolved resource manage-ment, research needs to explore the extent to which, between departments, the potential benefits of more efficient and effective resource utilization are being realized in relation to departmental differences in degrees of devolu-tion of authority. Similarly, with reference to the purchaser/provider split, it is important to examine the forms which this takes between departments, and identify the factors associated with its more effective implementation within different service areas. For ensuring maximum effectiveness, different systems are required for different services, with their different work processes and client or customer groups.

Strategies for managing change

Much of the impact of the 'new management' systems within local author-ities will, of course, depend on the ways in which the transition from the 'old' to the 'new' is planned and managed. This research raises a number of questions about effective change management. The effective planning and management of change is essential in order to gain the maximum commit-ment of middle managers and to ensure that they will adopt new work practices. Barset's 'change management programmes' have been consider-ably successful in transforming the behaviour of managers. Most of them, however, could identify areas where the management of change had been inadequate, and where potential benefits for the organization as well as for individuals had been only partially realized. Barset's change policies and practices – which have been praised in a number of Local Government Management Board publications – suggest a number of 'good practices' which could usefully be followed by other public sector organizations.

First, managers differ in their own personal preferences for working in relatively stable or dynamic work role environments and in the extent to which they enjoy their work (Nicholson and West 1988). It is essential, when recruiting and redeploying staff, to use selection methods which will ensure the appointment of those with the appropriate preferences for working within relatively flexible work environments. Managers' attitudes to embracing changing working practices are also likely to be influenced by the degree to which they possess the necessary competences for discharging new responsibilities. Clearly, an authority can achieve much by ensuring that adequate training in the newly required skills and knowledge is provided *in advance* of managers taking on new duties. Training to develop skills in time management, delegation, information processing etc. can be of immense value in helping them to cope with the problems which frequently accompany public sector change, of 'doing more with less', which can lead to increasing work pressures and stress, and longer hours. Managers are also more likely to be committed to change, and to adopt changing work roles, if they perceive that enhanced intrinsic and/or extrinsic rewards are likely to be gained from the new practices. Thus, the likely impact of changes on managers' personal work values should be assessed when change is planned. It may be more difficult to maintain extrinsic reward opportunities, especially those concerned with job security and promotion opportunities. Authorities need to focus on changing a culture emphasizing traditional hierarchical promotion to one where lateral opportunities for personal development are emphasized. More advice and assistance on career planning can also be helpful. If redundancies are likely, systems which reduce uncertainties, and provide counselling and help with finding alternative employment etc., can soften the pain for affected staff. Job insecurities are more likely to be experienced by provider rather than purchaser managers. The former may feel undervalued compared with the latter, who may be seen as more secure, and more extensively involved in high-status corporate activities such as strategy formulation and planning.

The responses of the managers in this study suggest that public sector managers' willingness to adopt proposed changes in their work practices is also likely to be influenced by other factors. The first is that the changes are perceived as arising from 'real' needs; that is, changes which will improve service delivery as opposed to externally imposed 'political' or doctrinaire requirements which can be seen to have little or no relevance to organizational performance. The second is that the aims and objectives of change are clearly explained and communicated at an early stage. The third is that appropriate procedures are implemented to involve managers in change planning and design as soon as possible. The fourth is that changes are 'paced' in order to avoid overload. Clearly, much depends on strong and coherent leadership from the top; on clearly disseminated, consistent and well argued communication which outlines useful and positive rationales for the planned changes, followed by procedures for ensuring that managers and staff throughout the authority are involved as much as possible. This should involve *real*, as opposed to *token*, consultation, not just at the outset, but on an ongoing basis. Continual monitoring and reinforcement – particularly of cultural and value-based changes – is essential to avoid 'drift' back into 'old' ways of doing things. Role model examples provided by senior management can be important; exhortations to adopt stringent 'value-for-money' practices will be resented and evaded if senior managers are not perceived to be behaving accordingly.

Little can be done by senior management or elected members about central government legislative prescriptions or requirements for particular changes. However, the way in which these are communicated, planned and implemented, with an emphasis upon the benefits, can help to overcome resistance to what may be perceived as 'unnecessary' change. Elected members and senior managers should be aware of the need to avoid 'unnecessary' change for change's sake. Even managers who are predisposed to 'dynamic' role prescriptions need time to consolidate and to reflect.

The future of the 'new managerialism' in local government

What is the future for local government managers with the election of a Labour government in May 1997? Certainly, the national structure of local government will be very different with the creation of the new unitary authorities. The traditional elected member committee structures and governance systems are likely to face changes with the possible introduction of measures to permit local authorities to experiment with elected mayors and cabinet-style executives (Doyle 1996). There are also proposals to introduce annual elections for a proportion of councillors (Labour Party 1997). In terms of the general role and function of local government, the Labour Party election manifesto stated that the party has a commitment to 'good' local government: 'Local decision-making should be less constrained by central government, and also more accountable to local people. We will place on councils a new duty to promote the economic, social and environmental well-being of their area. They should work in partnership with local people, local business and local voluntary organisations. They will have the powers necessary to develop these partnerships' (Labour Party 1997: 34).

It would appear that (for both the existing and the new authorities) the shift during the 1990s towards community and consumer choice and participation in policy-making and service delivery, and towards better service standards and quality – as well as better value for money – will continue. The emphasis may move away from Leach *et al.*'s (1994) and Stoker's (1996) 'business' values element of the 'new managerialism' towards those which are underpinned by citizen- and customer-based 'market' and 'community' value clusters. The core features of the Labour government's approach to local government would certainly seem to reflect the 'hybrid' model of public sector management identified by Ferlie *et al.* (1996), in that they combine elements of a more business-like orientation (albeit with a greater emphasis on service standards and quality as well as cost-cutting measures) with some of the more traditional 'public administration' values. The 'learning organization' component of the 'new managerialism' – with its emphasis on flexibility, bottom-up as well as top-down innovation and 'willingness to experiment' – also appears to be gaining ground (Clarke 1996: 94; Ferlie *et al.* 1996). But the question of which particular combination of such 'new' managerialist elements is likely to result in the most effective levels of performance by local authorities clearly requires further research in the light of the problems identified with various aspects of the 'new managerialism' in its present forms.

Certainly, a key feature of the Labour government's policies is to instruct local authorities to achieve particular standards of service delivery which would be compared with those set by other similar authorities. These could involve annual service delivery plans and objectives similar to those drawn up under the exercise undertaken recently in Wales by the new unitary authorities: 'nearly all the Welsh plans outlined an overall mission for each council, supported by a comprehensive range of objectives for each service ... Most ... went beyond current statutory requirements in publishing their plans. Councils conducted extensive consultations with organisations ranging from the private sector, chambers of commerce, training and enterprise councils to health authorities, voluntary organisations, fire and police authorities and the public' (Pike 1997a: 14). Such standards clearly include a continuing emphasis on the 'service user focused "revolution"' (Page 1996), including extensive consultation with local community groups, agencies and consumers undertaken through such devices as newsletters, service guides, surveys, user forums, citizen's juries, customer panels and the like (Labour Party 1997). This focus would appear to be justified given the primary emphasis placed on local government as a 'service provider' by the general public. Recent surveys suggest that 'quality of services', 'responding to local people's wishes' and 'cost of services' were the three most important factors taken into account when people were asked about deciding the structure of local government for their particular area (Page 1996). Interestingly, such surveys also demonstrate rising levels of satisfaction with local government performance since 1988.

Yet this 'responsive service' focus is unlikely to be accompanied by a return to any traditional notion of the local authority as a direct provider.

While Labour intends to abolish the compulsory element of competitive tendering in 1999, there will be a legal requirement for authorities to demonstrate 'best value' practice for the public (Pike 1997a). They will have to make continuous improvements in service costs and quality as an alternative to CCT, although Labour does not intend to set 'minimum' national service standards.

There will also be a continuing focus on 'partnerships' in terms of local authorities working with voluntary and private sector organizations to adopt a very wide variety of different service delivery methods to meet the new required quality standards. These will also operate between central and local government institutions, with more consultative relationships between the two government levels (Pike 1997b; Labour Party 1997). General levels of central government funding for local government are, however, unlikely to be increased, and it is not clear to what extent Labour will remove the spending 'caps' currently set for each authority. In addition, despite the commitment to central/local partnerships, it is evident that 'the basic framework, not every detail, of local service provision must be for central government ... The Audit Commission will be given additional powers to monitor performance and promote efficiency. On its advice, government will where necessary send in a management team with full powers to remedy failure ... Although crude and universal tax capping should go, we will retain reserve powers to control excessive council tax rises' (Labour Party 1997: 34).

Thus, local government managers will continue to be subjected to increasingly tight resource constraints, with continuing demands from both central and local government for more and higher service standards, and the continuation of mixed economy forms of service provision – although there will be greater scope for choice over the latter between individual local authorities. Within this relatively hostile environment of having 'to do more with less', local authorities may well tend towards the adoption of increasingly centralized control systems in attempting to counter the potentially fragmenting impact of the current CCT requirements and the forthcoming requirements to set clear service cost and quality standards. They may implement more rigorous and extensive performance measures and controls, especially within the context of the continuing need for contracts and service level agreements to regulate service delivery, and for strategic planning systems to coordinate fragmented delivery systems. Such central management control will be facilitated by the growing use of sophisticated computerized management information systems, which, as yet, are only in their infancy in many authorities. Utilization of these may lead to a fuller realization of the fragmented 'network' organization associated with the 'enabling' local authority. Increasingly, local authority workforces are likely to become subdivided into a relatively secure and privileged group of 'core' managers involved in strategic planning and purchasing of services, and a less secure category of employees responsible for service provision, who are at risk from job losses should contracts not be secured from 'enabling' authorities.

Managers, then, will need to continue to enhance their skills to function in this changing local government environment. Yet they will be operating, under the Labour government, within a more sympathetic political climate, in the sense of an acknowledgement of the importance of the welfare state and public service provision. There may well be more emphasis on the development of non-competitive, as opposed to market, forms of service provision, where trust and collaboration can be more firmly established between purchaser and provider functions. This may help to reduce a growing gap between policy making and the execution of service delivery; strengthen local public accountability; and render more rewarding the work of local authority middle managers. What is certain is that the work environment of local government managers will continue to change. The election of a Labour government does not herald a return to the 'security' and routinized bureaucratic practices of the past. Even were this to be contemplated by politicians, the results of this research suggest that it would be resisted by practising local government managers. For the majority of them, the 'new managerialism' is no longer rhetoric but the reality of their employment within local government in the late 1990s.

Appendix 1: Methodology

A case study approach was chosen for this research because it has the potential to provide valuable insights into the complex socio-political processes which characterize behaviour in organizations. These are difficult to elucidate through the use of 'at a distance' methods such as surveys (Crompton and Jones 1988: 72; Bryman 1989). Barset County Council was selected for the case study because it represents an authority which is 'critical' in the sense of this term as used by Goldthorpe *et al.* (1969: 31).Thus, the authority was chosen on the grounds that, given its extensive and nationally recognized adoption of the 'new managerialism', it would present an 'as favourable as possible' organization for examining the impact of such systems on managerial behaviour. The authority presented a 'best possible chance' for studying these managerial behaviour changes, in that if changes did not occur in this 'critical' organization, then they were unlikely to be occurring to a significant degree elsewhere. The findings of this research can therefore be seen as illustrative of wider trends affecting middle managerial work behaviour in other comparable local authorities.

Stage one of the research involved the analysis, from within Mintzberg's (1973, 1983, 1989) models of organization design and managerial roles, of the formally prescribed structural and managerial changes which had occurred in the authority since the mid-1980s – the onset of adoption of the 'new' management model. Non-participant observation, semi-structured interviews with senior managers and perusal of a large range of internal documents were used to assess the authority's progression towards the 'ideal-type' new managerialist structures and systems. The second stage of the research involved semi-structured interviews of about two hours' duration with 48 middle managers. Middle managers were defined as those managers who had first-line managers/supervisors reporting to them, and who reported in turn to more senior managers (Dopson and Stewart 1990a, b). Largely open-ended questions about the impact of Barset's formally prescribed changes in policies and managerial role prescriptions on their work behaviour were put to the managers, plus a short, self-administered questionnaire to assess job satisfaction levels. The managers were drawn from two direct service departments (Social Services and Highways) and two indirect service departments (Finance and Commercial Services). An outline of these departments' functions, budgets and size are provided below. Given that local authorities are highly differentiated organizations, these departments were chosen on the assumption that the responses of these managers, within their four very different contexts, would vary in terms of their experiences of the impact of BCC's new management prescriptions on their role behaviour.

Selected departments: approximate number of employees, revenue budgets and functions at the time of the research

The *Social Services Department* has a revenue budget of over £50 million and about 5000 full-time equivalent staff. It is responsible for the provision of a variety of home-based, community and residential care services for children and families, elderly people, people with learning and physical disabilities and people with mental health problems.

The *Highways Department* is responsible for the provision of highways and transportation services, which include: transportation planning; public transport support; the planning, design, construction and maintenance of roads and footways; traffic management and road safety; waste management and regulation. It employs over 800 full-time equivalent members of staff, and has a revenue budget of over £8 million.

The *Commercial Services Department* has over 2000 full-time equivalent employees, but receives no public funding; it generates its own income from product/services sales. The business units, many operating under compulsory competitive tendering regulations, provide services which include printing, cleaning services, office furniture and equipment, lease cars, catering services and vehicle maintenance.

The *Finance Department* has a revenue budget of about £4 million, with just over 200 full-time equivalent staff employed within the county's Corporate Finance Department. About 400 staff are devolved to the various service departments. The services provided by Corporate Finance include management and review of corporate financial processes, ensuring compliance with financial control procedures and standards and supporting departmental finance services. The devolved departmental finance sections carry out a similar range of services at departmental levels, and also assist budget-holder line managers.

Appendix 2: Management approaches: past and present

	Past (Say 1960–1975)	Present (Say 1979→)
Era	Rising expectations	Limited resources
Strategies	Allowable growth	Real cuts
	Big is best	Small is best
	Economies of scale	Economy through managers who have recognized responsibility for activities, budgets etc.
Structures	Fragmented	Central corporate direction
	Service/committee based	Delegated management
Key systems	Allocation of resources	Strategic planning to adapt and take advantage of demographic shifts
	Detailed bureaucratic and universal controls, particularly of inputs	Concentration on control of outputs in broad terms
	Financial control in 'real terms' (i.e. inflation costs accepted)	Cash planning (i.e. if inflation exceeds expectations, activities are cut)
Key skills	Professional	Managerial
	Administrative	Political (small p)

	Past (Say 1960–1975)	*Present (Say 1979→)*
Style	Bureaucratic	Experimental
	Safe (i.e. documentary cover for action; 'Yes, Minister' levels of protection)	Innovative: participative (i.e. selective in the use of resources and therefore involving risk-taking)
Staff	Heavy at the centre	Lean at the centre (or should be)
	Limited use of technology; limited freedom to managers to manage	Intensive use of technology; maximum freedom to manage

Source: local authority document; identity withheld to protect confidentiality.

References

Ackroyd, S. (1996) 'Organisation contra organisations: professions and organisational change in the United Kingdom', *Organisation Studies*, 17(4), 573–97.

Ackroyd, S., Hughes, J. and Soothill, K. (1989) 'Public sector services and their management', *Journal of Management Studies*, 26(6), 603–19.

Argyris, C. (1964) *Integrating the Individual and the Organisation*. New York: Wiley.

Audit Commission, Local Government Training Board and Institute for Local Government Studies (1985) *Good Management in Local Government*. Luton: Local Government Training Board.

Audit Commission (1988) *The Competitive Council*. London: HMSO.

Audit Commission (1989a) *Better Financial Management*. London: HMSO.

Audit Commission (1989b) *People Management: Retaining and Recruiting Professionals*. London: HMSO.

Audit Commission (1989c) *More Equal than Others: the Chief Executive in Local Government*. London: HMSO.

Audit Commission (1990) *We Can't Go on Meeting Like This*. London: HMSO.

Audit Commission (1991) *People Management: Human Resources in Tomorrow's Public Services*. London: HMSO.

Audit Commission (1995) *Paying the Piper: People and Pay Management in Local Government*. London: HMSO.

Bains Report (1972) *The New Local Authorities: Study Group on Local Authority Management Structure*. London: HMSO.

Baker, W.E. (1992) 'The network organisation in theory and practice', in N. Nohria, and R.G. Eccles (eds) *Structure, Form and Action*. Boston: Harvard Business School Press.

Barham, K. and Rassam, C. (1989) *Shaping the Corporate Future*. London: Unwin Hyman.

Bass, B.M. and Avolio, B.J. (1990) 'The implications of transactional and transformational leadership for individual, team, and organisational development', *Research in Organisational Change and Development*, 4, 231–73.

Blake, B., Bolan, P., Burns, D. and Gaster, L. (1991) *Local Budgeting in Practice*. Bristol: School for Advanced Urban Studies.

Blau, P.M. (1955) *The Dynamics of Bureaucracy*. Chicago: University of Chicago Press.

Blau, P.M. and Scott, W.R. (1963) *Formal Organisations*. London: Routledge and Kegan Paul.

Blumenthal, B. and Haspeslagh, P. (1994) 'Towards a definition of corporate transformation', *Sloan Management Review*, Spring, 101–6.

Brignall, S. (1993) 'Performance measurement and change in local government: a general case and a childcare application', *Public Money and Management*, October–December, 23–30.

Brooke, R. (1989) *Managing the Enabling Authority*. Harlow: Longman.

Broussine, M. (1988) *Local Authority Chief Officers and Their Private Sector Counterparts: Are They the Same or Different?* Bristol: Bristol Polytechnic.

Broussine, M. (1992) 'Private and public management compared', in Bristol Business School, *Public Services Management, Reader No. 1*. Bristol: University of the West of England.

Bryman, A. (1989) *Research Methods and Organisation Studies*. London: Routledge.

Buchanan, D.A. (1992) 'High performance: new boundaries of acceptability in worker control', in G. Salaman, S. Cameron, H. Hamblin, P. Iles, C. Mabey and K. Thompson (eds) *Human Resource Strategies*. London: Sage.

Buckland, Y. and Joshua, H. (1992) 'Nottingham into the 1990s – managing change in a district council', *Public Money and Management*, July–September, 21–5.

Burns, T. and Stalker, G.M. (1961) *The Management of Innovation*. London: Tavistock.

Burrell, G. and Morgan, G. (1979) *Sociological Paradigms and Organisational Analysis*. London: Heinemann.

Butcher, H. (1990) *Local Government and Thatcherism*. London: Routledge.

Cameron, K., Kim, M. and Whetton, D. (1987) 'Organisational effects of decline and turbulence', *Administrative Science Quarterly*, 32(2), 222–40.

Campbell, A. (1991) *The Role of the Centre: the Need for Review*. Luton: Local Government Management Board.

Caulfield, I. and Schultz, J. (1989) *Planning for Change: Strategic Planning in Local Government*. Harlow: Longman.

Child, J. (1972) 'Organisation structure, environment and performance: the role of strategic choice', *Sociology*, 6(1), 1–22.

Child, J. (1984) *Organisation: a Guide to Problems and Practice*. London: Harper and Row.

Clarke, J. (1994) 'Leisure and the new managerialism', in J. Clarke, A. Cochrane and E. McLaughlin (eds) *Managing Social Policy*. London: Sage.

Clarke, M. (1988) *Chief Officers: Roles, Dilemmas and Opportunities*. Luton: Local Government Training Board.

Clarke, M. (1996) *Renewing Public Management: an Agenda for Local Governance*. London: Pitman.

Clarke, M., Greenwood, R. and Stewart, J. (1985) *'Excellence' and Local Government*. Luton: Local Government Training Board.

Clarke, M. and Stewart, J. (1988) *Managing Tomorrow*. Luton: Local Government Training Board.

Clarke, M. and Stewart, J. (1990) *Developing Effective Public Service Management*. Luton: Local Government Training Board.

Clarke, M. and Stewart, J. (1994) *Influence and Influencing (Executive Summary)*. Luton: Local Government Management Board.

Clegg, S.R. (1990) *Modern Organizations*. London: Sage.

Cochrane, A. (1994) 'Managing change in local government', in J. Clarke, A. Cochrane and E. McLaughlin (eds) *Managing Social Policy*. London: Sage.

Cockburn, C. (1977) *The Local State*. London: Pluto Press.

Collard, R. (1992) 'Total quality: the role of human resources', in M. Armstrong (ed.) *Strategies for Human Resource Management*. London: Kogan Page.

Collard, R. and Dale, B. (1989) 'Quality circles', in K. Sisson (ed.) *Personnel Management in Britain*. Oxford: Basil Blackwell.

Cook, P. (1993) *Local Authority Financial Management and Accounting*. Harlow: Longman.

Coulson-Thomas, C. and Coe, T. (1991) *The Flat Organisation: Philosophy and Practice*. Corby: British Institute of Management.

Crompton, R. and Jones, G. (1988) 'Researching white collar organisations: why sociologists should not stop doing case studies', in A. Bryman (ed.) *Doing Research in Organisations*. London: Routledge.

Davies, M. (1986) *The Future Role and Organisation of Local Government*. Birmingham: University of Birmingham, Institute of Local Government Studies.

Davis-Smith, R. (1987/8) 'New technology as an emerging issue', in *Emerging Issues*. Leicester: Society of Chief Personnel Officers.

Dawson, S. (1986) *Analysing Organisations*. Basingstoke: Macmillan.

Deakin, N. and Walsh, K. (1996) 'The enabling state: the role of markets and contracts', *Public Administration*, 74, 33–48.

Deal, T.E. and Kennedy, A.A. (1982) *Corporate Cultures*. Reading, MA: Addison-Wesley.

Donaldson, L. (1992) 'Key to the community chest', *Personnel Today*, 24 March, 24–5.

Dopson, S. and Stewart, R. (1988) *Changing Functions of Lower and Middle Management, Management Research Papers*. Oxford: Oxford-Templeton College.

Dopson, S. and Stewart, R. (1990a) 'What is happening to middle management?', *British Journal of Management*, 1, 3–16.

Dopson, S. and Stewart, R. (1990b) 'Public and private sector management; the case for a wider debate', *Public Management*, Spring, 37–40.

Douma, S. and Schreuder, H. (1991) *Economic Approaches to Organizations*. Hemel Hempstead: Prentice Hall.

Doyle, P. (1996) 'Mayors or nightmares', *Public Policy and Administration*, 11(3), 47–50.

Elcock, H. (1993) 'Local government', in D. Farnham and S. Horton (eds) *Managing the New Public Services*. London: Macmillan.

Elcock, H. (1996) 'Local government', in D. Farnham and S. Horton (eds) *Managing the New Public Services*, 2nd edn. London: Macmillan.

Elcock, H., Jordan, G., Midwinter, A. and Boyne, G. (1989) *Budgeting in Local Government: Managing the Margins*. Harlow: Longman.

Ellis, T. and J. Child (1977) 'Placing stereotypes of the manager into perspective', in D.S. Pugh and R.L. Payne (eds) *Organisational Behaviour in Its Context*. Farnborough: Saxon House.

Farnham, D. (1993) 'Human resources management and employee relations', in D. Farnham and S. Horton (eds) *Managing the New Public Services*. London: Macmillan.

Farnham, D. and Giles, L. (1996) 'People management and employee relations', in D. Farnham and S. Horton (eds) *Managing the New Public Services*, 2nd edn. London: Macmillan.

Farnham, D. and Horton, S. (1993) 'The new public service managerialism', in D. Farnham and S. Horton (eds) *Managing the New Public Services*. London: Macmillan.

Farnham, D. and Horton, S. (1996) 'Public service managerialism: a review and evaluation', in D. Farnham and S. Horton (eds) *Managing the New Public Services*, 2nd edn. London: Macmillan.

Fayol, H. (1949) *General and Industrial Management*. London: Pitman.

Ferlie, E., Pettigrew, A., Ashburner, L. and Fitzgerald, L. (1996) *The New Public Management in Action*. Oxford: Oxford University Press.

Fincham, R. and Rhodes, P.S. (1992) *The Individual, Work and Organisation*. London: Weidenfeld and Nicolson.

Flynn, N. (1993) *Public Sector Management*, 2nd edn. Hemel Hempstead: Harvester Wheatsheaf.

Flynn, N. (1994) 'Control, commitment and contracts', in J. Clarke, A. Cochrane and E. McLaughlin (eds) *Managing Social Policy*. London: Sage.

Fowler, A. (1988a) *Personnel: the Agenda for Change*. Luton: Local Government Training Board.

Fowler, A. (1988b) *Human Resource Management in Local Government*. Harlow: Longman.

Fowler, A. (1995) *Human Resource Management in Local Government*, 2nd edn. London: Pitman.

Francis, A. (1994) 'The structure of organisations', in K. Sisson (ed.) *Personnel Management*. Oxford: Blackwell.

Franklin, B. (1988) *Public Relations Activities in Local Government*. Croydon: Charles Knight Publishing.

Fulop, L. (1991) 'Middle managers: victims or vanguards of the entrepreneurial movement', *Journal of Management Studies*, 28(1), 25–44.

Gaster, L. (1993) *Organisational Change and Political Will: a Study of Decentralisation and Democratisation in Harlow*. Bristol: School for Advanced Urban Studies Publications.

Geeson, T. and Haward, J. (1990) 'Devolved management – the Berkshire experiment', *Local Government Studies*, January/February, 1–9.

Gibson, J. (1992) 'From Poll Tax to Council Tax: the implications of the changes in the system of local government finance', in S. Leach, J. Stewart, K. Spencer, K. Walsh and J. Gibson (eds) *The Heseltine Review of Local Government*. Birmingham: University of Birmingham, Institute of Local Government Studies.

Glynn, J. (1993) *Public Sector Financial Control and Accounting*. Oxford: Blackwell.

Goffee, R. and Scase, R. (1986) 'Are the rewards worth the effort? Changing managerial values in the 1980s', *Personnel Review*, 15(4), 3–6.

Goffee, R. and Scase, R. (1992) 'Organisational change and the corporate career: the restructuring of managers' job aspirations', *Human Relations*, 45(4), 363–85.

Goldthorpe, J.H., Lockwood, D., Bechhofer, F. and Platt, J. (1969) *The Affluent Worker in the Class Structure*. London: Cambridge University Press.

Gouldner, A. (1954) *Patterns of Industrial Bureaucracy*. New York: Free Press.

Gouldner, A. (1957) 'Cosmopolitans and locals: towards an analysis of latent social roles, 1', *Administrative Science Quarterly*, 2, 281–306.

Gray, A. and Jenkins, B. (1993) 'Markets, managers and the public service: the changing of a culture', in P. Taylor-Gooby and R. Lawson (eds) *Markets and Managers: New Issues in the Delivery of Welfare*. Buckingham: Open University Press.

Gray, A. and Jenkins, B. (1995) 'From public administration to public management: reassessing a revolution?', *Public Administration*, 73, 75–99.

Greenwood, R. (1987) 'Managerial strategies in local government', *Public Administration*, 65, 149–68.

Greenwood, R. and Stewart, J.D. (1986) 'The institutional and organisational capabilities of local government', *Public Administration*, 64, 35–50.

Greenwood, R., Stewart, J. and Clarke, M. (1984) *'Excellence' and Local Government*. Luton: Local Government Training Board.

Greenwood, R., Walsh, K., Hinings, C.R. and Ranson, S. (1980) *Patterns of Management in Local Government*. Oxford: Martin Robertson.

Greenwood, R. and Warner, A. (1985) *Part I on Strategic Style, Attributes of Excellence, and Structural Design. Part II, Local Authority Structures, 1984–5: Paper LP 8/85*. Birmingham: University of Birmingham, Institute of Local Government Studies.

Gyford, J., Leach, S.N. and Game, C. (1989) *The Changing Politics of Local Government*. London: Unwin Hyman.

Hadley, R. and Young, K. (1990) *Creating a Responsive Public Service*. Hemel Hempstead: Harvester Wheatsheaf.

Hales, C. (1986) 'What do managers do? A critical view of the evidence', *Journal of Management Studies*, 23(1), 88–115.

Hales, C. (1993) *Managing through Organisation*. London: Routledge.

Hambleton, R. (1978) *Policy Planning and Local Government*. London: Hutchinson.

Handy, C. (1976) *Understanding Organisations*. Harmondsworth: Penguin.

Harrow, J. and Willcocks, L. (1990) 'Public services management: activities, initiatives and limits to learning', *Journal of Management Studies*, 27(3), 281–304.

Haynes, R.J. (1980) *Organisation Theory and Local Government*. London: Allen and Unwin.

Hender, D. (1993) *Managing Local Government Services*. Hemel Hempstead: ICSA Publishing.

Henley, D., Lilierman, A., Perrin, J., Evans, M., Lapsley, I. and Whiteoak, J. (1992) *Public Sector Accounting and Financial Control*. London: Chapman and Hall.

Hepworth, N.P. (1980) *The Finance of Local Government*. London: Allen and Unwin.

Herzberg, F. (1966) *Work and the Nature of Man*. New York: Staples Press.

Hinings, C.R. and Greenwood, R. (1988) *The Dynamics of Strategic Change*. Oxford: Blackwell.

Hoggett, P. and Bramley, G. (1989) 'Devolution of local budgets', *Public Money and Management*, Winter, 9–13.

Holtham, C. (1987) 'Financial management: opinions survey', *Public Finance and Accountancy*, 10 July, 3–19.

Hood, C. (1991) 'A public management for all seasons', *Public Administration*, 69 (Spring), 3–19.

Hood, C. (1995a) 'Emerging issues in public administration', *Public Administration*, 73 (Autumn), 183–95.

Hood, C. (1995b) 'Contemporary public management: a new global paradigm?', *Public Policy and Administration*, 10(2), 104–17.

Hood, C., Peters, G. and Wollmann, H. (1996) 'Sixteen ways to consumerize public services: Pick 'n' mix or painful trade-offs?', *Public Money and Management*, October–December, 43–50.

Horngren, C. and Sundem, G. (1993) *Introduction to Management Accounting*. Englewood Cliffs, NJ: Prentice Hall.

Huczynski, A. and Buchanan, T. (1991) *Organisational Behaviour*. London: Prentice Hall.

Hulme, G. (1994) 'Achieving greater success in government', *Public Money and Management*, January/March, 51–7.

Hutchinson, S. and Wood, S. (1995) 'The UK experience', in *Personnel and the Line: Developing the New Relationship*. London: Institute of Personnel and Development.

Issac-Henry, K. and Painter, C. (1991) 'The management challenge in local government: emerging themes and trends', *Local Government Studies*, May/June, 69–90.

Jackson, D. and Robson, D. (1989) *A Vast Co-operative System? Volume 2*. Bolton: Public Administration Research Centre.

Jackson, P.M. (1993) 'Public service performance evaluation: a strategic perspective', *Public Money and Management*, October–December, 9–14.

Johnson, T.J. (1972) *Professions and Power*. London: Macmillan.

Jordan, G. (1994) 'Re-inventing government: but will it work?', *Public Administration*, 72 (Summer), 271–9.

Kanter, R.M. (1984) *The Change Masters*. London: Unwin Hyman.

Katz, D. and Kahn, R.L. (1966) *The Social Psychology of Organizations*. New York: John Wiley.

Kay, C. and Malone, S. (1989) *Cost Centre Management*. Luton: Local Government Training Board.

Keeling, D. (1972) *Management in Government*. London: Allen and Unwin.

Kerley, R. (1994) *Managing in Local Government*. Basingstoke: Macmillan.

Kinnie, N. (1991) 'Human resource management and changes in management control systems', in J. Storey (ed.) *New Perspectives on Human Resource Management*. London: Routledge.

Knowles, R. (1977) *Modern Management in Local Government*. Woking: Barry Rose (Publishers) Ltd.

Labour Party (1997) *New Labour: Because Britain Deserves Better*. London: Labour Party.

Laffin, M. (1986) *Professionalism and Policy: the Role of the Professions in the Central–Local Government Relationship*. Aldershot: Gower.

Laffin, M. and Young, K. (1990) *Professionalism in Local Government*. Harlow: Longman.

Langan, M. and Clarke, J. (1994) ' Managing in the mixed economy of care', in J. Clarke, A. Cochrane and E. McLaughlin (eds) *Managing Social Policy*. London: Sage.

Lawrence, P.R. and Lorsch, J.W. (1967) *Organization and Environment*. Boston: Harvard University Press.

Lawson, R. (1993) 'The new technology of management in the personal social services', in P. Taylor-Gooby and R. Lawson (eds) *Markets and Managers: New Issues in the Delivery of Welfare*. Buckingham: Open University Press.

Leach, S., Stewart, J. and Walsh, K. (1994) *The Changing Organisation and Management of Local Government*. Basingstoke: Macmillan.

Leach, S., Walsh, K., Game, C., Rogers, S., Skelcher, C. and Spencer, K. (1993) *Challenge and Change: Characteristics of Good Management in Local Government*. Luton: Local Government Management Board.
Lessem, R. (1989) *Global Management Principles*. Hemel Hempstead: Prentice Hall.
Levacic, R. (1993) 'Markets as coordinating devices', in R. Maidment and G. Thompson (eds) *Managing the UK: an Introduction to Its Political Economy and Public Policy*. London: Sage.
Likert, R. (1961) *New Patterns of Management*. New York: McGraw-Hill.
Local Government Information Unit (1990) *Information Briefing*. Luton: Local Government Training Board.
Local Government Management Board (1991) *Achieving Success: a Corporate Training Strategy*. Luton: Local Government Management Board.
Local Government Management Board (1992a) *Citizens and Democracy – Empowerment: a Theme for the 1990s*. Luton: Local Government Management Board.
Local Government Management Board (1992b) *Corporate Approaches to People Management*. Luton: Local Government Management Board.
Local Government Management Board (1993a) *A Portrait of Change: Interim Report*. Luton: Local Government Management Board.
Local Government Management Board (1993b) *Managing Tomorrow: Panel of Inquiry Report*. Luton: Local Government Management Board.
Local Government Management Board (1993c) *The 2345th Resource: Information*. Luton: Local Government Management Board.
Local Government Management Board (1993d) *Information Management: Implications of Local Government Restructuring*. Luton: Local Government Management Board.
Local Government Management Board and MORI (1994a) *Employee Attitudes in Local Government*. Luton: Local Government Management Board.
Local Government Management Board (1994b) *Joint Staff Watch: Changes in Employment (England and Wales) 1975–1993*. London: Local Government Management Board.
Local Government Training Board (1984) *First Line Managers in Local Government*. Luton: Local Government Training Board.
Local Government Training Board (1988a) *Going for Better Management*. Luton: Local Government Training Board.
Local Government Training Board (1988b) *The Enabling Council*. Luton: Local Government Training Board.
Local Government Training Board (1990a) *Information Management in Local Government*. Luton: Local Government Training Board.
Local Government Training Board (1990b) *Squaring up to Better Management*. Luton: Local Government Training Board.
Local Government Training Board and Local Authorities Conditions of Service Advisory Board (1990) *Employment Strategies*. Luton: Local Government Training Board.
Lockwood, J., Teevan, P. and Walters, M. (1992) *Who's Managing the Managers*. Corby: Institute of Management.
Lowndes, V. (1992) 'Decentralisation: the potential and the pitfalls', *Local Government Policy Making*, 18(4), 53–63.
Lowndes, V. and Stoker, G. (1992a) 'An evaluation of neighbourhood decentralisation, part 1: customer and citizen perspectives', *Policy and Politics*, 20(1), 47–61.

Lowndes, V. and Stoker, G. (1992b) 'An evaluation of neighbourhood decentralisation, part 2: staff and councillor perspectives', *Policy and Politics*, 20(2), 143–52.

McGregor, D. (1960) *The Human Side of Enterprise*. New York: McGraw-Hill.

Macrae, N. (1982) 'Intrapreneurial now', *The Economist*, 17 April, 47–52.

Mansfield, R. and Poole, M. (1991) *British Management in the Thatcher Years*. Corby: British Institute of Management.

Maslow, A.H. (1943) 'A theory of human motivation', in V.H. Vroom and E.L. Deci (eds, 1970) *Management and Motivation*. Harmondsworth: Penguin.

Maud Report (1967) *Committee on Management in Local Government Report, volumes 1–5*. London: HMSO.

Merton, R.K. (1968) *Social Theory and Social Structure*. New York: Free Press.

Mintzberg, H. (1973) *The Nature of Managerial Work*. Englewood Cliffs, NJ: Prentice Hall.

Mintzberg, H. (1983) *Structure in Fives: Designing Effective Organizations*. Englewood Cliffs, NJ: Prentice Hall.

Mintzberg, H. (1989) *Mintzberg on Management*. New York: The Free Press.

Miles, R.E. and Snow, C.C. (1978) *Organizational Strategy, Culture and Process*. New York: McGraw-Hill.

Moizer, P. (1991) 'Performance appraisal and rewards', in D. Ashton, T. Hopper and R.W. Scapens (eds) *Issues in Management Accounting*. Hemel Hempstead: Prentice Hall.

Morgan, G. (1986) *Images of Organization*. London: Sage.

Morris, R.J.B. (1990) *Local Government Ground Rules*. Harlow: Longman.

Mueller, R.K. (1991) 'Corporate wisdom: how to tap unconventional wisdom', in J. Henry (ed.), *Creative Management*. London: Sage.

Napier, S. (1994) 'Jobs to go in wake of council scandal', *Kentish Gazette*, 9 June.

Nichols, G. (1995) 'Contract specification in leisure management', *Local Government Studies*, 21(2), 248–62.

Nicholson, N. and West, M. (1988) *Managerial Job Change: Men and Women in Transition*. Cambridge: Cambridge University Press.

Norton, A. (1991) *The Role of Chief Executive in British Local Government*. Birmingham: University of Birmingham, Institute of Local Government Studies.

Nulty, H. (1994) *All Authorities in England and Wales: Changes in Distribution*. London: Local Government Management Board.

Osborne, D. and Gaebler, T. (1992) *Reinventing Government: How Entrepreneurial Spirit Is Transforming the Public Sector*. Reading, MA: Addison-Wesley.

Ouchi, W.G. (1981) *Theory Z: How American Business Can Meet the Japanese Challenge*. Reading, MA: Addison-Wesley.

Page, B. (1996) 'Perceptions of local government: what do the public really think about local government?', *Public Policy and Administration*, 11(3), 3–17.

Palmer, A.J. (1993) 'Performance measurement in local government', *Public Money and Management*, October–December, 31–6.

Peters, T. (1987) *Thriving on Chaos*. London: Macmillan.

Peters, T. (1992) *Liberation Management*. London: Macmillan.

Peters, T. and Austen, N. (1985) *A Passion for Excellence*. New York: Random House.

Peters, T. and Waterman, R.H. (1982) *In Search of Excellence*. New York: Harper and Row.

Pfeffer, J. (1981) *Power in Organisation*. London: Pitman.

Pike, A. (1997a) 'Delivery goals "can help local services"', *Financial Times*, 28 May, 14.

Pike, A. (1997b) 'Twin boost for local authorities', *Financial Times*, 4 June, 9.

Preston, A.M. (1991) 'Budgeting, creativity and culture', in D. Ashton, T. Hopper, and R.W. Scapens (eds) *Issues in Management Accounting*. Hemel Hempstead: Prentice Hall.

Prior, D., Stewart, J. and Walsh, K. (1995) *Citizenship: Rights, Community and Participation*. London: Pitman.

Purcell, J. (1992) 'The impact of corporate strategy on human resource management', in G. Salaman, S. Cameron, H. Hamblin, P. Iles, C. Mabey and K. Thompson (eds) *Human Resource Strategies*. London: Sage.

Radley, S. (1992) *A Glimpse of the Future: Social and Economic Trends for Local Government in the 1990s*. Luton: Local Government Management Board.

Ranson, S. and Stewart, J. (1994) *Management in the Public Domain*. London: Macmillan.

Rawlinson, D. and Tanner, B. (1990) *Financial Management in the 1990s*. Harlow: Longman.

Reed, M. (1996) 'Expert power and control in late modernity: an empirical review and theoretical synthesis', *Organisation Studies*, 17(4), 573–97.

Rice, A.K. (1963) *The Enterprise and Its Environment*. London: Tavistock.

Robbins, S.P. (1990) *Organization Theory: Structure, Design and Applications*. Englewood Cliffs, NJ: Prentice Hall.

Roethlisberger, F.J. and Dickson, W.J. (1939) *Management and the Worker*. Cambridge MA: Harvard University Press.

Rose, M. (1975) *Industrial Behaviour: Theoretical Developments since Taylor*. Harmondsworth: Penguin.

Rowbottom, R. (1974) 'Professionals in health and social services organisations', in D. Billis, G. Bromley, A. Hey, and R. Rowbottom (eds) *Organising Social Services Departments*. London: Heinemann.

Scase, R. and Goffee, R. (1989) *Reluctant Managers*. London: Routledge.

Schein, E. (1978) *Career Dynamics: Matching Individual and Organizational Needs*. Reading, MA: Addison-Wesley.

Schlesinger, L.A. and Oshry, B. (1984) 'Quality of work, life and the manager: muddle in the middle', *Organisational Dynamics*, 13, 5–19.

Scrivens, E. (1991) 'Is there a role for marketing in the public sector', *Public Money and Management*, Summer, 17–23.

Selznick, P. (1948) 'Foundations of the theory of organizations', *American Sociological Review*, 13(1), 25–35.

Selznick, P. (1966) *T.V.A. and the Grass Roots*. New York: Harper and Row.

Sieber, S. (1981) *Fatal Remedies: the Ironies of Social Intervention*. New York: Plenum.

Sisson, K. (1994) 'Personnel management: paradigms, practice and prospects', in K. Sisson (ed.) *Personnel Management*, 2nd edn. Oxford: Blackwell.

Skelcher, C. (1992) *Managing for Service Quality*. Birmingham: University of Birmingham, Institute of Local Government Studies (draft).

Smith, V. (1990) *Managing in the Corporate Interest*. Berkeley: University of California Press.

Society of Information Technology Managers (1991) *IT Trends in Local Government*. Northampton: Northamptonshire County Council.

Solomons, D. (1965) *Divisional Performance: Measurement and Control*. Homewood, IL: Richard D. Irwin.

Spence, P. (1990) 'The effects of performance management and performance related pay in local government', *Local Government Studies*, July/August, 1–6.

Spencer, K. (1992) 'Public service, citizen and consumer charters', in S. Leach, J. Stewart, K. Spencer, K. Walsh and J. Gibson (eds) *The Heseltine Review of Local Government*. Birmingham: University of Birmingham, Institute of Local Government Studies.

Spencer, L. and Welchman, R. (1991) *Twice as Good to Go Twice as Far*. London: Social and Community Planning Research.

Stewart, J. (1986) *The New Management of Local Government*. London: Allen & Unwin.

Stewart, J. (1988a) *Decentralised Organisation and Management in Local Government, Occasional Paper*. Birmingham: University of Birmingham, Institute of Local Government Studies.

Stewart, J. (1988b) *Understanding the Management of Local Government*. Harlow: Longman.

Stewart, J. (1992) *Managing Difference: the Analysis of Service Characteristics*. Luton: Local Government Management Board.

Stewart, J. (1996) 'A dogma of our times – the separation of policy-making and implementation', *Public Money and Management*, July–September, 33–40.

Stewart, J. and Ranson, S. (1988) *Management in the Public Domain – a Discussion Paper*. Luton: Local Government Training Board.

Stewart, J. and Walsh, K. (1992) *Change in the Management of Public Services*. Luton: Local Government Management Board.

Stewart, R. (1982) *Choices for the Manager: a Guide to Managerial Work and Behaviour*. Englewood Cliffs, NJ: Prentice Hall.

Stewart, R. (1991) *Managing Today and Tomorrow*. London: Macmillan.

Stoker, G. (1988) *The Politics of Local Government*. Basingstoke: Macmillan.

Stoker, G. (1989) *New Management Trends*. Luton: Local Government Training Board.

Stoker, G. (1991) *The Politics of Local Government*, 2nd edn. London: Macmillan.

Stoker, G. (1996) 'The struggle to reform local government: 1970–95', *Public Money and Management*, January–March, 17–22.

Stoker, G., Oppenheim, F.W. and Davies, M. (1988) *The Challenge of Change in Local Government: a Survey of Organisational and Management Innovation in the 1980s*. Birmingham: University of Birmingham, Institute of Local Government Studies.

Storey, J. (1992) *Developments in the Management of Human Resources*. Oxford: Blackwell.

Tapscott, D. and Caston, A. (1993) *Paradigm Shift: the New Promise of Information Technology*. New York: McGraw-Hill.

Taylor, F.W. (1947) *Scientific Management*. New York: Harper and Row.

Thompson, G., Frances, J., Levacic, R. and Mitchell, J. (eds) (1991) *Markets, Hierarchies and Networks*. London: Sage.

Thompson, P. (1992) 'Public sector management in a period of radical change: 1979–1992', *Public Money and Management*, July–September, 33–41.

Tiernan, S., Flood, P. and Wally, S. (1994) *Managing without Traditional Structures*. Limerick: University of Limerick.

Tighe, C. (1992) 'Tiers are shed as councils cut back', *Financial Times*, 14 December.

Townley, B. (1989) 'Employee communication systems', in K. Sisson (ed.) *Personnel Management in Britain*. Oxford: Blackwell.

Tyson, S. and Jackson, T. (1992) *The Essence of Organizational Behaviour*. London: Prentice Hall.

Vize, R. (1997) 'Labour set to scrap CCT in April 1999', *Local Government Chronicle*, 2 May, 1.

Vroom, V.H. (1964) *Work and Motivation*. New York: Wiley.

Walsh, K. (1989) *Marketing in Local Government*. Harlow: Longman.

Walsh, K. (1991) *Competitive Tendering for Local Authority Services*. London: HMSO.

Walsh, K. (1992) 'The extension of competitive tendering', in S. Leach, J. Stewart, K. Spencer, K. Walsh and J. Gibson (eds) *The Heseltine Review of Local Government*. Birmingham: University of Birmingham, Institute of Local Government Studies.

Walsh, K. (1995) *Public Services and Market Mechanisms*. Harlow: Longman.

Walton, R.E. (1985) 'From control to commitment in the workplace', *Harvard Business Review*, 63, 77–84.

Watkins, J., Drury, L. and Preddy, D. (1992) *From Evolution to Revolution: the Pressures on Professional Life in the 1990s*. Bristol: University of Bristol.

Watson, T.J. (1986) *Management, Organisation and Employment Strategy*. London: Routledge and Kegan Paul.

Weber, M. (1947) *The Theory of Social and Economic Organization*. New York: Oxford University Press.

Weber, M. (1991) 'Legal authority in a bureaucracy', in G. Thompson, J. Frances, R. Levacic and J. Mitchell (eds) *Markets, Hierarchies and Networks*. London: Sage.

Wheatley, M. (1992) *The Future of Middle Management*. Corby: Institute of Management.

Widdicombe, D. (Chairman) (1986) *The Conduct of Local Authority Business, Report of the Committee of Enquiry into the Conduct of Local Authority Business*. London: HMSO.

Williams, A., Dobson, P. and Walters, M. (1989) *Changing Culture*. London: Institute of Personnel Management.

Williamson, O.E. (1975) *Markets and Hierarchies: Analysis and Antitrust Implications*. New York: The Free Press.

Williamson, O.E. (1985) *The Economic Institutions of Capitalism*. New York: The Free Press.

Wilson, D.C. and Rosenfeld, R. (1990) *Managing Organizations*. Maidenhead: McGraw-Hill.

Young, K. (1996) 'Reinventing local government', *Public Administration*, 74, 347–68.

Young, K. and Davies, M. (1990) *The Politics of Local Government since Widdicombe*. York: Joseph Rowntree Foundation.

Young, K. and Mills, L. (1993) *A Portrait of Change*. Luton: Local Government Management Board.

Zaleznik, A. (1977) 'Managers and leaders: are they different?', *Harvard Business Review*, 54, 67–78.

Index

In Search of Excellence (Peters and
    Waterman), 9, 12, 27
'individual' leadership, 43
influencing behaviour, 59
informal structures, 24–5
informal systems (information), 97, 98
information
    culture (open), 46–7, 48–9, 91,
        97–8, 111–16
    systems, 51, 97–8, 110–16, 119,
        125–6, 134–5, 169
    technology, 13, 36, 45, 46–9, 82, 84
informational roles, 32, 35–6, 38,
    45–9, 96–8, 114, 118, 157–8
inspirational leadership style, 88, 89,
    91, 95, 157, 159
Institute of Local Government Studies,
    3
inter-agency cooperation, 107–11, 158
internal business units (IBUs), 77–8,
    92
internal markets, 4–5, 13, 67, 85, 100,
    107, 115, 119, 137, 143
    see also quasi-markets
internal provider units, 77
interpersonal roles, 32, 33–5, 38,
    42–5, 74, 118, 157
intrinsic rewards, 146, 147, 166
Issac-Henry, K., 14, 43, 51

Jackson, D., 43
Jackson, P. M., 14, 15
Jackson, T., 155
Jenkins, B., 8, 105, 158, 159, 160,
    161, 163, 165
job roles, 10–12
    motivation/morale and, 144–56
job satisfaction, 59–62, 63, 143, 144,
    146
    decreased levels, 150–6
    increased levels, 147–9
job security, 72, 164, 169–70
    changing managerial roles and,
        59–64
    motivation/morale and, 144–7,
        152–6
Johnson, T. J., 19, 41
Jones, G., 171
Jordan, G., 158, 159
Joshua, H., 14, 43

Kahn, R. L., 25
Kanter, R. M., 27, 33, 35, 36
Katz, D., 25
Kay, C., 17, 18
Keeling, D., 3
Kennedy, A. A., 22
Kerley, R., 10, 41
Kinnie, N., 37
knowledge (standardization), 29, 31
Knowles, R., 2

Labour government/party, 1, 6, 63,
    167–70
Laffin, M., 2, 3, 12, 24, 42, 70, 79
Langan, M., 19, 52, 106
Lawrence, P. R., 21, 25
Lawson, R., 8
Leach, S., 7, 10, 12, 14, 23, 24, 28,
    46, 61, 63, 146, 150, 168
leadership roles, 32–4
    Barset County Council, 67, 70, 72,
        73, 74, 87–95, 157, 159
    ceremonial roles, 42–3, 95–6
leadership skills, 43–4
leadership styles
    charismatic, 88, 89, 91, 95, 157,
        159
    consultative, 34, 35, 37, 89, 91, 93,
        157
    directive, 34
    inspirational, 88, 89, 91, 95, 157,
        159
    participative, 89, 91, 93, 157, 159
    transactional, 34, 67, 88
    transformational, 34, 43–4, 67, 70,
        72, 73, 88–90, 92, 94
learning organizations, 44, 72, 168
    continuous improvement, 12, 28,
        127, 142
legal-rationality, 22
Lessem, R., 22
Levačić, R., 47, 105, 164
liaison roles, 32–3, 35, 96–8, 107–11,
    114, 157–8
Likert, R., 25
line managers, 33, 43, 49, 51, 70, 84,
    94–5, 123, 124, 132, 133, 139
Local Authorities Conditions of Service
    Advisory Board (LACSAB), 11,
    12, 14, 57

WHATEVER HAPPENED TO LOCAL GOVERNMENT?

Allan Cochrane

In the 1980s British local government was at the eye of the political storm. Councils were blamed for overspending and central government was blamed for threatening to bring an end to local democracy. In 1990 a new local tax – the poll tax – proved so unpopular that it helped to bring an end to Margaret Thatcher's reign as Prime Minister. But what has really happened to local government over the last fifteen years? What do the changes tell us about the nature of British politics in the 1990s? And what do they mean for the future direction of local government?

These questions are at the heart of this book, which argues that it is necessary fundamentally to reappraise the ways in which we understand local government. Allan Cochrane develops a wide ranging argument, drawing on material from across the traditional divisions created by academic disciplines and theoretical systems to show that local government in Britain will never be the same again. It needs to be seen as just one element in a more complex local welfare state, which is itself being transformed to fit in with a new (business-led) agenda for welfare.

Contents
Introduction – Local government as welfare state – The 'end' of local government? – From state to market? – Towards the 'enabling' authority? – Post-Fordism and local government – Restructuring the local welfare state – From local government to local state: the impact of restructuring – References – Index.

160pp   0 335 19011 1 (Paperback)

ENABLING OR DISABLING LOCAL GOVERNMENT

Steve Leach, Howard Davis and Associates

- What are the main underlying patterns in the changes which central government have introduced in relation to local government over the past 10–15 years?
- What are the major choices of direction facing local authorities, in working out how to respond to these (and other) changes?
- What is the significance of local government reorganization within this overall pattern of change, and how is it likely to turn out?

Over the past ten years or so there has been an unprecedented amount of change in the world of British local government: for instance the growth of Compulsory Competitive Tendering; the opportunity for schools to opt out of local authority control; the new responsibilities for community care; the introduction of the community charge (or poll tax) and its subsequent replacement with council tax. And now local government is in the throes of a major and controversial reorganization. There have been several books which have described such changes but this one represents the first systematic attempt to draw out the overall implications of these changes for the future role of local government as an institution. It argues that there are major strategic choices of direction facing local authorities, and that these choices will shape management structures and many other aspects of local choice. The book provides a clear framework of analysis to enable readers to understand the forces at work in this particularly turbulent and unstable period of local government's history, and to see where they are leading.

Contents
Introduction – Part 1: Dimensions of change and choice – The fragmentation of community government – The dimensions of analysis – Local government reorganization – The role of the market and the growth of competition – Locality and community – Part 2: Services and activity areas – Personal social services for older people – The changing role of local authorities in housing – Police reform – Urban regeneration – Conclusion – References – Index.

192pp   0 335 19348 X (Paperback)   0 335 19545 8 (Hardback)

CLASS
Richard Scase

Of all the concepts used by sociologists for describing and explaining social relation-ships, social class is probably the most ambiguous, confusing and ill-defined. This is despite the fact that the development of sociology as an academic discipline has been intimately connected with class related issues. In this book Richard Scase offers a highly accessible introduction to the analysis of social class. Against a back-ground of the failure of Soviet and East European state socialism he highlights the enduring importance of social class in Western capitalist society, which is charac-terized by relations of exploitation. He concludes that whilst Marxist categories continue to be invaluable, Marx's ideas for abolishing class must, towards the end of the twentieth century, be seen to be utopian.

Contents
Preface – The relevance of class – Class and stratification: patterns of rewards – Class and stratification: patterns of opportunity – Class and stratification: some collective responses – Conclusion – Bibliography – Index.

112pp   0 335 15625 8 (Paperback)